The Russian Violin School

The Russian Violin School

The Legacy of Yuri Yankelevich

TRANSLATED AND EDITED BY

MASHA LANKOVSKY

OXFORD
UNIVERSITY PRESS

Oxford University Press is a department of the University of Oxford. It furthers
the University's objective of excellence in research, scholarship, and education
by publishing worldwide. Oxford is a registered trade mark of Oxford University
Press in the UK and certain other countries.

Published in the United States of America by Oxford University Press
198 Madison Avenue, New York, NY 10016, United States of America.

CIP data is on file at the Library of Congress
ISBN 978-0-19-991762-4 (pbk); 978-0-19-991760-0 (hbk)

9 8 7 6 5 4 3 2 1

Paperback printed by Webcom Inc., Canada
Hardback printed by Bridgeport National Bindery, Inc., United States of America

CONTENTS

FOREWORD

This first form of this book was published in Moscow in 1983 under the title *Pedagogicheskoe Nasledie* (Pedagogical Legacy). Compiled by Yuri Yankelevich's sister, Elena Yankelevich, ten years after Yuri Yankelevich's passing, the Russian version of the book consisted of two methodological texts by Yuri Yankelevich and various supplemental essays by Yankelevich's students and colleagues. The book was reedited and reprinted in Russian in 1993, 2002, and 2009. In 1999 the book was translated into French as *Yuri Yankelevitch et l'ecole russe du violon*. The English translation of the book in the present volume, *The Russian Violin School: The Legacy of Yuri Yankelevich*, is based on the 2009 Russian edition and retains the two methodological texts by Yuri Yankelevich and the original essays by Maya Glezarova and Vladimir Grigoryev. In lieu of the other supplemental material the companion website www.oup.com/us/therussianviolinschool to this book provides updated biographical information on Yankelevich's students, selected video interviews, the original essay by Gregory Zhislin and further resources. Aside from the introduction and unless otherwised specified, all material is translated from the original Russian to English.

ACKNOWLEDGMENTS

With great gratitude to Yuri Yankelevich's nieces, Irina and Nataliya Lifshits, for making the publication of this edition possible and for continuing the commitment of their mother, Elena Yankelevich, to preserving Yankelevich's legacy. I would also like to thank all of Yankelevich's students and assistants who have generously shared their experiences and assisted with the supplementary materials, including Alexandre Brussilovsky (who released the French translation), Dmitry Sitkovetsky, Mikhail Bezverkhni, Lydia Dubrovskaya, Irina Medvedeva, Ilya Grubert, Lev Markiz, Vladimir Landsman, Eugenia Chugaeva, and Maya Glezarova.

I thank my violin teacher Boris Roninson for introducing me to this branch of the Russian Violin School, and my violin teacher for five years at Indiana University, Nelli Shkolnikova. One of Yankelevich's first students to receive international recognition, Nelli Shkolnikova was extremely faithful to Yankelevich's principles, and it was she who many years ago first handed me Yankelevich's book with the dream that it would one day be available in English. It is to her memory I dedicate this translation.

Translation is often a painstaking process, and I am extremely grateful to my family, friends and colleagues for their advice and support. Thanks to Andrew Maillet for preparing the musical examples, and to all the editors at Oxford University Press and Newgen Knowledgeworks for steering this book through completion. I thank my doctoral advisers Jane Palmquist and Joseph Straus who supported this project since the beginning; and all the readers of my drafts, including Mai Kawabata, Michael Appleman, Greg Erickson, and my mother, Tatiana Putilina, without whose love this project would also not be possible.

NOTE ON TRANSLITERATION

For the most part in this book, transliterated terms are spelled according to the table provided by the US Board on Geographic Names, except for proper names that are familiar to readers in other spellings. For ease in accessing further research, the transliteration consistent with the Library of Congress is also provided for names and titles in the bibliography (although for clarity, double capitalization is omitted). English translations of Russian titles in the notes and bibliography are the translator's own.

ABOUT THE COMPANION WEBSITE

www.oup.com/us/therussianviolinschool

Oxford University Press has created a website to accompany *The Russian Violin School: The Legacy of Yuri Yankelevich*. The site provides extended biographical information on Yankelevich's students as well as interviews and additional resources.

The Russian Violin School

Introduction

Yuri Yankelevich and the Russian Violin School

MASHA LANKOVSKY ∎

Yuri Yankelevich was one of the preeminent Russian violin teachers of the twentieth century. He taught at the Moscow Conservatory from 1936 to 1973 and produced an exceptional number of outstanding students, including over forty prize-winners in international competitions. Yankelevich was keenly interested in the methodology of violin playing and teaching and contributed a significant number of musical editions and pedagogical texts (the latter are translated in English in this volume for the first time).

As an heir to the rich traditions of violin playing in Russia, Yankelevich was particularly influenced by the violin teachers Lev Tseitlin, Konstantin Mostras, and Abraham Yampolsky who helped establish the Moscow Violin School following the Russian Revolution of 1917. Because of limited communication with the West during the Soviet years, the methodological approach of these teachers has largely remained unknown outside Russia. Despite the huge success of many Soviet violinists in international competitions, few were allowed to travel freely outside of Russia and little was known of the methodology behind their playing. This lack of information has often led to vague and imprecise characterizations of what became known as the "Russian Violin School" in the West. Yankelevich's scholarly works shed light on the pedagogy of the Moscow and Soviet Violin Schools and reveal a modern analytical and individual approach, which incorporates elements of psychology and physiology as well as detailed analysis of the most efficient techniques, all in the service of artistry and individual expression.

THE RUSSIAN VIOLIN SCHOOL

Naturally, as a representative of the Moscow and Soviet Violin Schools, Yuri Yankelevich also represents the more generally known Russian Violin School. Although the term "Russian Violin School" is in common use, it eludes a fixed definition. The history of violin playing in Russia is a fascinating combination of both foreign and native elements over the course of many centuries. Instead of attempting to define the Russian Violin School, it is easier to understand it as a broad term that encompasses a variety of different, although often overlapping, branches.

Most commonly today, the Russian Violin School in the West refers to the influential legacy of Leopold Auer (1845–1930), a Hungarian who taught in St. Petersburg from 1868 to 1917.[1] Among Auer's students were some of the twentieth century's most renowned violinists, including Jascha Heifetz, Mischa Elman, Nathan Milstein, and many others. Following the Russian Revolution of 1917, Auer and many of his students fled Russia and went on to establish successful careers in the West. Because these violinists left before the fall of the Iron Curtain, they were able to achieve significant international renown and pass on their traditions to audiences outside of Russia.

Meanwhile, largely helped by a sociopolitical emphasis on culture and support for the arts, violin playing continued to flourish inside the Soviet Union. One influential figure who established his own branch of the Russian Violin School was Pyotr Stolyarsky (1871–1944). Based in Odessa, Stolyarsky studied with Josef Karbulka (a student of the Czech violinist Otakar Ševčík) and Emil Młynarski (a student of Leopold Auer). Stolyarsky became known for his exceptional ability to teach young children, and he opened his own school in Odessa that was soon renowned as a wunderkind factory. Many of Russia's most famous violinists, including David Oistrakh, Boris Goldstein, Elizaveta Gilels, Mikhail Fichtengolz, and many others, began their studies with Stolyarsky before continuing at the St. Petersburg or Moscow conservatories.

Although Auer and many of his famous students left Russia following the Revolution, Auer's legacy continued to thrive in the Soviet Union through his students who remained and his former assistants Ioannes Nalbandyan (1871–1942) and Sergei Korguyev (1863–1938). As Moscow replaced St. Petersburg as the capital, the Moscow Conservatory in particular built a formidable string faculty that was interested in the methodological analysis of violin playing and teaching. This became known as the Moscow or Soviet Violin School, and among its founding teachers were Lev Tseitlin (1881–1952, a student of Leopold Auer), Abraham Yampolsky (1890–1956, a student of Sergei Korguyev), and Konstantin Mostras (1886–1965. a student of Boris Sibor, who in turn was a student of Auer). Following his studies with Nalbandyan, Yuri

Yankelevich became a student of Abraham Yampolsky and served as his assistant for seventeen years.[2] Yankelevich was greatly interested and influenced by the pedagogical work of these teachers, and through his thirty-seven years of teaching at the Moscow Conservatory he exemplified the methodology of this particular branch of the Russian Violin School.

Just as it is difficult to pinpoint the Russian Violin School historically, it is also difficult to pinpoint it methodologically. One distinguishing feature commonly assigned to Auer's school is the so-called Russian bow hold, a term first used by Carl Flesch, probably because he observed this bow hold in Heifetz and Elman. In the Russian bow hold, the right hand holds the bow with a deep grip, the right elbow is held high, and the right wrist is raised. However, not all of Auer's students held the bow in this manner, and there is no evidence to suppose that Auer taught his students to hold the bow this way. Some suggest that this bow hold could have been inherited from Henryk Wieniawski and even possibly Niccolò Paganini himself. Boris Schwarz points out that Auer himself seems to have used the Franco-Belgian grip and that "every Auer student was virtually free to choose his own posture; some played with a high elbow, others left it low, some pressed the index finger above the second joint, others below."[3] Auer himself claimed that there should be no exact rules in how to hold the violin and bow, but that it should be an individual matter based on physical and mental laws that are impossible to analyze.

Despite Auer's phenomenal success as a teacher and his published pedagogical treatises, he never established a concrete methodology. Even Jascha Heifetz once remarked, "I was never able to say what the so-called 'Auer method' was even though I studied with him."[4] Indeed, what appears to emerge from Auer's legacy is not a rigid set of rules, but rather the nurturing of a creative and productive atmosphere among his students. Auer stressed the need to uncover individualism in the student from musical, technical, and psychological points of view. It is precisely this attention to psychology and individuality that found its way into the methodologies of many teachers of the Moscow Violin School.

Very quickly the Moscow Violin School began producing outstanding students. At the Ysaÿe International Violin Competition in 1937, the international jury was stunned when five of the six top prizes were awarded to Soviet violinists, all of whom had studied at some point at the Moscow Conservatory. From 1917 to 1966, 128 out of the 151 Russian prize-winners at major international competitions had studied at the Moscow Conservatory. The success of these musicians was largely a result of a concentrated pedagogical initiative in a collaborative and supportive structure.

The years immediately following the Russian Revolution witnessed a surge of creative energy, scientific experimentation, and educational reforms. In the mid-1920s the Moscow and St. Petersburg Conservatories were restructured, and the progressive younger faculty were in search of new solutions and fresh approaches. In 1932 the Central Music School was established, which provided a direct link to the Moscow Conservatory. This allowed children to receive expert guidance right from the start. There was no clear division between "master teachers" and "beginning teachers," since many of the same faculty served at both institutions.

Soon after joining the faculty of the Moscow Conservatory, Lev Tseitlin helped establish the conductor-less orchestra Persimfans that flourished for ten years and represented the ambitious energy of its time.[5] Many of the musicians in Persimfans were on the faculty of the Moscow Conservatory and rehearsals took place in the Great Hall of the conservatory. Because there was no conductor, the musicians in all sections spent time meticulously discussing and deciding on phrasing, bowings, fingerings, tempi, and so on. The rehearsals turned into methodological symposiums, and the constant discussion formulated a new pedagogical outlook and innovative ways of teaching. The orchestra sat in a circular foundation with Tseitlin in the middle. Next to Tseitlin sat Abraham Yampolsky, and at the second stand were Dmitri Tsyganov and Konstantin Mostras. All of these violinists subsequently became leading professors at the Moscow Conservatory and were fundamental in establishing the Moscow Violin School.

Mostras taught at the Moscow Conservatory from 1922 to 1965 and headed the violin department from 1936 to 1950. He was deeply committed to the analysis of violin playing and teaching, and in 1931 he instituted a course at the conservatory devoted exclusively to violin methodology. Mostras contributed over four hundred original etudes, transcriptions, and editions to the violin literature and authored a number of pedagogical texts, including *Intonation on the Violin, Rhythmic Discipline of the Violinist, Dynamics in Violin Playing, A System of Practicing at Home for the Violinist,* and *24 Caprices for Violin Solo by N. Paganini: Methodological Commentary.*[6] Extremely analytical and scientific in his approach, Mostras was interested in the psycho-physiological side of playing and teaching, and he introduced the concepts "pre-hearing" and "pre-feeling." Mostras's ideas not only were influential on the Moscow Violin School but also were passed on to his student Ivan Galamian (1903–1981), who would go on to become of the most important violin teachers in the United States.

The teacher who exerted the most influence on Yankelevich was Abraham Yampolsky, who taught at the Moscow Conservatory from 1926 to 1956. Yampolsky was acclaimed for his acute pedagogical intuition and the great number of superb musicians who came out of his studio, including Leonid Kogan, Julian Sitkovetsky, Igor Bezrodny, Boris Goldstein, Elizaveta Gilels, and a host of others. Elaborating on Mostras's pedagogical ideas, Yampolsky paid attention to cultivating sound and stressed the connection between mental conception and physical execution. He believed that the performer's main role is to make any music, even the most complex, understandable and convincing to the listener. Yampolsky contributed numerous editions of the standard repertoire, including an edition of the forty-two Kreutzer etudes that includes not only recommendations on studying the etudes but also more difficult variations for some of them.

Naturally, there were also many other teachers who comprised the Soviet Violin School, including the renowned David Oistrakh who taught a host of outstanding violinists. However, Yampolsky, Mostras, and Tseitlin exerted a particularly strong influence on Yankelevich because of their detailed analysis of pedagogical problems. Also, both Yampolsky and Mostras devoted their entire musical careers to teaching rather than performing. In his writings, Yankelevich constantly makes reference to Tseitlin, Mostras, and Yampolsky. He not only synthesized their work but also, through his own pedagogical experience and insight, continued the traditions of this school through the next generation.

YURI YANKELEVICH'S LEGACY

Yuri Yankelevich was born into the cultured family of a renowned Omsk lawyer, who was also an amateur violist and a founder of the Omsk Philharmonic Society. Yankelevich's mother was an accomplished pianist, and the young boy grew up with chamber music resounding in the home. Yankelevich made quick progress studying the violin with Anisim Berlin, a student of Auer's who had moved to Omsk.[7] In 1924 the family moved to Leningrad (as St. Petersburg was named at the time), and Yankelevich entered the Leningrad Conservatory as a student of Ioannes Nalbandyan. Yankelevich soaked in the creative atmosphere at the conservatory, and he recalled with fondness the deep impressions made by Alexander Glazunov's chamber music classes and meetings with other faculty, including Sergei Korguyev. Outside the conservatory, Yankelevich was also influenced by the rich artistic cultural life of 1920s Russia, especially by such luminaries of the theater and opera as Ivan Yershov, Fyodor Chaliapin, and Alexander Ostuzhev. The influence of opera on Yankelevich is not coincidental, for one of the most characteristic traits not only of Yankelevich's methodology but indeed of the entire Russian Violin School is the idea that the violin should "sing."[8] In 1928 Yankelevich began his graduate studies in Moscow with Abraham Yampolsky, who was to have a profound effect on Yankelevich's future career. Yankelevich was appointed assistant concertmaster of the Moscow Philharmonic in 1930, but gradually he felt himself more and more drawn to pedagogy. Playing in itself did not provide him with complete satisfaction, and as his colleagues would often approach him for tips or fingerings he found his recommendations to be successful, inspiring him as a pedagogue musician. Yankelevich recalls how, in following studies with Yampolsky, "I began to be consciously drawn to pedagogy, to the cognitive aspects of the theory and practice of violin playing.... From Yampolsky I understood that violin playing is not a miracle, not 'alchemy,' but a science and that besides inspiration there exist objective rules, which, when combined with serious work, can accomplish a great deal."[9]

In 1932 Yankelevich started teaching at the Central Music School and the specialized high school (uchilische).[10] In 1936 he became Yampolsky's assistant, and his life was then forever tied to the Moscow Conservatory. After seventeen years as Yampolsky's assistant, Yankelevich was given his own class at the conservatory in 1953.

The first of Yankelevich's students to achieve international recognition was Nelli Shkolnikova, who won first prize at the Jacques Thibaud competition in 1953. Nelli Shkolnikova started studying with Yankelevich when she was still a child and when Yankelevich was still Yampolsky's assistant. The pedagogical talents of Yankelevich became widely recognized as more and more outstanding students emerged from his studio. In the coming years, forty of his students were awarded prizes at international competitions, including Irina Bochkova, Victor Tretyakov, Vladimir Spivakov, Gregory Zhislin, and many more (a list of Yankelevich's students is found in Appendix A).

In addition to teaching soloists, Yankelevich also nurtured generations of chamber musicians, orchestral musicians, and teachers. Throughout his career, Yankelevich taught close to two hundred students through his pedagogical activities at the Moscow Conservatory, the Gnessin Institute, the Moscow uchilische (specialized high school), and the Central Music School. He also conducted methodological lectures and seminars in Moscow, throughout the former Soviet Union, and in a limited number of visits abroad (the latter included masterclasses and lectures in Japan, Germany, and Czechoslovakia).[11]

The scope of Yankelevich's pedagogical and methodological activities reflected his desire to constantly share his knowledge. He never belonged to that category of teachers who try to "guard" their professional secrets. He worked very closely with his assistants, consulting with them and granting them considerable autonomy, while still maintaining a cohesive and programmed course of study for each individual student. Many of Yankelevich's assistants, including Maya Glezarova, Zinaida Gilels, Evgenia Chugaeva, and Felix Andrievsky, worked closely with him for decades and became recognized teachers in their own right. The pedagogical model of utilizing assistants not only made it easier to develop a unified and comprehensive methodology but also allowed a deep and thorough exploration of each methodological element.

Yankelevich was extremely methodical in his own work, and his archives contain more than thirty notebooks filled with his observations. He treated pedagogy as serious and disciplined work. "I work like a slave all my life," he would say. "I leave the conservatory at 11 pm or later, and then I continue working at home. It is important to not just listen to the student, but really to work with them. A teacher who just hears the student play and simply corrects the notes with 'play like this here, and like this there. Now play this again'— that is not work."[12] Indeed, at times there were some who criticized him for being overly analytical and pedantic. Studying with Yankelevich (and with some of his assistants) unquestionably required a certain discipline and perseverance. And yet, as his own texts reflect, his rigor and work ethic arose solely from his desire to serve the music and was free of ego. His humility allowed his mind to be open, and he was constantly questioning and investigating new ideas. Above all, he believed it is the teacher's responsibility to uncover and bring out the individual qualities in every single student.

Yankelevich's students were distinguished not only by their impeccable quality of technique but also by their sophisticated and comprehensive musical taste and understanding. Contrary to some assumptions about the Russian Violin School, Yankelevich, just like Abraham Yampolsky before him, saw technique solely as a tool for musical expression. He believed that absolutely all elements of playing the violin must be directed toward a final musical goal. "The performer should be in possession of all technical skills, but at the same time he or she must first develop an understanding of music and delve into the composer's intent. Basically, this means that one not only needs to possess *the tools* to speak, but most importantly one needs to know *what* to say."[13]

Yankelevich always took into consideration the psychological and physiological aspects of playing the violin. This was reflected not only in his approach to solving technical problems (e.g., conditioning appropriate motor and nerve reflexes) and choosing repertoire (e.g., analyzing and taking into account the student's character) but also in his desire to cultivate the student's independence and individual personality. He was interested in teaching not only how to play the violin but also how to *think* about playing the violin. The following words of Abraham Yampolsky particularly resonated with Yuri Yankelevich:

In practice, we [teachers] are obliged to spend a lot of time working on formal perfectionism, working on intonation, technical aspects, etc. . . . In the process of preparing a student we often overlook the isolated, exceptional moments in the student's performance. We don't notice these sparks, since our attention is turned to correcting all kinds of deficiencies. At the same time, we become accustomed to hearing the same piece played dozens of times in the traditional way and subconsciously cultivate a certain aural inertia. Any divergences from the general norm give us the impression of something strange and illogical. If this occurs in the student's performance we immediately try to correct him or her, instead of carefully listening and trying to discern that which is valuable and creative, and may be embedded in the artistic intentions of the student.[14]

These exact sentiments are reflected in Yankelevich's comments to one of his students:

> For me it is very valuable when you express your ideas, when I feel you have thought about things and have ideas and conceptions of your own; let them even be wrong, for we can correct them together, but starting from wrong ideas we can work our way to the right ones. If you will always be waiting for the teacher to supply you with a ready-made idea, one that is already developed, already "chewed on" that you just have to swallow, then you will be utterly helpless when you need to work on your own without a teacher.[15]

Yankelevich possessed an incredible pedagogical intuition that enabled him not only to pinpoint students' weak points but also, more importantly, to determine each student's individual strengths. He lived through his students, creating a close-knit atmosphere in his studio akin to family. This move away from a teacher-centric model of learning to a dialectical model of learning may even be traced back to Leopold Auer. Grigoryev writes how one of Auer's remarkable innovations was to create a system whereby the teacher and the student are learning together.[16] And this idea directly passes through to the Moscow Violin School, for Mark Lubotsky describes how, in Yampolsky's pedagogy, a process of "reincarnation" would occur, where "the teacher would proceed from the creative 'I' of the student."[17]

For this reason, Yankelevich's "school" does not embody one style of playing, one specific positioning, or a single type of technique. Yankelevich himself said that, for him, the idea of a "school" is defined not by a similar way that students play but by a shared embrace and understanding of various musical styles, a high quality of tone production, and the beauty and mastery of efficient motor skills.

YANKELEVICH'S METHODOLOGICAL WORKS

The two texts by Yuri Yankelevich translated in this book illustrate both his extremely detailed analytical and methodological side as well as his flexible and broad understanding of music as an active, living process. Details of his methods and his psycho-physiological approach are thoroughly discussed in chapter 3 by Maya Glezarova and chapter 4 by Vladimir Grigoryev. All these texts not only offer invaluable practical advice on overcoming specific difficulties but also illustrate the fascinating thought process of a great pedagogical mind. Certain themes are consistently present. These include the importance of understanding the violin as a singing and "vocal" instrument, the interconnectivity between the parts and the whole (this applies to both technical elements such as positioning and musical elements such as form and style), the importance of creating an individually catered plan of study for each student, a scientific analysis of every element of technique in order that it may serve in a clearly envisioned musical context, and viewing each problem not as an isolated matter but as part of an inseparable chain connecting every stage and component of violin playing.

Yankelevich's works stand alongside texts by Carl Flesch, Ivan Galamian, and Leopold Mozart as some of the most insightful treatises in the history of the instrument. In "Setting Up the Violin and Bow Hold," instead of simply prescribing rules on how the instrument should be positioned, Yankelevich analyzes the different possibilities and places them in historical context, discussing the pros and cons of various points of view. He then offers practical suggestions that take into account the individual constitution of each student and provide the optimal conditions to accomplish all the tasks the music requires with the minimal amount of tension.

Similarly, in "Shifting Positions in Conjunction with the Musical Goals of the Violinist," Yankelevich analyzes the technique of shifting in historical context and addresses the various suggestions and arguments encountered in the methodological literature. In this extremely detailed and thorough work, Yankelevich addresses every element of shifting, always in light of how the technique may best serve the performer's musical goals. Following a general presentation of how we understand the positions, Yankelevich goes on to analyze the role of the ear and reflexes, the elimination of tension, and the optimal movements in all parts of the hand while shifting. He then classifies different types of shifts and makes a detailed analysis of each type of shift. For the basis of his analysis, Yankelevich conducted oscillographic readings in the acoustic laboratory of the Moscow Conservatory of different shifts performed by the leading violinists of the day. He also addresses shifts that incorporate harmonics and open strings, shifts in double stops, and the coordination between shifting and bowing. In conclusion he presents a summary of general principles that may be used in performance and pedagogical practice. This work originated as Yankelevich's doctoral dissertation in 1955. Following his defense, the head of his dissertation committee, David Oistrakh, wrote the following: "This work will help many of our teachers (especially those further away on the 'periphery') since there are still many conflicting opinions in the field that sometimes even block the development of violin methodology and pedagogy."[18]

Maya Glezarova worked closely as Yankelevich's assistant for over twenty years. In chapter 3 she describes key elements of Yankelevich's methodology as well as providing examples of the long-range individual repertoire plans he would create for his students. Vladimir Grigoryev, drawing on his observations of Yankelevich's seminars and lessons, provides a comprehensive examination of Yankelevich's pedagogy, addressing tone production, exercises, intonation, vibrato, fingerings and bowings, repertoire, and his general approach to methodology. (Additional resources and commentaries from Yankelevich's students may be found at the companion website to this book.)

Forty years after Yankelevich's passing, his work and his legacy remain relevant largely because he was never dogmatic in his principles. He encouraged an approach to learning that was as flexible as it was comprehensive. Yankelevich's legacy lives on through the playing and teaching of his students and his "grand-students" all over the world. With the present publication of his works in English, it is hoped that his legacy will continue through to many more generations of violinists to come.

NOTES

1. When Leopold Auer was appointed as Henryk Wieniawski's successor in St. Petersburg, he continued the long tradition of prominent foreign musicians working in Russia. One of the first violinist composers to settle in Russia was Luigi Madonis (1690-1779), who was born in Venice but lived and worked in St. Petersburg from 1733. Later, famous European violinists such as Pierre Rode, Louis Spohr, Charles de Bériot, Henri Vieuxtemps, Heinrich Ernst, Henry Schradieck, and Jan Hřimaly all spent some time working in Russia. However, outside the Imperial Court and before the openings of the Moscow and St. Petersburg Conservatories, violin playing was also widespread in circles of aristocratic intelligentsia, artisans, and serfs in the peasant populations. The most comprehensive text that addresses violin playing in Russia from its origins through the 1860s is Israel Markovich Yampolsky's *Russkoe Skripichnoye Iskusstvo* (Russian Art of the Violin) published in 1951. Yampolsky describes the often-competing worlds of peasant string traditions and foreign guest violinists at the Imperial Court. This divide was bridged by Russia's first great virtuoso, Ivan Khandoshkin (1784–1804), who was born into a family of serfs but whose musical talent allowed him to engage in a career at the Imperial Court. Another influential Russian violinist was Aleksey Lvov (1798–1870), who composed a number of violin pieces as well as a pedagogical treatise with a set of twenty-four caprices.

2. The family name Yampolsky appears often among twentieth-century Russian string players, and it is important not to confuse Israel and Abraham Yampolsky. Abraham Yampolsky's (the violin teacher referenced here) brother was Mark Yampolsky (1879–1951), a cellist, fellow member of the Persimfans Orchestra, and professor at the Moscow Conservatory. Mark's son was Israel Yampolsky (1905–1976), who studied the violin with his uncle, Abraham Yampolsky. Israel Yampolsky later became a prominent musicologist and wrote *Russkoe Skripichnoe Iskusstvo* (Russian Art of the Violin) and *Principles of Violin Fingering*, among other publications. Of no relation to this family is Philip Yampolsky (1874–1957), a student of and former assistant to Leopold Auer. Interestingly enough, for a short while Philip Yampolsky taught Abraham Yampolsky (in St. Petersburg) as well as Leonid Kogan (in Dnepropetrovsk). Leonid Kogan later continued his studies in Moscow as a student of Abraham Yampolsky. Unless otherwise noted, the single name "Yampolsky" will hereafter refer only to Abraham Yampolsky.

3. Boris Schwarz, *Great Masters of the Violin* (New York: Simon & Schuster, 1983), 421.

4. Ibid.

5. "Persimfans" stood for *Pervyi Simfonicheskii Ansambl'* (lit., "The First Symphonic Orchestra Ensemble").

6. These English titles are translated by the editor; the original Russian titles are found in the bibliography.

7. Anisim Berlin (1896–1961) was also the grandfather of acclaimed cellist Nathalia Gutman.

8. Yankelevich himself was in possession of a fine baritone voice. Not only would singers sometimes attend his classes at the conservatory but also he was sometimes invited to serve on the jury of competitions for singers.

9. Tatiana Gaidamovich, "Zhizn' pedagoga v tvorchestve ego uchenikov" (The Pedagogue's Life through the Creative Work of His Students), in Yuri Yankelevich, *Pedagogicheskoe nasledie* (Pedagogical Legacy), 4th ed., (Moscow: Muzyka, 2009), 326.

10. The Central Music School provided a ten-year course of study to students aged seven through eighteen, combining intensive musical training with regular schoolwork. The *uchilische* or music high school was a parallel five-year music-intensive program for students aged fifteen through nineteen.

11. Impressions of his trips to Japan and the GDR are found in his essay "Na muzykal'nyh seminarakh v IAponii i Gdr" (At Musical Seminars in Japan and the German Democratic Republic), *Masterstvo muzykanta-ispolnitelia* (1972).

12. Gaidamovich, "Zhizn' pedagoga v tvorchestve ego uchenikov," 331.

13. Elena Yankelevich, "Professiia—pedagog" (Profession—Pedagogue), in *Pedagogicheskoe nasledie* (Pedagogical Legacy), 4th ed., Yuri Yankelevich (Moscow: Muzyka, 2009), 412.

14. Abraham Yampolsky, "O metode raboty s uchinikame" (On Methods of Working with Students), in *Voprosy skripichnogo ispolnitel'stva i pedagogiki, sbornik statei* (Matters of Violin Performance and Pedagogy, a Collection of Articles), ed. S. Sapozhnikov (Moscow: Muzyka, 1968), 18.

15. Excerpt of comments recorded on tape during a lesson, found in Elena Yankelevich, "Professiia—Pedagog" (Profession—Pedagogue), 411.
16. Tatiana Gaidamovich, ed., *Muzykalnoe ispolnitelstvo i pedagogika* (Musical Performance and Pedagogy) (Moscow: Muzyka, 1991), 89.
17. Mark Lubotsky, "A. I. Iampolskii—Muzykant, Pedagog, Vospitatel" (A. I. Yampolsky—Musician, Pedagogue, Mentor), *Sovetskaya Muzyka* 24, no. 11 (1960): 117–23.
18. Gaidamovich, "Zhizn' pedagoga v tvorchestve ego uchenikov," 330.

1

Setting up the Violin and Bow Hold

YURI YANKELEVICH ▪

In studies of the positioning of a violinist's hands and arms, one discovers a variety of individual ways of adapting to the instrument.[1] It is not uncommon to find that these seemingly different approaches yield practically the same beneficial results. However, to conclude from this, as is sometimes done, that positioning lacks norms and therefore requires no direction would be unfounded and detrimental to violin pedagogy. General norms and standards in positioning a violinist's hands and arms do exist, and they are based upon objective principles of physiology, anatomy, and mechanics. Before moving to an account of the various views on positioning, it is first necessary to understand and define the term itself.

The violinist's position should not be regarded as something constant or static. One must not forget that it has changed historically. It is well known that the chin once supported the violin on the right side of the tailpiece rather than on the left. Clearly this determined the corresponding positions of the left and right hands. In the old German schools it was customary to position the right arm so the shoulder pressed against the torso of the body.[2] To master this position, students were advised to hold a book underneath their arm while practicing. Today this method seems absurd, but it was used in its time and was derived from the designated way of holding the instrument.

Changes in position and posture did not occur spontaneously over the course of history, but were a product of evolving aesthetic ideas and styles. The emerging need to extend the violin's range and to command control over the entire fingerboard made it necessary to free the left arm. This required the repositioning of the chin from the right side of the tailpiece to the left side, with a resulting change in the position of the entire body. As violin technique developed further and the left hand became increasingly mobile, a steadier hold of the instrument was required. This was provided with the invention of the chin rest. In this manner, the aesthetic requirements of an era determine changes in artistic styles. Each style then determines the corresponding technique, which is made possible only with the appropriate positioning. Consequently the positioning, in adjusting to the new requirements, must also change.

The manner of holding the instrument also changes in the process of playing, according to specific technical and artistic demands. Numerous examples can illustrate how the left hand changes shape while executing chord changes, extensions, and chromatic sequences. These examples clearly show that the violinist's position is dynamic in nature, closely linked to the demands made upon the motor apparatus. The process of selecting efficient methods of movement modifies the positioning.

Nonetheless, one often encounters examples of "fetishism" in a number of positioning matters. The works of Ion Voiku, B. Mikhailovsky and others are characteristic in this respect; they advocate specific positions that are to a certain degree removed from the demands of live playing.[3] Occasionally, similar views are even encountered among highly respected authorities. For example, Joseph Joachim, discussing the problems of shifting in his *Violinschule*, indicates the necessity of maintaining, while shifting, the same hammerlike position of a finger on the string, as observed when the finger is placed in a fixed position.[4] Yet, to any violinist, it is clear that accomplishing this requirement will automatically provoke constraint and tension that necessarily impinges the freedom of movement.

Undoubtedly, the issue of an efficient setup can only be examined with regard to its immediate relationship to those movements for which it was created and whose freedom it must guarantee. At the same time, one must not forget that in musical performance the criteria for establishing correct movements should be determined solely in consideration of the quality of sound that is subsequently produced.

The term "prospective positioning" is often encountered in pedagogical practice. Relative to what was mentioned earlier, the prospective positioning of a violinist is determined by how that positioning can accommodate the entire range of movements a violinist will require in his or her future development. Teachers at music schools find themselves in a particularly challenging situation, since they mostly work with beginners and only occasionally with more advanced students.[5] However, in establishing a student's position, the teacher needs to know not only how to hold the bow and how to move it in the beginning stages of study but also how it will need to be used later in performing, say, the Brahms concerto. This means the teacher needs to look far ahead and possess great insight, sensibility and a profound understanding of the instrument.

We have already mentioned that a violinist's movements are not purely mechanical and isolated from sound. A relaxed motion produces a pleasing sound, while a tense motion is incapable of producing a good tone and creates obstacles that block the development of technique. When discussing the relationship between movement and sound, it is necessary to emphasize that sound is not an abstract concept. The quality of tone may only be determined in conjunction with specific musical material. Since the character of the musical material determines the character of the sound, at this point we are confronted with broader issues of musical context. It goes without saying that in the early stages of working with pupils on sound quality, the demands are elementary, that is, the focus is on absence of scratchiness and production of a full and supple tone. However, when speaking of the interpretation of a musical composition, the sound can be determined only in context. Consequently, such seemingly different concepts as positioning, movement, sound, and musical content turn out to be links in one and the same chain, and it becomes obvious that problems in positioning may have considerably greater consequences than might initially appear.

In pedagogical practice it is not uncommon to encounter dogmatic approaches to setting up the violin and bow hold. In these instances, teachers advocate certain positions without taking into consideration a student's hand structure and individual way of adapting to the instrument. As an example, one can compare the directions in the methodical literature concerning any specific issue, such as the position of the left-hand thumb.

In Leopold Mozart's violin treatise, it is stated that the thumb of the left hand must be held closer to the second or even the third finger.[6] Bartolomeo Campagnoli advocates that the thumb must be placed opposite the second finger, playing the note B-natural on the G string.[7] Leopold Auer indicates that the position of the thumb be determined by the second finger playing the note F-natural on the D string (i.e., one half-step lower).[8] Joachim recommends that the thumb be held opposite the first finger, playing the note A on the G-string (i.e., yet another half-step lower).[9] The Belgian pedagogue Gustave Koeckert, assistant to the violinist S. Thomson (celebrated for his rare virtuosity), presents a more extreme point of view, asserting that the thumb must be slanted back towards the scroll of the violin.[10] Viktor Valter recommends the reverse, indicating that the thumb must be held as far away from the scroll as possible and slanted toward the body of the violin.[11]

All of the expressed opinions belong to respected authorities holding important places in the history of violin playing. These contradictory opinions naturally lead to the puzzling question: Who is correct? It turns out that all these authors are, to a certain extent, both correct and incorrect. Each found the positioning for himself that proved to be the most efficient. However, to turn an individual solution to a problem into a general rule (i.e., to dogmatize) is incorrect.

In pedagogical practice, we often encounter instances when the pedagogue justifies directions in the following way: "this is correct because this is how I was taught" or "this is the way so-and-so plays" (here follows the name of some famous artist). The following situation is a good example. In the early years of David Oistrakh's career, posters with his photograph were published that showed his index finger stretching far up on the bow stick. Today it's hard to tell whether the photograph caught a corresponding moment in the artist's playing or was a photographic distortion, but in any case, this position of the hand is not characteristic of Oistrakh's playing. Nonetheless, this photograph served as a model that was copied by many students and a considerable number of violin pedagogues.

Boris Struve's work *Typical Forms of Positioning the Hands of Instrumentalists* provides interesting material relating to this topic.[12] The author attempts to determine the connection between different types of positioning and the individual's particular anatomical structure. An example characteristic of the author's method of analysis is the question of a high or low position of the right elbow, an issue that provokes many arguments in pedagogical practice. Struve suggests that the correct position of the elbow (high or low) be determined by the anatomical structure of the arms, in particular by the shoulder joints. Observations show that in a relaxed arm hanging "by the seams," the shoulder, upper arm, and elbow do not always align in the same position. In some individuals the elbow falls close to the body; in others the elbow falls significantly away from the body. Therefore, in the first case the most natural position of the elbow will be lower, while in the second case it will be higher.

In pedagogical practice it is not always easy to determine the most effective positioning for each student. Sometimes a student's individual characteristics are not immediately apparent. This is why a teacher must carefully observe the process of a student's adaptation to the instrument and, avoiding dogma, try to find methods that are most organic to the student.

In the course of studying the violin, one often hears discussion of "natural" movement and positioning. This prompts the question: What is meant by "natural"? Considering the position of the violinist's left arm with the elbow twisted under the violin, we would have to admit that this position in itself is unnatural, since it would rarely be encountered in everyday life. This is proved when the student's left arm tires almost immediately in the beginning lessons, precisely because of the awkward nature of this position.

The fundamental idea in Voiku's famous work *The Formation of a Natural System of Violin Playing* is to move away from this unnatural positioning of the left arm and to create a more natural position.[13] The author's mistake lies in the fact that the positioning of the left hand he proposes, one that corresponds closely to its use in everyday life, cannot fulfill all the motor functions that are indispensable to the process of playing the violin. For this reason Voiku's system is unusable in practice. Consequently, when discussing "naturalness" in violin playing, one must proceed not from the natural position of the arms in everyday life but from the arms' most natural position under specific professional conditions.

Any activity, and violin playing in particular, is impossible to accomplish entirely free of tension; in other words, any physical activity requires certain minimal efforts. At the same time, from a professional point of view, tension is understood as the excessive effort that produces constraint and limits artistic possibilities. It is not uncommon to find instances when technical limitations are consequences of severe tension, such as the excessive pressure of the fingers on the string and the extreme gripping of the neck of the violin with the left hand. It must be noted that in pedagogical practice we are constantly confronted with contradictions between the demand for relaxed movements and recommended methods that make relaxed movements impossible to achieve.

Regarding tension, one must never forget that the human organism is a unified system. No matter where an area of tension may originate and appear, it will always limit the freedom of movement in the arms. Therefore, achieving free movement in, say, the left hand is impossible without simultaneously freeing the right arm and maintaining a relaxed condition of the shoulders and torso. A necessary condition to attaining a natural position and relaxed movement in the arms turns out to be a steady and natural position of the body. This, in turn, depends largely on how the legs are positioned and the weight of the torso is distributed.

In the methodical literature there is no concurring opinion on how to determine the correct positioning of the legs. The older classical texts often provide illustrations showing the legs of the violinist standing in ballet's "third position." It would make more sense to consider distributing the weight of the body equally between both legs. Moreover, the legs should not be drawn too close together or too far apart, but placed approximately at the width of the shoulders.

To ensure the shoulder region remains relaxed, it is necessary to determine the correct position of the head. Often, one sees the instrument positioned with the head inclined too far to the left and the violin supported on the edge of the chinrest. Regarding this issue we may recall the advice of Lev Tseitlin. Tseitlin, who himself held the violin extremely freely, recommended starting from the regular, natural position of the neck, head, and shoulders. From there, the chin needs to be only slightly lowered and the instrument is securely fixed with the left side of the jaw. Such a position allows for the most freedom in the arms and upper torso.

The stability of the instrument plays an important role in allowing free movement in the arms, especially the left arm. This is why the effective use of a chinrest and pad is extremely important.[14] The chinrest should be not too high, but deep enough so that the chin may lie on it securely, allowing the violin to be held confidently. If the chinrest is too flat, the chin must squeeze down in order to hold the violin, and this causes tension in the muscles of the neck.

Opinions differ regarding the use of shoulder pads. One may name a great number of violinists who play without a pad, including such prominent performers as Jascha Heifetz and Leonid Kogan. Likewise, certain pedagogues teach their students to play without a pad. Nevertheless, one cannot deny that using a pad creates more advantageous conditions for holding the instrument and eliminates unnecessary tension that arises from lifting the shoulder. Without a pad the shoulder will inevitably lift, even for those with broad shoulders, and especially for those with sloped shoulders. Also, one cannot always use outstanding violinists such as Heifetz or Kogan as reference points since they possessed uniquely individual ways of adjusting to the instrument. The difficulties involved in performing contemporary works require conditions that provide maximal freedom in the left arm.

There are two points of view on the positioning of the violin while it is being played. According to the first, widespread in practice, the instrument is held with only one point of support; the violin is securely fixed between the chin and the collarbone, thus completely freeing the left hand. The more outspoken proponent of the second point of view is L. Nemirovsky, who believes the instrument should be held with two points of support.[15] One of these points is constant (the violin rests on the collarbone without using a cushion and without lifting the shoulder), and the second point is variable (the left hand). This method is practical for playing in one position, or for shifting from a lower position to a higher position. Yet it presents serious difficulties in shifting down from a higher position to a lower one. In this case all violinists playing without a pad are obligated to resort to lifting the shoulder. However, Nemirovsky suggests that lifting of the shoulder be avoided by using auxiliary movements of the thumb. He recommends that the thumb move to a lower position in advance of the shift and provide a pivot point for the consequent displacement of the entire hand. Thus, holding the violin with two points of support requires constant, extra preparatory movements of the thumb that present additional technical difficulties. When performing fast passages it is almost impossible to manipulate the thumb quickly enough. Consequently those playing without a pad are still compelled to lift the shoulder to secure the violin.

Practically, the question regarding the effectiveness of a pad should be answered in the following manner: the pedagogue should choose a chinrest and pad of the appropriate height for each student and begin studies under these conditions. Eventually, when the student can play with facility in all positions, and the teacher sees that the student's individual particularities allow him or her to do without a pad, it may be removed. Note that even Kogan also used a pad in his early years of study.

Another important factor is the height at which the instrument is held. In his treatise Leopold Auer notes that the violin must be held sufficiently high to allow for smooth shifts between positions.[16] At first glance it would seem there is no logical connection between shifting and raising the violin. Yet, after giving this matter some thought, we discover Auer's opinion is perfectly justified. This is proved by a simple experiment. It is enough to sit on a chair, holding the violin so that the elbow rests on the table, with the first finger placed on any string in first position. If one shifts to third position keeping the same posture, the violin will rise. This is understandable since the arm, with the elbow glued to the table, can only move in a circular motion. When shifting down, the violin will correspondingly lower. This is why it becomes clear that in practice a performer requires supplementary corrective movements to direct the hand in a straight line rather than a circle. These auxiliary movements are accomplished by slightly raising the elbow and simultaneously stretching the shoulder away from the body (when shifting to lower positions) and by lowering the elbow and drawing the shoulder closer to the body (when shifting to higher positions).

When learning how to shift, beginners often make two contrasting mistakes: either they raise the violin too high, or they drop it too low. The analysis presented above explains the origins of these errors. When the violin is lifted too high, the shoulder and elbow fail to make the corrective supplementary movements; and when the violin is lowered, the supplementary movements are made excessively. Auxiliary movement in the shoulder is also observed when the left hand shifts positions in the upper area of the fingerboard. In this case, instead of moving up and down, the shoulder moves right and left. Thus, it turns out that movements in the shoulder are necessary to allow the hand to move freely along the fingerboard and for the violin to remain in a normal position.

Consequently, Auer's recommendation is understandable. When the violin is held too low, the shoulder and elbow are cramped against the violinist's torso and unable to move, whereas a higher position of the violin allows the necessary corrective movements to be completed easily, both vertically and horizontally. A high position of the violin also ensures the bow moves straight, for if the violin is held too low the bow will slide to the fingerboard, creating a bad habit that is subsequently hard to get rid of.

The degree to which the violin is directed to the player's right or left side is also significant. It is difficult to overestimate the importance of this for the right arm. When the violin is held too far to the left, the right arm must extend forward. Otherwise the bow will not lie perpendicular to the string and the sound will suffer. If the violin is held inclined too far to the right, in order for the bow to be perpendicular, the right wrist must bend in an excessively high manner. This is especially uncomfortable for those with long arms. Very often tightness in the right arm, a lack of flexibility in the wrist, and consequent difficulties in executing various bow strokes, are all caused precisely because of such an incorrect positioning of the instrument. In this case, moving the instrument to the left will immediately release the right arm, allowing it to move naturally and freely. The positioning of the instrument must be determined on an individual basis, taking into consideration the length of the student's arms. For those with shorter arms the violin should be directed more to the right; for those with longer arms, more to the left.

Likewise, the angle of inclination of the violin is extremely important. This is regulated by the height of the pad; the higher the pad, the greater the angle of inclination, and the lower the cushion, the flatter the violin will lie. The correct level of inclination should be determined by the position of the left elbow. If the violin is held too flat (i.e., entirely parallel to the floor), the left elbow will need to move excessively to the right, creating an unnatural position (we have already noted the unnatural position of the violinist's left elbow in general, and it is only made worse with a flat positioning of the violin). A flat positioning of the violin also causes the up-bow on the G string to be incorrectly directed down toward the floor, a problem often encountered in beginners. On the other hand, if the violin is inclined too much, it becomes difficult for the fingers of the left hand to fall at the correct angle and may cause them to slide off the E string.

Turning to the matter of holding the bow, it is first necessary to determine the correct placement of the fingers in relation to the frog. Many teachers recommend resting the thumb against the protruding part of the frog.[17] In some instances violinists will even fit their thumb into the niche of the frog.[18] A more efficient hold is achieved by placing the thumb on the bow stick next to the frog. Often players with shorter arms have difficulties drawing the bow to the tip and will hold the bow a little above the frog. For example, Leopold Auer, who had short arms, held the bow this way. Beginners, for whom the bow is too heavy, may also have a tendency to hold the bow like this. Instinctively trying to lighten the bow, students will move their hand up from the frog, thereby shortening the heavier left side of the stick. This bow hold may also be used if the weight of the bow itself is distributed incorrectly.

Often, if the bow is too long for the student, teachers will advise the student not to draw the bow to the very tip. Instead, the teacher will tie a piece of string to the bow, marking where the movement should end. Tseitlin recommended shortening the amount of bow used by moving the right hand up from the frog. This not only shortens the bow but also lightens it; thus it should be considered the more sound advice. However, it is certainly better to match the student with a bow that is the correct length and weight, so as not to resort to such measures. The positioning of the hand on the bow affects the placement of the thumb in relation to the frog. Consequently, the thumb should be held on the stick and not in the niche of the frog, as is often recommended.

The positioning of the thumb in relation to the other fingers of the right hand is another controversial issue. Struve, in his work that we have already cited, claims the position of the thumb on the bow must be determined by the structure of the saddle joint between the thumb and the other fingers.[19] This may be seen when the hand is clenched into a fist and each person's thumb takes on a different position. Consequently, for some violinists it is more natural to hold the thumb opposite the middle finger and for others to hold it opposite the ring finger. Naturally, in-between positions may also exist. Nonetheless, it is important to note that Struve's point of view is not the only one. The artistic goals associated with various styles also play an important role. With this in mind, let us compare the opinions of Tseitlin and Yampolsky. Yampolsky suggested placing the thumb opposite the middle finger; Tseitlin suggested placing the thumb almost opposite the ring finger, that is, between the middle and ring fingers. As noted above, these differences are assumed to originate from the corresponding anatomical hand structure of each violinist. These different ways of holding the bow produce different results.

The artistic goals of Tseitlin, in his playing as in his teaching, were oriented toward a large, full sound and a grandiose style of playing. His recommended bow hold allows greater pressure on the bow, ensuring more contact between the bow and the string. At the same time this position of the fingers, to a certain extent, impairs the execution of light bow strokes. Yampolsky strove for versatility in bow technique and the mastery of elegant strokes—hence the alternate method of holding the bow.

The correct position and function of the thumb is extremely important for the freedom of the right hand. As a rule, the thumb should be slightly bent at the frog. In the process of drawing the bow from the frog to the tip, the thumb gradually straightens. Drawing the bow in the opposite direction, from the tip to the frog, the thumb gradually reverts to its bent position.

Teachers often demand from their students that the thumb always be bent, incorrectly assuming that this means it is relaxed. In reality, a constantly bent or "rigid" position of the thumb produces tension in the other fingers, causing stiffness. It is essential for the fingers on the bow to be free to perform light auxiliary movements during bow changes and to accomplish a variety of strokes. To achieve this freedom, the thumb and all the other fingers must be attached to the stick flexibly like a joint, no matter what part of the bow is used. If the thumb is fixed in any one position (bent or straight), all the other fingers will be limited in their movements.

When playing at the tip, constrained movements in parts of the right arm are often explained by tension in the thumb. However, there are instances when violinists freely command the bow in spite of the thumb being held straight or even indented in the opposite (concave) direction. For example, this is the way Auer and Kogan held the bow, and clearly it didn't trouble them. This is explained by the fact that some people, because of their particular hand structure, have joints that are especially supple and flexible. This flexibility allows them to perform all the necessary movements in spite of a concave thumb. But it is clear that this position should be regarded more as an exception.

Consequently, when determining the role of the thumb, it is important to proceed from the fact that the thumb must ensure free movement in the other fingers on the bow. The position of the other fingers can be deep or shallow depending, to a certain extent, on their length. The fingers should not be spread too close together or too far apart. The technique of holding the bow with the fingertips, as was recommended in the past, is not used anymore since it does not produce a large sound. The fingers on the bow must be curved, and their normal position should permit the weight of the arm to transfer to the stick, letting the sound flow naturally. One often encounters the position where the fingers of the right hand are tensely extended with the knuckles sticking up. This defect is easily corrected by curving the fingers, giving them a rounded shape.

It is especially important to pay attention to the round position of the little finger on the bow while playing at the frog. This position of the little finger fulfills an important function when drawing the bow and allows the other fingers to be positioned naturally. However, pedagogues often will not pay enough attention to the position of the little finger or make do with its initial defects in positioning. This consequently leads to innumerable difficulties in mastering right-hand technique. When the bow nears the frog, the little finger must balance the weight of the bow in its curved position. Because it is difficult for beginners to keep the little finger round while balancing the weight of the bow, the little finger will often straighten and stiffly press against the stick. This impairs the correct functioning of all the other fingers. A good positioning should ensure that the little finger is able to execute all the necessary bending and straightening motions while simultaneously balancing the weight of the bow.

When drawing the bow from the middle to the tip, it is not necessary to keep the little finger on the bow. Since the bow's center of gravity is distributed differently, the bow lies naturally on the string and doesn't require the little finger for balance. However, in practice, many teachers often demand that the little finger still be kept on the bow even when playing at the tip. In most cases this causes the wrist to bend excessively, especially for those with short arms.

It is important to remember that such "extreme positions of the wrist," as Yampolsky called them (referring to when the wrist is excessively high at the frog and pushed down at the tip), greatly limit freedom of movement in the right arm. The wrist should be slightly bent at the frog and perhaps slightly indented at the tip. If the wrist indents too much at the tip, it becomes difficult to get out of this position to play an up-bow. In this case, the natural movement of the forearm is replaced by movement of the upper arm when playing détaché in the upper half of the bow. Consequently, only violinists with very long arms are able to keep the little finger relaxed on the bow when playing at the tip.[20]

It is essential to comprehend the main differences in positioning the hand at the frog and at the tip. At the frog the fingers are slightly bent; at the tip they are straighter. Likewise, the thumb is curved at the frog and straight at the tip, and naturally the angle of the wrist in relation to the bow is sharper at the tip. When the bow is held freely, the transition from one position to the other should occur effortlessly. A tense grip causes the fingers to remain fixed in one position, limiting the freedom of movement.

The correct position of the index finger on the bow is very important. When the index finger is held too deeply (with the first phalange lying on the stick), the flexibility of the wrist is constricted, especially at the frog. In his treatise Flesch presents three ways of holding the bow: the old German school, holding the bow with the tips of the fingers; the Franco-Belgian school, where the bow is held a little deeper, and the Russian school, where the bow is held deeper still (although it still does not go beyond the joint connecting the first and second phalanges of the index finger).[21]

Of course there are other individual ways of holding the bow, but they are not typical for use as reference points. Some violinists, for example, hold the bow very deeply, in contradiction to the general rules. It would seem that this would cause cramped playing at the frog. Yet, even in this situation, good violinists can master all the necessary bow strokes by compensating with a high position of the elbow, allowing the wrist to move slightly differently. This example once again shows that all elements in positioning are intertwined and underlines the necessity of working them out carefully to avoid hasty conclusions.

The bow stick should be slightly tilted toward the fingerboard. This is because the string provides more resistance to the bow near the bridge and is "softer" near the fingerboard. Moreover, the strings are not drawn parallel to the fingerboard—they are lower at the nut and significantly higher at the bridge. Thus, when the bow is tilted, it meets with the most resistance, and the string is able to withstand greater pressure. Consequently, it becomes possible to make greater dynamic changes while maintaining a good quality of sound. It is interesting to note that, in playing the cello, the bow stick is similarly inclined toward the fingerboard according to the same principles, even though the positioning of the instrument and right hand are completely different.

Observing the bow move from the frog to the tip, one finds that the angle of inclination is greater at the frog and less at the tip. This is explained by the fact that at the frog, the sound is produced mostly with the weight of the arm and bow, and it is unnecessary to use the entire stretch of bow hair. Conversely, at the tip, it is necessary to exert more pressure and use more bow hair to sustain a full sound. This explains why the bow is tilted less at the tip. In playing *piano* it is not necessary to use all the bow hair. However, when playing *forte* and increasing the pressure without changing the angle of the bow, the hair will compress naturally, lying completely on the string.

The angle of inclination of the bow is also related to the performer's habit of tightening the bow: the tighter the bow, the greater the angle, and vice versa. The artistic goals of the performer play an important role in determining the tension of the hair. As an example one can compare the interpretative styles of such leading violinists as Fritz Kreisler, Pablo de Sarasate, and Karol Gregorowicz. Kreisler played with an extremely tight bow that was tilted at a significant angle. He generally did not employ extremely broad strokes, but his sound was full and intense, distinguished by its richness and expression. Sarasate did not significantly tighten the bow. His sound came almost exclusively from the weight of the bow (he played with a heavy bow), and he used long, light strokes. Gregorowicz, who possessed incredible lightness and freedom in the right hand, played in a manner similar to Sarasate. It is rumored that while warming up he would play the prelude from Bach's E Major Partita using the entire bow almost up to tempo.

Turning to the question of drawing the bow, it is necessary to clearly understand which parts of the arm are involved in making sure the bow moves freely and in which sequence they proceed. In this respect the general rule that separate parts of the arm should not move in isolation is confirmed. Analyzing the movement of the bow from the frog to the tip, we find that it begins with an immediate straightening of the wrist. Consequently the forearm becomes involved, and at the tip the shoulder moves forward a little, with a slight auxiliary motion. This shoulder motion must indeed be auxiliary and not created artificially (the student shouldn't pay special attention to this motion in order to avoid caricature-like exaggerations). If the arms are perfectly relaxed, this will occur naturally.

When the bow is drawn from the tip to the frog, the process occurs in reverse. First the forearm moves as the shoulder slightly withdraws. Then the shoulder follows through as the wrist simultaneously bends. When the frog is reached, the fingers curve to maintain the correct direction of the bow. Only the interaction of all these movements can ensure the bow is drawn in a straight line.

In order to better understand these consecutive movements, such pedagogues as Konstantin Mostras and Hugo Bekker suggested the following clever method: while the teacher holds the bow, the student slides his or her hand along the stick, as on a track, making note of the correct corresponding movements. This helps the student overcome the usual errors in the early stages of bowing, such as moving the arm too far backward or forward. In running the hand along the stick of the bow, the student cannot grip the stick with the fingers. This helps overcome an inborn reflex to grasp the bow and cultivates a relaxed hold and freedom in bowing.

Taking into account the difficulties that beginners commonly encounter in playing at the frog, Mostras recommends starting the bow strokes at the middle of the bow, and then widening in both directions (tip to the frog). One may also recommend starting the strokes with an up-bow.

Now it is necessary to touch upon the problem of bow changes. It makes sense to focus on this after the regular strokes are stable and drawn correctly and freely. Because the problem of changing the bow unnoticeably is delicate and complicated, it is often consciously put aside during the beginning stages of study. The opinion that one cannot immediately demand smooth bow changes is correct. However, pedagogues often incorrectly apply this example to other problems. Thus, it is not uncommon to hear teachers assert that it is impossible to demand beginners to play in tune, since out-of-tune playing is seemingly natural in the early stages of study. Under these circumstances the student will never play in tune, as is often proved in practice. The student's ear must be tuned to both intonation and tone quality from the earliest stages of teaching.

Incidentally, in practice, these two issues often become separate from one another; the student may correct notes that are out of tune while paying no attention to an unpleasant sound. However, if the student is educated to be demanding of him- or herself, it will consequently make the teacher's work easier. Most importantly the student must be taught to listen to him- or herself.

This is essential not only for developing good intonation but also for improving the tone quality.

Auxiliary movements in the fingers (the so-called *fingerstriche*) play an important role in achieving imperceptible bow changes. It is, of course, possible to change the bow without the *fingerstriche*; however it makes sense to use it. In this stroke, the upward motion of the hand is broken into two components. At the end of an up-bow at the frog the arm stops, but the fingers keep moving up. As the movement reaches a "dead end" (when the fingers stop on the bow), the arm has already begun moving in the opposite direction. This makes the connection less angular and consequently less audible.

The ability to change bows inaudibly is essential to cantilena playing. To a great extent this ability determines the general level of right-hand technique and overall quality of sound, and it requires a great deal of work. This is why it is necessary to practice moving the bow slowly and playing (or "holding") long notes.

A change of bow might be audible for two reasons. The first, primarily concerning the change at the frog, is usually caused by the arm changing direction too late. In order to avoid an audible gap, the arm movement should occur with the help of the connecting finger-stroke, at the very last moment of the up-bow. The other reason, as the violinist Myron Poliakin points out, is the loss of contact with the bow hair at the point of change. In summary, this article essay has presented some expedient principles of positioning that create favorable conditions for developing necessary skills in playing the violin. These are the principles used by the author in his pedagogical practice.

NOTES

1. The term "positioning" in this context is a translation of the Russian word *postanovka*. *Postanovka* derives from the Russian verb *postavit'* (to place, put, arrange) and refers to the setup of the arms, hands, and body when establishing the violin and bow hold. This term is translated throughout the text interchangeably as "positioning" or "setup." —*Translator's note.*

2. The term "shoulder" is used in the anatomical sense, meaning the shoulder bone (specifically the section of the arm from the shoulder to the elbow joint). This term often leads to confusion, since even in specialized methodological works the "shoulder" may refer to both the shoulder bone and the shoulder in the everyday sense of the of the word. *The shoulder bone referred to in this context is the humerus bone. —Translator's addition in italics.*

3. Ion Voiku, *Postroenie estestvennoi sistemy skripichnoi igry (tekhnika levoi ruki). Perevod s Nem. V. N. Rimskogo-Korsakova* (The Formation of a Natural System of Violin Playing (Left-Hand Technique), trans. V. N. Rimsky-Korsakov

(from the German) (Moscow: n.p., 1930); B. Mikhailovsky, *Novii put' skripa-cha* (New Directions for the Violinist) (Moscow: n.p., 1934). The first name of B. Mikhailovsky is unknown as is further information about Ion Voiku, who appears not related to the recognized Romanian violinist of the same name Ion Voicu (1923 – 1997) —*Translator's note.*

4. Joseph Joachim and Andreas Moser, *Violinschule* (Berlin: N. Simrock, 1905).

5. The term "music school" implies a beginning or preparatory school, as opposed to a college or university. —*Translator's note.*

6. Leopold Mozart, *Osnovatel'noe skripichnoe uchilishche/perevod s nem* (Fundamental Violin Treatise) (translated from German) (Saint Petersburg, n.p., 1804).

7. Bartolomeo Campagnoli, *Neue Methode der fortschreitenden Fingerfertigkeit* (Leipzig: Breitkopf und Härtel, 1797).

8. Leopold Auer, *Graded Course of Violin Playing: A Complete Outline of Violin Study for Individual and Class Instruction* (New York: Carl Fischer, 1926).

9. Joachim and Moser, *Violinschule.*

10. Gustave Koeckert, *Rationelle Violintechnik* (Leipzig: Breitkopf & Härtel, 1909).

11. Viktor Valter, *Kak uchit' igre na skripke* (How to Teach Violin Playing), 3rd ed. (St. Petersburg: n.p., 1910).

12. Boris Struve, *Tipovye formy postanovki ruk u instrumentalistov: Smichkovaia gruppa* (Typical Forms of Positioning the Hands of Instrumentalists: Bowed Instrument Group) (Moscow: n.p., 1932).

13. Voiku, *Postroenie estestvennoi sistemy skripichnoi igry (tekhnika levoi ruki). Perevod s Nem. V. N. Rimskogo-Korsakova.*

14. The term "pad" here is taken to also include the abundant variety of cushions and shoulder rests that are placed between the violin and shoulder. Yankelevich's students used a metal shoulder rest covered in nylon that was slanted toward the shoulder. —*Translator's note.*

15. L. Nemirovsky, *Mekhanicheskie i psikhologicheskie momenty v osnovnykh prie-makh skripichnoi tekhniki* (Mechanical and Psychological Moments in Violin Technique) (Moscow: n.p., 1915).

16. Leopold Auer, *Moia shkola igry na skripke* (Violin Playing as I Teach It) (Moscow: Muzyka, 1965); and *Interpretatsiia proizvedenii skripichnoi klassiki* (Violin Masterworks and Their Interpretation) (Moscow: n.p., 1964).

17. The author is referring to the top section of the frog where it connects to the bow stick. —*Translator's note.*

18. The author is referring to the U-shaped hollow at the top of the frog. —*Translator's note.*

19. Struve, *Tipovye formy postanovki ruk u instrumentalistov.*

20. As an example one can refer to the famous violinist Joseph Szigeti, who had such long arms that when playing at the tip, his forearm was perpendicular to his shoulder (an angle most violinists encounter at the middle of the bow). This explains why Szigeti never needed to lift his little finger; it never caused him any difficulties.

21. Carl Flesch, *Iskusstvo skripichnoi igry* (The Art of Violin Playing) (Moscow, n.p., 1964).

2

Shifting Positions in Conjunction with the Musical Goals of the Violinist

YURI YANKELEVICH ■

The problem of shifting positions is one of the most important problems in violin playing and requires a thorough and multifaceted study. Studying this or any other technical problem is not productive without constantly focusing on and submitting to musical goals. This is precisely the basis of the following work, which discusses various methodological matters associated with shifting and also analyzes shifts in specific musical contexts.

The range of questions related to shifting is quite diverse. The following detailed analysis of these questions attempts, where possible, to list and classify various views on the subject in the methodological literature, both past and present. The result of this analysis is a series of suggestions that have been tested many times in this author's pedagogical practice. These suggestions may form the basis for creating a more rational method for teaching beginners in addition to correcting problems that were previously established.

1. GENERAL PERCEPTION OF THE POSITIONS. DIFFERENT SYSTEMS OF DIVIDING THE FINGERBOARD AND THEIR MODIFICATIONS IN THE EVOLUTION OF VIOLIN PLAYING.

A *position* is defined as that part of the fingerboard on which the position of the first finger on any string corresponds to a particular interval in relation to the open string. Thus, a second equals first position, a third equals second position, a fourth equals third position, and so on. The general number of positions on the fingerboard comes to between ten and twelve, and of these the more commonly used are the first seven. Dividing the fingerboard into positions is, to a certain degree, relative. Thus, depending on the tonality, the interval determining first position could either be a minor, a major, or an augmented second. Likewise, the interval determining second position could be a diminished, a minor, a major, or an augmented (in tonalities containing the notes B♯, F×, etc.) third. Third position could be determined by a diminished, a perfect, or an augmented fourth, and so on. The interval determining the position remains constant only in those circumstances when the tonic of the major scale is played on the G string with the first or fourth finger. In this case, the transfer of the first finger across the perfect fifths is consistent over the course of the two octaves that comprise the position. This also applies to major scales in first position starting on the open string.

The system of dividing the fingerboard into positions changed considerably as violin playing evolved. In Carlo Tessarini's treatise from 1750, the fingerboard was divided into three principal positions.[1] The first of these corresponds to today's accepted second position, the second to today's third position, and the third to today's seventh position.[2] The division of the fingerboard into only three positions is explained by a primitive idea of how the left hand can move along the fingerboard. For example, according to this treatise, in order to reach seventh position the whole arm needs to move directly from third position, that is, shifting from the note D played with the fourth finger on the E string to the subsequent note E played with the first finger.

In Leopold Mozart's treatise published in 1756, we already find the idea of positions to be more developed.[3] Mozart speaks of many positions (corresponding to those in use today) and calls them "fingerings." He differentiates the odd positions from even positions in respect to their practical use, describing odd positions as using a "whole fingering," and even positions as using a "half fingering."

In accordance with the level of violin technique of his time, Mozart considers scalar passages to be the primary means of moving the left hand. Thus he refers to movements that incorporate shifts and are not scalar sequences as being exceptional circumstances and the most difficult. In scalar sequences, Mozart recommends using alternating fingers, generally the first and second fingers, and in some cases the third and fourth fingers. Mozart considers it possible to use both "fingerings" (i.e., the "whole" and "half") and introduces a special term for this called "mixed fingering." The examples of mixed fingerings that Mozart provides are associated with the successive use of odd and even positions in sequential passages.

In 1797 Bartolomeo Campagnoli 's treatise appeared, in which he similarly divided the fingerboard into "whole" and "half" fingerings.[4] By dividing the fingerboard this way it became necessary to speak of first, second, third, and so on whole fingerings and of first, second, third, and so on half fingerings, which naturally was a bit cumbersome. Clearly for this reason Campagnoli also categorized each position with a letter that corresponded to the highest note in that position. Thus, Campagnoli labeled second position as half finger-ing or C fingering, third position as whole fingering or D fingering, fourth position as half fingering or E fingering, fifth position as whole fingering or F fingering, and so forth.

Louis Spohr considered the division of the fingerboard into half and whole fingerings very confusing. In his treatise he resolutely advocates the terminol-ogy adopted by the French school of naming the different positions of the hand as first, second, third, and so forth.[5] This logical idea of naming the positions according to their order along the fingerboard has remained until this day. However, this has not at all changed the conditional nature of a true under-standing the positions, and in this respect all attempts to define their essence have not yet been successful.

For example, Joseph Joachim defines first position by the so-called place-ment of the second, whereby the first finger of the left hand is placed on the string at the interval of a second from the open string in a given key.[6] This could be a major second (in D and G major), a minor second (in E♭, A♭ major, etc.), and an augmented second (in C♯ major on the three lower strings). In this respect we may speak of three different positions of the left hand in first posi-tion: low, normal, and high.

Leopold Auer, in contrast to Joachim, views the positions as unrelated to the tonality.[7] Using the position of the hand in C major as an example, Auer does not recognize that the intervals (in relation to the open string) that form the basis for these positions may vary. Yet it is clear that if, for example, in second position on the G string the first finger is placed on the note B♮, then the interval from the open string is a major third, while if the first finger plays the note F♮ on the D string then the interval that determines the position becomes a minor third (a major third on the D string would already be characteristic of an ele-vated placement). Thus, Auer's suggested system also does not remove the dis-crepancies associated with characterizing the positions and their framework.

Karl Davidov presents an interesting system of dividing the fingerboard in his cello treatise.[8] While Auer used the key of C major in constructing his sys-tem of positions across all strings, Davidov determined the positions accord-ing to the major tonality of each individual string (see Example 2.1).

In practice, however, it is difficult to imagine a case where each string adheres to its own tonality. Naturally, when the tonality changes, the structure

Example 2.1

Example 2.2

Example 2.3

of Davidov's system inevitably falls apart and thus this system also turns out to be conditional.

These examples show that the systems we examined are not able to clearly differentiate one position from another. On the one hand, various placements of the hand may correspond to one position as in Example 2.2. On the other hand, an identical placement of the hand may belong to different positions if the notes are enharmonically substituted. This is obvious in Example 2.3 taken from Flesch's treatise, in which Flesch poses the question—is the hand in second or third position?[9]

Thus it becomes understandable why many pedagogues search for new ways to divide the fingerboard. One such attempt is an interesting system suggested by Israel Yampolsky.[10] This system is based not on the diatonic scale (which determines the positions according to whole and half-steps) but on the chromatic scale. Yampolsky arrives at the completely justified conclusion that, since "the chromatic alternation of a note by a half-step with the same finger (such as the first or fourth which form the borders of the position) inevitably creates a change in the hand's placement, it is essential to reexamine and define the current systems of dividing the fingerboard." Yampolsky writes:

The enharmonic substitution of a note or a series of notes retaining an identical fingering, is not sufficient grounds for categorizing them in another position. For example:

Example 2.4

Yet the common system categorizes both these examples as belonging to different positions, as though the hand changes its location, while in reality it does not.[11]

According to Yampolsky's suggested system, each position is clearly delineated from another only by one specific tonality in that position, that in which the first finger lies on the tonic on the G string.[12] Yet, other tonalities may require a combination of positions, and an augmented fourth would need to replace the perfect fourth between the first and fourth fingers. Thus the chromatic half-step system of determining positions also turns out to be conditional.

In practice there are numerous examples where musical and technical considerations require the hand to be placed on the fingerboard in a way that cannot be defined by one specific position, taken in the normal sense of spanning a fourth (see Examples 2.5–2.7).

Often, we use a position of the hand where the distance between the first and fourth fingers creates the interval of a fifth. The widespread use of this technique allows us to speak of a "fifth-wide" (alongside a "fourth-wide") position

Example 2.5 Brahms: *Violin Concerto, mvt. 1.*

Example 2.6 Kreisler: *Recitativo and Scherzo.*

Example 2.7 Khachaturian: *Violin Concerto, mvt. 3.*

of the hand. There are numerous examples of a fifth-wide position of the hand throughout the literature (see Examples 2.8–2.11).

Example 2.8 Rimsky-Korsakov: *Concert Fantasia on Russian Themes.*

Example 2.9 Rimsky-Korsakov: *Scheherazade.*

Example 2.10 Glazunov: *Violin Concerto.*

Example 2.11 Tchaikovsky: *Violin Concerto, mvt. 1.*

A fifth-wide position presents difficulties only for violinists with small hands, and even then only in the lower positions. It creates no difficulties in the higher positions, and in the very highest positions it turns out to be even easier than a fourth-wide position. In his treatise, Carl Flesch cautions against the fourth-wide position turning into a fifth-wide position when practicing stretches between the first and fourth fingers.[13] However, this should not be understood as a rejection of the commonly used fifth-wide position, but simply as a caution against the overuse of stretches that may distort the perception of distances on the fingerboard, which nonetheless are still based on the fourth-wide position.

It is significant that Otakar Ševčík, in his numerous exercises aimed at a multifaceted development of violin technique, advises studying not only fourth-wide but also fifth-wide positions (see Example 2.12)[14]

Example 2.12 Ševčík: *School of Violin Technique, opus 1, book 2.*

In each position it is possible to play notes lying outside the limits of that position. The higher the position, the greater the possibility of playing notes lying outside the position. This is done using one of two techniques—either the so-called *extension* (i.e., stretching the first finger down or the fourth finger up; see Examples 2.13 and 2.14) or by sliding the finger along the string (see Example 2.15).

Example 2.13 Popper (Auer): *Spinning Song.*

Example 2.14 Paganini: *Caprice No. 3.*

Example 2.15 Rimsky-Korsakov (Zimbalist): *The Golden Cockerel Fantasy.*

When the note lying in another position is reached with the help of an extension, then the wrist and forearm may lean slightly in the direction of the extended finger as in Example 2.16.

Example 2.16 Vitali (Charlier): *Chaconne.*

However, in this case the first finger stays in place. It is necessary to emphasize that there is a big difference between this leaning movement of the hand and that which takes place when shifting positions, since in the latter case the entire arm moves, including the forearm, wrist, and fingers.

As illustrated earlier, it is possible to place the fingers in different positions while retaining the same placement of the hand. In cases of enharmonic substitution (where theoretically the designation of the position should change), the fingers and the hand remain practically in the same place.

At the same time the opposite phenomenon may be observed: moving the fingers a half-step could either be accompanied by an entire displacement of the hand (forearm, wrist, and fingers) or may only involve sliding a finger in the framework of the same position (as in a chromatic scale). Taking all this into account, one may readily agree with Jean Delphin Alard's idea that a position be defined as that placement of the hand that, without changing, permits all the required notes in a phrase or passage to be executed.[15]

David Oistrakh presents a particularly interesting point of view. He suggests envisioning the positions as zones, with a zone encompassing all the possible placements of the hand in one position—low, normal, and high. This characterization unites both types of fingering, since the outer limits of the zone would be defined by a fifth-wide position. Oistrakh did not associate the fifth-wide position only with arpeggios; in practice he often used this position in diatonic sequences by sliding one of the fingers a half-step.

Consequently, in practice it is the movement of the entire arm in carrying out specific musical tasks that is important and not the numerical delineation of positions. Konstantin Mostras expressed this aptly when he remarked that, for a violinist who has mastered the instrument, it does not matter to which positions the notes belong since playing is directly connected to the sonic realization of musical thought. Many competent violinists experience difficulties if asked to shift, for example, from the second finger in first position on the E string to the fourth finger in ninth position. Yet, at the same time this shift is easily accomplished if the positions are not named and only the pitches are given.

We may conclude that all systems of dividing the fingerboard to this day are entirely relative, and any search for new systems is counterproductive. This is especially so considering that actual musical performance is never tied to the necessity of classifying the positions, although the latter may serve a purpose in the beginning stages of study.

2. SHIFTING AND THE PROBLEM OF INTONATION. THE AURAL PERCEPTION OF INTERVALS AND ITS ROLE IN DEVELOPING A SENSE OF DISTANCE ON THE FINGERBOARD.

Clean intonation is absolutely essential to artistic interpretation, for otherwise neither the beauty of sound, finesse of a phrase nor clarity of form can produce their desired effect. Turning to the matter at hand, it is necessary to first analyze the general rules that establish the basis for clean intonation while shifting. Similar to any other untempered instrument, the particularity of the violin naturally allows free intonation. This leads each performer to develop a personal intonation determined by the individual interpretation of the music (this is convincingly proven by Nikolai Garbuzov).[16]

The ear determines accurate intonation. This is why precisely the ear must guide the accuracy of movements in the left hand, with the assistance of the corresponding muscular sensations that arise. A *conditioned reflex for distance* is created in the process of mastering shifting. This means that corresponding coordinated relationships are established between the perception of a sound and the movement of the hand that enables the desired note to be attained in the new position. The correct movement is determined by the accuracy of the pitch attained. A discrepancy between the actual and conceived sound requires a repetition of the movement until an accurate movement develops that leads to clean intonation. It should be noted that when shifting from one position to another, accurate intonation is established not so much through the immediate action of the fingers as it is by the movement of other parts of the arm—the wrist, forearm, and shoulder. Coordinated relationships are also established between all these movements.

Flesch believed that to achieve clean intonation, the arrival note in the new position must be lengthened so that it may be checked and corrected.[17] However, it is difficult to agree with this approach. Such a method makes it impossible to cultivate a "reflex for accurate arrival," since the sensation of distance covered by the arm is not studied and thus not secured. In contrast, Mostras's opinion related to the study of conditioned reflexes may be considered more correct.[18] Mostras notes that it is not enough to just correct the faulty note. Instead, the shift needs to be repeated many times in order to more reliably remember the interval and the nature of the movement.

The distance between the fingers widens and narrows depending on which part of the fingerboard the notes are located. As a result of the coordinated reflexes that are established, an automatic feeling for the change in distance between the fingers develops, which leads to accurate intonation even in large and quick shifts. This is all a part of *knowing the fingerboard*. This also explains why some violinists with highly developed aural-motor coordination have the ability to play in tune on smaller violins. Consequently, the decisive point determining accurate intonation while shifting turns out to be establishing coordination between the movement of the left hand and the ear, which controls and directs these movements.

The use of any kind of supportive devices during studies that replace aural regulation should be seen as underestimating the role of the ear. Excluding the ear to any extent and orienting the student to use, even if only temporarily, alternate supporting elements hinders the natural development of aural-motor coordination, which is one of the most important elements in violin playing.

However, there are some who recognize the use of these kinds of "supportive" devices (an example is feeling the body of the violin with the palm of the hand when shifting to third position). This kind of approach is notably expressed in the method of August Leopold Sass.[19] Proceeding from a purely mechanical observation of where the fingers "press," Sass replaces aural perception and aural control of intonation with the marking of the fingerboard! For example, when setting up the beginner's left hand, Sass indicates that the first finger should be at the nut, the second finger approximately 44 millimeters from the nut, the third finger at 79 millimeters, and the fourth finger at 93 millimeters. It is perfectly clear that such indications may only be considered as examples of sterile mechanics.

3. PARTICULARITIES OF MOVING THE LEFT HAND ALONG THE FINGERBOARD AND CHANGING POSITIONS IN VARIOUS PARTS OF THE FINGERBOARD—IN SEARCH OF THE MOST EFFICIENT TECHNIQUES.

A clear understanding of efficient procedures and correct movements should lie at the root of all technique. In this light, let us examine the movements associated with shifting positions. Shifting is of paramount importance in practice and requires an appropriate analysis of the principal movements of the left hand and arm.

Ideas about the character and nature of left-hand motion developed rather peculiarly and inconsistently in violin pedagogy. For example, in the early treatises such as Campagnoli's, we find an indication describing ascending movement as beginning with the index finger, and then the thumb and rest of the hand immediately follow.[20] Campagnoli's opinion was founded purely on outward appearances rather than on any kind of serious analysis. This may be explained by the state of violin pedagogy in his time, when methodological matters were only starting to develop. But it is surprising that some imprecise, and even erroneous, ideas about left-hand movement are still encountered today, even among well-known pedagogue violinists.

In this regard, one may first cite Siegfried Eberhardt.[21] In his study of exercises for changing positions, Eberhardt notes that the wrist and fingers, which seem at first glance to play a leading role, are in reality not involved in arriving accurately at the note. Therefore, instead of being active they should simply passively follow the direction of the arm. However, Eberhardt's opinion cannot be considered correct in all cases. This is easily illustrated by analyzing the movement of the hand in the highest positions where precisely the wrist is the active component.

Gustave Koeckert presents an opposite point of view.[22] In his violin method, Koeckert states that the movement of shifting in fact originates from the wrist joint; the movement starts in the wrist and then later the arm becomes involved. However, one also cannot agree with Koeckert. In determining the wrist as the leading component and the arm as passive, he applies this principle to all positions, while in reality it may only be considered correct in the higher positions.

Flesch, who gave this matter a lot of attention, believed that shifting involved covering a specific, strictly determined distance. In the lower positions (up until the fourth) only the forearm is involved, whereas in the higher positions the shoulder, wrist, and thumb are included. In an article from 1947, P. Radmall almost identically reinstates this point of view presented by Flesch in 1923.[23] L. Nemirovsky also sides with Flesch by noting that in the first three positions the wrist and forearm move together, "isolated from the shoulder."[24]

It is easy to see the inaccuracy of this opinion by performing the following experiment: Sit at a table and hold the violin in normal playing position, with the elbow fixed against the table and the first finger placed, say, in first position on the note B on the A string. Then shift from first to third position (i.e., moving the first finger to the note D) and note that the violin will move upward. By fixating the elbow on the table, we isolate the shoulder from being involved in the hand's movement from first to third position. Corresponding regulatory movement in the shoulder is necessary for the violin not to move. This regulatory movement should either allow the elbow to lower when moving from first to third position or, conversely, to rise when moving back from third to first position.

Thus it becomes clear that the most efficient way to move the hand in the lower part of the fingerboard is by using the forearm together with obligatory involvement of the shoulder. The particularity of this movement is that the shoulder's role is purely auxiliary, only regulating the direction of the primary movement. The wrist and fingers, which may appear to be directly producing the motion, in reality are simply being guided. It is the forearm that plays the principal role in this movement and determines its correct direction along the fingerboard.

Inadequate attention to these principles may create a whole series of difficulties in working on specific problems. For example, it is a common mistake to lift the violin when shifting in the first four positions. This lifting is simply explained by an insufficient or lacking involvement of the shoulder. Similarly, the opposite phenomenon of lowering the violin may be observed, which is caused by an overly active shoulder. These problems make shifting more difficult and restrict freedom and agility. Moreover, the wavering position of the violin affects the stability of the bow on the strings and creates unfavorable conditions for the right arm, especially when calm and smooth movements of the bow are required, such as in legato passages.

This analysis of the movement of the left hand and arm in the first four positions illustrates the necessity of involving the shoulder and strictly coordinating the movement of the shoulder and the forearm. However, it should be understood that the shoulder movement, though important, is only an auxiliary element in the general movement of the arm. While it should not be restricted, it should also not be overemphasized.

In his eight-volume work on violin playing, Leopold Auer recommends a high position for the violin, which provides considerable freedom for the fingers of the left hand in fast passages and while shifting.[25] Without going into the efficiency of this recommendation, we will simply note that a high position of the violin, achieved by slightly drawing the left arm away from the body, allows the shoulder to be free and able to participate in the aforementioned general movement of the arm during shifts. It is interesting that even in Campagnoli's old treatise, which states that the left arm should be drawn close to the torso, there are indications that it should move away from this position only when shifting positions.

When analyzing the nature of each movement, it is necessary to understand not only what the individual components of the movement are but also the respective role that each component plays. Thus, if the forearm plays the leading role in shifting and instead the player tries to use extra movements in the fingers, the result is a loss of agility. For in this case, each finger, rather than fulfilling only one function (i.e., dropping onto the string), instead is obligated to fulfill another active role by also anticipating the movement of the arm and wrist.

However, the forearm plays the leading role only in the first four positions. When shifting in the upper part of the fingerboard, the movements of the forearm are absent since the body of the violin stops the forearm from moving closer to the torso. In this case the wrist must be very active, and its flexibility accommodates the required changes of position.

It is simple to determine whether only the wrist is involved when shifting in the upper part of the fingerboard by using the same experiment mentioned earlier. Hold the violin in playing position with the elbow fixed on the table, as explained in the first experiment, and place the first finger on the note E^3 on the E string (seventh position) and shift to the note B^3 on the same string (ninth position). In this case we notice that the shift is accomplished easily. However, if we then try to put the fourth finger down in the new position on the note E^4, we find it impossible. For the fourth finger to reach the fingerboard it becomes necessary to lift the elbow from the table and free the shoulder. The shoulder then makes the supportive motion inward (in the direction of the right arm), allowing all the fingers to find their necessary position on the string. The extent of this shoulder movement increases as the distance of the shift widens. When moving from high positions to lower ones in the same area (approximately fifth position), the shoulder makes an opposite movement to the left.

Consequently, both the shoulder and the wrist are involved when changing positions in the upper part of the fingerboard. As already noted, the forearm almost doesn't move in the upper part of the fingerboard, since it is restricted by the body of the violin. The forearm moves only slightly in tandem with the shoulder motion. The main movements in this case are those of the wrist. Similar to shifts in the lower part of the fingerboard, the fingers simply follow. The shoulder movement, ensuring normal finger action in the attained position, is purely supportive. Thus, the shoulder is involved in both the lower and upper parts of the fingerboard. In the first case it lifts and lowers, and in the second case it moves to the right or the left.

The following chart illustrates the combination of the separate components of movement in the left hand in different parts of the fingerboard (see Table 2.1).

Table 2.1. Separate components of movement in the left hand in different parts of the fingerboard.

	Lower part of the fingerboard	Upper part of the fingerboard
Leading element	Forearm	Wrist (hand)
Guided element	Wrist (hand) and fingers	Fingers
Supportive element	Shoulder (vertical movement)	Shoulder (horizontal movement)

Our analysis of separate components of movement in the left hand in different parts of the fingerboard reveals the reasons for the contradictions found in the specialized literature, including in the views of Koeckert, Eberhardt, and others. These contradictions turn out to be based on exaggerating the role of one element (and generalizing it for all parts of the fingerboard) and underestimating the roles of other elements.

After examining the different components of shifting movement in the left hand in both the lower and the upper sections of the fingerboard, it is also necessary to determine the movement that connects these different placements of the hand. When shifting in the upper positions, this connection is made by moving the left shoulder inward (to the right), allowing for the aforementioned movement of the wrist. This shoulder movement causes the wrist to lift slightly above the fingerboard while simultaneously the thumb comes under the neck of the violin. Meanwhile, the base of the index finger draws away from the fingerboard. Naturally, when gradually shifting from the upper part of the fingerboard to the lower, these movements are reversed. Also, the connecting movement of the shoulder toward the right should occur not together with the shift but slightly earlier, effectively becoming a preparatory movement.

In large shifts that require big swings in the arm, the shoulder assumes the leading role. In contrast, small shifts, such as those between adjacent positions, may occur only by moving the wrist. In the latter case the forearm and shoulder are kept practically immobile, and sometimes even just the finger moves, with the wrist barely involved. However, the decision to use these small movements largely depends on the musical context. Thus, when shifting to an adjacent position and remaining there for a while, it is better to move the entire arm and not just the finger or wrist (see Example 2.17).

Example 2.17 Wieniawski: Etude.

If the subsequent music requires a quick return to the initial position, then it is more effective to shift with the finger or the wrist without moving the thumb or forearm. It is important to keep in mind that the performer's individual adaptation plays a big role in accomplishing these kinds of shifts.

In those cases where it is necessary to make many small consecutive shifts in one direction, the general principle of moving the hand and arm remains the same as already described for different sections of the fingerboard. The only difference is more complex work in the fingers.

In sequential changes of position (such as scales), all the placements of the hand we examined are connected. However, when shifting immediately from a low position to a much higher one (or the opposite), we observe corresponding changes in how the hand moves. Thus, for example, when making the shift in Example 2.18, the hand, while still in half position, already assumes that shape that allows it to easily come around the body of the violin for a quick shift. Conversely when making a "leap" immediately from a high position to a low one, the hand retains the shape it assumed in the initial high position for practically the entire duration of the shift. Only when approaching the lower position does it assume the shape corresponding to the new position. This occurs especially when an intense and expressive sound is required, such as in Example 2.19.

Example 2.18 Paganini: *Witches's Dance.*

Example 2.19 Spohr: *Concerto No. 9, mvt. 1.*

The change in shape of the left hand is rather particular when playing a chromatic glissando with one finger. The hand does not miss one point of the fingerboard, passing either from a high position to a low position or, less commonly, from a low position to a high position. However, an analysis of this movement shows that in its essence it is similar to that movement that takes place in immediate shifts or "leaps" that connect the outer notes of the chromatic glissando. The only difference is that it occurs in slow motion.

Thus we have illustrated that the more effective processes of playing consist of different placements of the left hand in the lower and upper sections of the fingerboard that are connected using the appropriate movements.

An alternate point of view brought forth by some pedagogues of the Czech school, such as Bedřich Voldan, Jan Marak, and Viktor Nopp, suggests that an identical position of the left hand be used in both high and low positions.[26] This means the shape of the hand in the higher positions should be retained in the lower positions, that is, keeping the elbow drawn out with the base of the index finger pulled away from the neck and the thumb drawn underneath the violin neck. However, this creates an entirely unnatural shape for the left arm in the lower positions. The drawn-out elbow creates tension in the muscles of the forearm and the shoulder, causing serious difficulties, and therefore this position is not effective. Consequently, the only way of facilitating and simplifying the movement of the hand along the fingerboard when shifting is to consider the natural particularities of the hand's shape in different parts of the fingerboard.

4. RELAXED MOVEMENT AS AN ESSENTIAL CONDITION FOR REALIZING ARTISTIC INTENTIONS. AN ANALYSIS OF THE REASONS RESTRICTING THE MOVEMENT OF THE LEFT HAND WHILE CHANGING POSITIONS.

The violinist's movements are inextricably connected to the music performed—they are determined by the music and they produce the music. According to Konstantin Stanislavsky, these movements are essentially connected to the artistic idea as *physical manifestations* of the *ulterior goal*. Naturally, movements that are awkward, rigid, and tense restrict the realization of the player's musical intentions. Consequently, developing efficient playing movements is a necessary condition for musical performance, and the perfection of these movements largely depends on how relaxed and free they are.

Analyzing the conditions of free movement in the left hand, it is important to note that it is impossible to achieve a free and relaxed left hand without also freeing the right hand, relaxing the shoulder, relaxing the body, and so on.[27] This is why left-hand technique cannot be studied in isolation from the right hand and from all the other processes involved in violin playing.

There is no doubt that many problems in left-hand technique not only originate in the immediate vicinity but also can occur because of other phenomena that determine the regulatory process of the central nervous system. This should always be taken into consideration, particularly when analyzing various problems in performance.

Of the main restrictions in moving the left hand freely along the fingerboard, there are firstly problems of a purely mechanical nature, which are easily determined by simple observation. Secondly, there are other problems that lie beneath the surface and are related to an incorrect feeling of the movement (which may appear perfectly "correct" on the outside).

A common problem belonging to the first category is when the arm is held too close to the torso. This restricts the movement of the shoulder and consequently the movement of the entire hand along the fingerboard. Thus this problem, which appears to be purely external and disrupting the movement of the left arm, also restricts movement in the wrist and fingers.

Another common mistake belonging to the first category is when the palm presses against the body of the violin in third position and in the upper parts of the fingerboard. In contrast to the previous problem, this technique has many supporters and is often recommended in the literature, and for this reason it requires closer examination.

In many treatises already mentioned, such as those of Louis Spohr, Charles de Bériot, Ferdinand David, Joseph Joachim, and Andreas Moser, we find directions that require a point of contact between the palm of the hand and the body of the violin in third position. The motivation behind this is to establish a more secure position of the hand in respect to intonation as well as to easily find a point of support when shifting from first position to third position. However, later treatises, in particular the Russian ones by Iosef Lesman and Alexander Rezvetsov, believe this method to be inefficient. Rezvetsov even believes that the palm should stay clear of the body of the violin not just in third position but also in fourth position, where it naturally comes into contact.

The underestimation of many pedagogues of the consequences of leaning the left hand against the body of the violin in third position results in a variety of problems that affect the function of the left hand. These include a change in the shape of the wrist, which causes a change in the shape of the fingers and consequently changes the angle at which they drop in third position. This affects not only finger mobility but also intonation. Indeed, this is often the reason for faulty intonation in third position. Furthermore, this technique makes shifting from third position to a higher position more difficult since a preliminary movement of the wrist away from the body of the violin is now required. If the palm is not pressed against the body of the violin, then the shift may be executed without this extra unnecessary movement.

It is interesting that Joachim's view on the subject was twofold. In his treatise he states that when performing, for example, scales on one string, the intermediate positions (such as the third when shifting between first and fifth) should be considered transitional, and the hand should not press against the body of the violin since this would affect the smoothness of the passage. We should note that leaning the wrist against the violin restricts movement in the left hand not only when the passage is transitional but also when it is the point of departure. And yet, remaining faithful to the traditions of the classic German schools (i.e., those of Spohr and David), Joachim only partially recognized the problems of this technique.

Voldan's opinion is representative of widespread similar ideas in the violin methodology. While rejecting the principle of pressing the wrist against the violin and understanding all the consequent problems, he nevertheless considers the possibility of using this technique in the more advanced stages of study.[28] However, a technique that is rejected in principle, and even considered detrimental in the early stages of study, clearly cannot be recommended to a more advanced violinist who has already overcome the problem of accurately arriving in third position.

Pressing the wrist against the violin bout in the higher positions also restricts free movement in the left hand. This method was recommended by Ion Voiku, who believed that the closer the wrist presses against the bout, the more stable the base for moving the fingers, and the more accurately and confidently the fingers move along the fingerboard.[29] But pressing the wrist against the violin greatly restricts its movement. This is why Voiku suggested moving the wrist away from the bout and transferring the point of support to the thumb when vibrating. However, Voiku did not consider that any kind of free movement in the wrist is impossible when it is pressed close to the body of the violin.

In complete contradiction to Voiku, Lesman advised not touching the body of the violin at all.[30] However, it should be noted that some contact with the body of the violin does not necessarily restrict movement in the hand and may be observed in practice. Attempting to not touch the body of the violin at all may cause another undesired result, with the wrist being forced to flex excessively in the other direction. Thus Lesman's opinion is also in need of correction.

We will now turn to problems in the second category, those based on an incorrect feeling of the motor processes. These problems are generally associated with the manner of holding the violin and excessive pressure of the fingers on the string.

One widespread problem that invariably restricts free movement in the left hand is when the thumb and index finger squeeze the neck of the violin. The difficulty lies in the fact that it is impossible for them to completely relax, otherwise the instrument will fall into the hollow between the fingers, which is not an optimal position. Therefore the most important moment in solving this problem is to establish the minimal degree of effort required to hold the violin neck. This should ensure an optimal shape of the hand for correct finger motion while simultaneously not restricting the motor process.

We should note that the degree to which the violin neck is squeezed relates directly to how the violin is held with the chin. When the violin is held insufficiently underneath the chin, all the functions of supporting the violin are transferred to the left hand, which inevitably results in excessive gripping of the neck.

Because of these objective difficulties associated with holding the violin, there have been many attempts in the methodological literature to create a new setup for the left hand that would allow an alternate point of support for the neck of the violin. For example, Campagnoli suggested that the neck of the violin should be held not in the hollow of the hand between the thumb and index finger but rather resting primarily on the thumb. This method requires the elbow to be brought quite far underneath the violin. This is why Campagnoli required the elbow to be held as close to the torso as possible, with the point of the elbow almost at the middle of the chest.

However, keeping the elbow in this position only increases the unnatural position of the left arm, which is already awkward in this respect.[31] Excessively drawing in the elbow also significantly restricts free movement of the left hand along the fingerboard. In addition, bringing the point of the elbow to the middle of the chest turns out to be physically difficult, if not impossible, for most people. If such a distinguished virtuoso as Campagnoli stressed this method, this is most likely explained by his purely individual adaptation to the instrument. We should also note that for Campagnoli and the violin schools of his time, it was not characteristic to search for the most natural positions.

To a certain extent Campagnoli's views are similar to those presented above by exponents of the Czech school, who suggested keeping the position of the left arm identical in all positions, not letting the base of the index finger come into contact with the neck and letting the thumb be the main point of support. Even in today's performance and pedagogical practice, we sometimes encounter the idea that the base of the index finger should not touch the violin neck.

This type of position is entirely suitable to facilitate freedom in vibrato (which naturally presupposes a less frequent change of position). However, such a position of the hand creates significant instability in placing the fingers on the string and has an adverse effect on intonation during frequent changes of position.

Voiku's treatise is based on the correct idea that only free and natural movements of the body can form the basis for a solid technique. However, in this work there are a series of erroneous conclusions. In particular, Voiku suggests eliminating the thumb's involvement as much as possible when holding the violin. He claims that the thumb is only significant in high positions when it presses against the concavity of the neck and becomes a support for the fingers during vibrato, when the wrist is drawn away from the bout. Otherwise the violin neck should rest on the cushion of the first joint of the index finger, which Voiku believes is the natural point of support.

However, this leads to a whole series of negative consequences. Firstly, in avoiding the grasp between the thumb and index finger, Voiku creates another point of tension at the base of the index finger. Thus, eliminating the thumb does not guarantee that the neck is not squeezed with the other fingers.

Secondly, using the cushion at the base of the index finger as a point of support creates unfavorable conditions for vibrato. Incidentally, it should be noted that Voiku largely avoids the question of vibrato in his work. This might not be a coincidence, and could stem from his recommended way of holding the instrument.

Thirdly, eliminating the thumb inevitably causes the point of support to be transferred to the palm of the hand in the higher positions, leading to the problems we have already examined.

Fourthly, the serious problem with Voiku's suggestion is that the movement of the fingers as they drop onto the strings is always different. This creates significant obstacles in developing unified and consistent movements. These problems with Voiku's method show that it does not accommodate the playing movements required and thus remains purely theoretical.

B. Mikhailovsky's views on the setup of the left hand likewise raise objections.[32] In order to avoid gripping the violin neck, Mikhailovsky recommends that the neck rest in the hollow between the thumb and index finger where it can lie completely relaxed, as if in a "sling." But this position hinders efficient movement along the fingerboard, since it completely disrupts the correct positioning of the fingers. The first finger appears to elongate, making it virtually impossible to normally place it a half-step above the open string, and the fourth finger, which is already the shortest, becomes even shorter. A correct setup should stem from the need to provide more favorable conditions for the fourth finger. The length of the fourth finger makes such a difference that many teachers even believe it is sometimes unfruitful to teach a child the violin if his or her fourth finger is much shorter than all the others. Thus, Mikhailovsky's setup, just like Voiku's, is detached from practical performance. Consequently it loses its main purpose of ensuring the most efficient movements, and it cannot be employed without causing difficulties for the performer.

It should be emphasized that all the violin treatises, except for those of Campagnoli, Voiku, and Mikhailovsky, recommended holding the violin neck between the thumb and index finger, and this is the most widely used technique in practice. For example, the classical treatise of the Paris Conservatoire by Pierre Baillot, Pierre Rode and Rudolphe Kreutzer indicates that the violin should be supported with the first joint of the thumb and the third joint of the index finger, and held with the minimal amount of pressure so it does not fall into the hollow between the thumb and finger.[33] Baillot's treatise from 1834 provides even more detail, indicating a space between the skin that connects the thumb to the index finger and the neck of the violin, which is big enough for "the point of the bow to pass through."[34] Other exponents of the traditional and contemporary French schools, such as Alard, Hubert Leonard, and Jules Charles Pennequin, held similar views.[35]

This all contradicts Mikhailovsky's reasons for rejecting the left-hand position he believes to originate in the German school, which he saw as outdated and no longer in practical use. The above material shows that not only the German schools but also the classical and modern French schools use precisely the positioning he rejects.

Two contradictory points in the methodological literature deserve attention. On the one hand, the manner of holding the violin between the thumb and index finger seems to have historically evolved and solidified. Yet at the same time this has not stopped the search for a different way of holding the violin. This is explained by the fact that the violin neck is often gripped, as already described, which significantly restricts the freedom of the fingers. Attempts to avoid this problem led to the search for alternate ways to hold the violin neck. At the same time, we see that these attempts were misdirected and structured in a purely formalistic way. This is why they were not only unable to ensure better conditions for the fingers but also ended up creating more problems.

After analyzing the mechanism of how the fingers move, it is easy to see that the most efficient conditions are indeed created by holding the violin neck between the thumb and index finger. For this reason it is irrational to reject this setup. However, it is necessary to find those conditions that allow the neck to be held in this manner freely without gripping and tensing the fingers.

Let us now turn to another aspect of left-hand technique. As we know, the technique of the left hand is based, on the one hand, on the vertical movement of the fingers dropping on the string and, on the other hand, on the horizontal movement of the entire hand along the fingerboard. Mastering violin technique largely depends on being in command of both these movements and being able to coordinate them. It follows that both these movements should primarily be developed in conjunction with each other.

However, the majority of violin methods, including those by Campagnoli and Auer and in particular those of the German violinists Joachim, Edmund Singer, Max Seifriz, Heinrich Kayser, and Richard Hofmann, require an excessive amount of time to be spent in first position.[36] During this time the student must master all sorts of complicated bowings, including virtuoso ones, in addition to difficult extensions, double stops, and so on. Working on this material in only one position develops the habit of holding the instrument too tight with the left hand. This contributes to excessive pressure of the fingers on the strings, which often causes heavy left-hand technique.

Because first position is studied for so long in most of the treatises of the past century, the instrument hold is developed in a way that almost fixates the left hand instead of ensuring its mobility. This is why subsequent difficulties occur when shifting, and may explain why some treatises, such as Joachim's, recommend avoiding shifts where at all possible.

These problems firstly have to do the creation of an incorrect perception as to how the violin should be held, that is, only with the left hand and without the participation of the chin. The student must develop an entirely different idea of how to hold the instrument when he or she needs to move the hand along the fingerboard. However, then not only must the new technique be mastered but also the old technique must be unlearned, which is naturally much more difficult and less effective. Besides, as already noted, the old way of holding the violin causes the fingers to grip the neck, which also restricts movement in the left hand. It is interesting that some exponents of this method understand the problems associated with it. Moser, for example, believes it necessary to overcome what he calls "the inertia of the left hand" when starting to learn the positions.[37]

We believe it absolutely essential to develop horizontal movement of the left hand along the fingerboard parallel to (and possibly earlier than) studying first position. Moving the thumb prevents development of the aforementioned problems, prepares the subsequent study of shifting, and has a positive effect on the general release of the left hand.

The following exercise may be recommended for a student who has not yet mastered the positions. As the right hand plays open strings, rhythmically dividing the bow into four to six quarter notes (mm equals 40), the left hand moves along the fingerboard with the same rhythmic pulse, shifting between first and third positions. This relatively simple exercise turns out to be extremely useful. From the very beginning the student realizes that neither the right hand nor the left hand remain motionless, and this helps immensely to further develop the necessary coordinated interactions. At the same time, the student gains a correct understanding of how to hold the instrument and of the specific role of the chin, collarbone, and wrist of the left hand.

This approach directly stems from the main ideas of Pavlov's physiological principles.[38] For the development of playing skills is nothing more than development of the corresponding conditioned reflexes. The development of these reflexes entirely depends on the conditions of their creation. Thus if one is developing the skill (reflex) of holding the neck freely, then those conditions that could cause the opposite reflex, such as gripping the neck, have to be eliminated. Otherwise, inevitably the gripping reflex also develops, which, as already noted, invariably happens since it stems from the inborn (unconditioned) reflex to grasp. Consequently, eliminating all the elements that block the necessary reflex is essential for its creation.

Furthermore, it is important to keep in mind that, if an undesirable reflex develops, work on the desired reflex takes longer and may, in some cases, be entirely impossible. This is why undesirable reflexes not only make matters more complicated but also can lead to harmful consequences. There are plenty of examples of this in pedagogical practice.

Finally, and most importantly, the conditions for developing the reflex must be determined by the reasons the reflex is being developed in the first place.

For example, if the goal is to move the left hand freely along the fingerboard, and the required reflex is to hold the violin neck freely, then this reflex should never be developed without the associated movements. Rather, the desired movements must be the obligatory condition for developing the reflex.

Consequently, the development of certain skills, such as specific conditioned reflexes, must always be preceded by a thorough and detailed analysis of those conditions in which the reflexes are to be developed, always taking into account the individual particularities of each student. Otherwise, the skills may not only be developed incorrectly but can also have negative consequences.

Another serious problem in this respect is excessive pressure of fingers on the string, which significantly restricts freedom in the left hand. This problem is also linked to an incorrect feeling that was not properly developed.

The problem is that in some methodological texts we find instructions requiring the fingers to press "sufficiently" to produce a pleasing sound. However, because the meaning of "sufficient" is never elaborated, the finger pressure is often exaggerated. This happens despite the fact that the aim of these instructions is to avoid "insufficient" pressure in the fingers. Many treatises, especially the German ones, use terms such as "firm," "strong," and so on. This naturally leads to more than just "sufficient" pressure and usually causes quite intense pressure of the fingers on the string. Furthermore, some treatises, such as those by Kayser, Reinhold Jockisch, Viktor Valter, and others, explicitly advocate strong finger pressure.[39] Jockisch, for example, recommends that the fingers be curved "like hammers" and that they drop to the string from a considerable height with considerable force. He believes the intensity of sound should be determined solely by the bow, and that the fingers in the left hand should always press onto the fingerboard *fortissimo*, even when playing *pianissimo*. It is difficult to agree with this. Not only is the excessive pressure of the fingers accompanied by excessive energy and tension, which restricts left-hand movement, but this also creates excessive counterpressure in the thumb, which is another very serious cause of gripping the violin neck.

In the methodological literature, there are many arguments and objections against strong finger pressure. Lesman, who writes in his 1914 treatise that the fingers should press quite strongly on the string, expresses a different opinion in his work in 1934: "The fingers should press the string as little as possible, only as much as needed to play. This is the only way to keep the fingers from assuming another separate function that would disrupt unified playing and lead to negative consequences."[40] Hugo Bekker shares the same opinion, and indications in his cello treatise are equally applicable to violin playing.[41] Bekker believes that the fingers should not press any more than is necessary to overcome to resistance of the string, otherwise serious physiological problems arise. Moreover, he notes that the sound's amplitude has nothing to do with the degree of finger pressure. Mostras examines this matter carefully in his lectures.[42] He illustrates how the degree of finger pressure is determined by the quality of sound and by how much resistance is required to keep the string from slipping under the fingers while it is bowed.

Of course, it would be entirely wrong to recommend any kind of universal rule concerning finger pressure on the string for all circumstances and in all parts of the fingerboard. On the contrary, we find that the character and degree of pressure depends on many factors. For example, finger pressure is significantly greater in the higher positions than in the lower positions because of the closer distance to the bridge and the consequent increase of space between the string and fingerboard. Furthermore, when playing with intense vibrato, especially in *forte*, the pressure of the fingers should considerably strengthen (in order to maintain the pitch). There is also an idea that finger pressure may sometimes increase when playing *piano*. When playing in a fast tempo the pressure of the fingers on the string, as a rule, releases to a certain degree.

These are enough examples to show that this matter cannot be resolved identically in all circumstances. However, considering the variety of circumstances it is important to remember that each technical problem is never a goal in itself, but only a means to achieving a sound that is associated with specific musical content. Consequently, in all cases without exception, the character and degree of finger pressure should be determined not by formal circumstances but solely by taking into consideration the musical context. Only control of the sound, which is determined by the music, can and should resolve technical problems, including the degree of finger pressure.

It is necessary to note that insufficient pressure of the fingers cannot ensure a full sound. Instead, insufficient pressure causes a feeble, vapid tone with extraneous noises when playing *piano* and even false intonation when playing *forte*. However, this problem is easy to notice, even by inexpert ears. On the other hand excessive finger pressure, which also negatively affects the sound by making it stiff, dry, and limited in the variety of timbres, is something that requires a more sophisticated and experienced ear to determine. This explains why excessive finger pressure is the more common problem in practice.

The pressure of the fingers on the string usually releases when shifting. This not only eases the movement of the hand along the fingerboard but also helps the quality of sound in terms of aesthetic considerations. The right hand clearly is also involved in creating the appropriate sound by releasing the pressure of the bow during the shift. Naturally, violinists who apply more finger pressure to the string are required to release the fingers considerably when shifting. Even Jockisch, an advocate of strong finger pressure, states that, when shifting, the sliding finger should just touch the string lightly without coming off, and it should press again fully only when it reaches the necessary position.[43] Yet this still does not validate his technique, since releasing and reapplying excessive pressure in itself restricts free movement in the left hand.

Voiku, on the other hand, recommends the opposite. He believes that finger pressure should not change at all during the shift and that the same degree of pressure should be maintained in both the initial and arrival positions. Yet this is not practical, since the movement becomes detached from the musical intention, which more often than not is incompatible with this kind of movement.

The degree of finger pressure depends, firstly, on the dynamics of the music and character of the shift; secondly, on the distance of the shift; and thirdly, on the tempo. This discussion clearly shows that the degree of finger pressure deserves serious attention. The maximum degree of freedom in moving the left hand requires the minimal amount of pressure of the fingers on the string. However, this minimal degree of pressure is determined by artistic considerations and the character of the music. Thus the ear needs to control the process of finding the most efficient technique.

When the student presses too hard, the following exercise is useful to help the student perceive the necessary degree of finger pressure. In third position, the second finger on the D string produces the natural harmonic on the note A. As this harmonic is played, the finger gradually begins to press down on the string, and the following changes occur: the harmonic stops sounding, then raspy and hissing sounds follow, and only then do we hear the note A^1. By noticing the exact moment at which the note is heard clearly, the student can determine how much excessive pressure he or she used in the past. This often helps nurture muscular sensations that are developed by consistently associating a sound with a movement, thereby creating the conditions for the sound to occur.[44] As already noted, the degree of finger pressure changes under different circumstances, but it should never be more than necessary. There are many opinions on how it is best to approach this matter.

Koeckert, for example, recommends lifting the fingers high above the string and dropping them with considerable force.[45] He believes that increasing the distance from the string generates more swing in the dropping finger and conserves the energy required to sufficiently press the string. However, this method does not achieve its purpose. Even if excessively lifting the fingers turns out to be, as Koeckert insists, less harmful than excessively pressing the string, it nonetheless restricts the motor capacity of the left hand and restricts the agility of the fingers.

Valter's treatise states the complete opposite.[46] Valter believed that the fingers should be held curved over the string and never lifted too high, as many teachers require, since the force of dropping the fingers is not as important as the force of pressing into the string.

In Eberhardt's treatise, we even find the need to differentiate the amount of pressure of each finger depending on its individual natural strength. According to Eberhardt, the degree of pressure needs to counterbalance the strength of the finger. Thus he recommends that the first and second fingers press less than the third and especially the fourth. However, it is also difficult to consider this method effective. Practice generally shows that excessively pressing or lifting the fingers inevitably worsens the quality of sound and generally has a restrictive effect on free movement, vibrato, and fast passagework. This problem is undoubtedly one of the main obstacles to moving the left hand easily along the fingerboard.

5. AN OPTIMAL SETUP. DEVELOPING CORRECT PLAYING MOVEMENTS.

We have already noted more than once that relaxed, efficient movements and complete command of the motor apparatus are essential conditions for playing the violin. In analyzing the conditions that determine the movements, it is important to examine the violinist's positioning or setup, since it significantly influences the origin of these movements and therefore playing in general. Great teachers always recognized the importance of a good setup. Even Leopold Mozart wrote of violinists "whose playing leaves a poor impression, because they limit themselves by their awkward hold of the violin and bow."[47] At the same time pedagogical practice clearly shows that determining the best setup is a difficult matter, leading to many disagreements and errors.

The principal error is that the violinist's positioning is sometimes treated as something fixed and self-contained. The aforementioned works by Voiku and Mikhailovsky provide examples of this. These authors examine positioning in an abstract way, disconnected from the demands of playing, and thereby turn it into a goal unto itself. Yet an efficient setup may be examined only in direct correlation to those movements for which it was created. The only factor determining the setup should be how it accommodates the necessary movements to produce the desired sound.

At the same time, one must consider that in the process of finding the optimal techniques, certain movements may cause the positioning to change and readjust. This is why positioning should never be considered as static; it is dynamic, just like all playing movements, and reflects the diversity of musical problems.

Another serious mistake is to dogmatize specific forms of positioning. An efficient setup should always take into account the individual characteristics of the performer, who in turn must also adapt to ensure the most efficient motor functions in any given circumstances. When we stress the importance of the player's individual characteristics in determining the positioning, it is important to emphasize that these characteristics are not important in their own right but only within the context of the musical goal, which they are entirely subservient to.

Turning directly to the setup of the left hand, we must note that the manner in which the instrument is held plays an essential role in ensuring free movement. The free movement of the left hand is naturally limited if it also needs to support the violin. This explains the many tendencies in violin pedagogy to support the violin only with the chin and collarbone, allowing the left arm to be entirely free. This technique is considerably widespread, and found many supporters in the Czech and German schools and was also recommended by the French school.[48] For the German school, this technique was a logical consequence of excessive finger pressure on the strings; since the left hand was already restricted by excess pressure, it was required (whenever possible) to be free from additionally supporting the instrument.

Another point of view insists that the violin should always be held with two points of support—between the chin and collarbone and between the thumb and index finger of the left hand. Nemirovsky was an ardent defender of this approach.[49] He wrote that the widespread practice of supporting the violin with the help of the shoulder or a pad (which he rejected) was based upon a "gross misunderstanding of the essence of the instrument" that it was "a deformity, disrupting the natural structure and habits of the body."[50]

At the same time, Nemirovsky correctly understood that without a "constant point of contact" (i.e., between the chin and collarbone) it is impossible to support the violin while shifting downward. For these cases he recommended auxiliary movement in the thumb preceding the shift, thereby creating an extra point of support.

Boris Struve had his own particular opinion on how the instrument should be positioned.[51] He conceded the possibility of holding the instrument both ways, that is, with one or two points of support. He believed that the choice should be based not on methodology but solely on the anatomical particularities and constitution of the player. For those violinists with sloped shoulders the rational positioning, according to Struve, is to hold the violin with two points of support. For if the violin were to be supported only in the chin area, the shoulder would lift significantly, and this in turn would cause tension in the left hand. However, for those with naturally high shoulders, Struve recommended holding the violin with one point of support. Meanwhile, just like Nemirovsky, Struve believed special coordinated movements in the thumb are necessary when shifting downward when the violin is held with two points of support. However, in those cases when this coordination is not enough, Struve did recommend using a pad.[52] On the one hand, the pad relieves the need to raise the left shoulder; and on the other, it allows the violin to be held with one point of support, thereby avoiding the extra movements in the thumb.

Without denying the importance of the constitutional particularities of the body, this should not be the sole determining factor. In reality, the two indicated ways of supporting the violin are closely intertwined. Every player will concede that the violin is held more firmly under the chin when shifting compared to when one is playing in a fixed position. In the latter case, some violinists even lift their head from the violin, proving the existence of two points of support at that instant. Those who heard Fritz Kreisler will recall that he often lifted his head away from the violin.

These examples show that it is wrong to insist on one static positioning. Similar to any other technique, the setup needs to be dynamic so it may correspond to the variety of musical tasks. This is particularly evident when shifting. The degree to which the violin is held with two points of support changes, depending on how much pressure is exerted by the chin. This, in turn, depends on the shift's direction (up or down), on the freedom and elasticity of the left-hand movement, and also on the degree of finger pressure on the strings and the opposite pressure of the thumb.

Alexei Lvov was a proponent of securing the instrument primarily with the chin and shoulder.[53] Lvov recommended holding the violin "almost at a right angle to the body," and securing it with the chin firmly enough so that the left hand could freely change position, barely holding the violin at all.

In practice, holding the violin tightly with the chin is often associated with lifting the left shoulder.[54] For example, this is the setup advocated by Valter and Nemirovsky.[55] The latter, as already noted, strongly advocated holding the violin with the chin but without using a pad.

Raising the left shoulder is neither efficient in providing constant support of the violin nor in temporary moments when the instrument needs to be firmly fixed with the chin. Additionally, raising the left shoulder causes tension in the muscles, which impacts free movement throughout the left arm and hand. Struve also shared this opinion, although he believed that the negative impact did not for some reason apply to those with high shoulders. Yet, practice shows that tension occurs in both cases, although it may manifest itself differently.

Mostras aptly notes that lifting the left shoulder changes the direction of the movement of the forearm. Thus, if normally the direction of the forearm's movement corresponds to the direction of the fingerboard, when the shoulder is raised then this movement strays from the fingerboard and requires special adjustment.

Since many violinists recognize the problems caused by lifting the left shoulder, various techniques of holding the instrument attempt to address this. The more common method in contemporary practice is to use a cushion or pad. We find this to be indisputably rational, since this entirely eliminates the need to lift the shoulder and allows the left arm to move freely. Regarding the cushion's negative effect on the sound of the instrument (incidentally, pressing the shoulder against the instrument without a pad also affects the sound), this may be avoided depending on the cushion's design.[56] At the same time it should be emphasized that using a pad does not mean the violin needs to be "rigidly fixed" in one position, as Nemirovsky implies. The pad is simply used to help free the left hand when it is necessary for the violin to be supported with the chin without lifting the shoulder (such as in descending passages, chromatic glissandi, big leaps, etc.).

It is important to recognize the problematic issues associated with supplementary movements of the thumb, which are inevitable when holding the violin according to Nemirovsky's method. According to this technique every shift requires two movements instead of one, and this can be restricting even when the most agile thumb movements have been mastered. Moreover, in observing violinists who hold the violin with two points of support, we find that supplementary thumb movements still give way to lifting the shoulder during fast passagework. This again confirms the validity of using a pad, not only to stop the shoulder from lifting but also to facilitate the general movement itself by avoiding supplementary action in the thumb. At the same time we should note that using a pad does not necessarily exclude using supplementary thumb movements. These may be useful in certain cases, though this largely depends on individual adaptation to the instrument.

Supplementary movements of the thumb are most commonly observed in cantilena, especially when the music requires the notes to be connected smoothly and expressively, such as in Example 2.20. In this case the preliminary preparation of the thumb provides the support for a smooth and stable transition.

Example 2.20 Tchaikovsky: *Violin Concerto, mvt. 1.*

As the tempo gradually accelerates, the supplementary movements of the thumb diminish. In a fast tempo, a new movement develops—the thumb moves together with the wrist and the fingers, led by the forearm. And sometimes cantilena passages also may be played without any help from the thumb. Abraham Yampolsky found supplementary movements of the thumb to be superfluous and even troublesome.[57] This was also the opinion of Auer, who affirmed that the thumb does not play an important role in shifting.[58]

However, no matter the opinion on using supplementary movements of the thumb, and in spite of the fact that treatises focus primarily on the thumb's auxiliary role in descending shifts, this is not the function that determines the thumb's primary purpose in ensuring free movement along the fingerboard. Therefore other functions of the thumb need to be examined, starting with an analysis of how it is positioned.

A detailed analysis of how to position the thumb immediately presents contradictory opinions. Leopold Mozart recommends holding the thumb closer to the second or even third finger rather than the first (i.e., opposite the note F or F♯ on the D string).[59] He believes that this allows greater possibilities for extending the fingers. Although many others, including Moser and Auer, share this opinion, we find it difficult to agree since moving the thumb forward in fact limits the possibilities of extending the little finger.

Campagnoli believed that the thumb should lie opposite "the note B♮ on the G string" (i.e., opposite the note F♯).[60] Auer believed that it should be opposite F♮.[61] In de Bériot's treatise, we find instructions indicating the thumb should be placed between the notes A and B♮ on the G string. This is the same opinion found in the treatise by Singer and Seifriz, although they also stress that the thumb should be more inclined to the A than to the B.[62] The treatise by Joachim and Moser claims that the thumb be opposite the index finger that is one whole step above the open string, (i.e., opposite A♮).[63] Valter and Koeckert take more extreme views on this matter. Valter recommends that the thumb be slanted with its tip pointed at the player and not the scroll, while Koeckert believes it should be turned as much as possible toward the scroll of the violin.

This all shows that in the existing methods there is no unanimous consensus on how the thumb should be positioned. This is likely not a coincidence, since it appears that a single, standard positioning of the thumb indeed cannot exist.

Since the thumb is not directly involved in playing, its positioning should be determined by the degree to which it accommodates the function of the other fingers. This is why the thumb's position depends upon a range of conditions: on the specific structure of the saddle joint that determines the direction of thumb,[64] on the length of the other fingers, on the difference in length between the thumb and the other fingers, on the width of the palm, and so on. It is important to remember, for example, that when technical difficulties occur because of a short little finger, the thumb should be pulled back toward the scroll of the violin further than usual, since the consequent turn in the wrist makes it easier for the little finger to function. Thus, violinists usually position their thumb according to the individual structure of their own hands. This explains why the authors of the aforementioned treatises recommended the thumb position that was most efficient for them personally. However, the pedagogue must consider not the structural particularities of his or her own hand, but rather those of the student's hand.

No matter how much the thumb's position is determined by the individual hand structure, it still must not be considered static. In conjunction with various tasks, the thumb changes position to ensure optimal conditions for activity in the left hand. The change in thumb position applies not only to the degree of proximity toward the scroll but also to the degree to which it slides under the neck of the violin. The extent to which the thumb slides below the neck largely depends on its length (the individual characteristics of the left hand also define where the index finger comes into contact with the violin neck—ranging from the base of the first phalange to almost where the first phalange meets the second). Certain students of Piotr Stólyarsky had a tendency to hold the thumb lower.

In analyzing the thumb's position, Flesch correctly noted that generally the violinist's thumb assumes two positions, depending on what part of the fingerboard is being played: the "normal lateral" position in the lower positions and the "low" position in the higher positions.[65] In special circumstances, such as in three- and four-note chords with finger extensions, the thumb may move under the neck of the violin even in the lower positions. However, for some violinists, such a "low" position of the thumb becomes the norm. This is associated with the base of the index finger leaving the neck of the violin and, as already noted, is characteristic of the Czech violin school. Such a position stems from the desire to retain an identical position of the left hand in both the lower and higher positions. According to Goby Eberhardt, Otakar Ševčík also recommended this "low" position of the thumb.[66]

The supportive role of the thumb becomes very clear when shifting in the upper positions. In these cases the thumb, as a rule, drops under the neck of the violin, and the wrist rises above the fingerboard, allowing the fingers to retain their necessary shape over the strings. Flesch suggested preparing to lower the thumb slightly ahead of time.[67] Nemirovsky advocated a similar opinion when analyzing shifts from first to fifth position. He recommended that in the initial (first) position the thumb already assumes the shape it will need in the fifth position, and it moves upward while retaining this shape.[68]

However, from our point of view, preparing the thumb this way is not always necessary. Sometimes the thumb may drop under the fingerboard at the same time as the hand moves along the fingerboard, sliding underneath the bottom of the neck. The point at which the thumb lowers depends on the player's individual adaptation and may consist of a variety of transitional movements.

When playing in the fourth or fifth positions, the thumb may assume one of two positions. It can either retain the same shape as in the lower positions, or move under the neck, as in the higher positions. The musical context and the hand's subsequent movement should determine which to choose.

Sometimes, when shifting from middle to high positions, the preparatory thumb movement is incorrect, and the thumb not only drops underneath the neck but also comes out to press against the junction of the neck and body of the violin. Sometimes this even occurs when shifting from first to third position. For example, when shifting is first introduced in Narcisse Augustin Lefort's treatise, the notes are to be separated by a pause during which the player should make the preparatory thumb movement, something the author calls "passage du pouce."[69] Yet this movement is irrational and entirely unnecessary. This type of extra thumb movement may still be justified when shifting from higher to lower positions by a desire to stabilize the instrument, which naturally drops slightly from under the chin as the hand moves down. However, since the instrument does not drop when shifting up, it is unnecessary to move the thumb forward and disrupt the unified gradual movement of the hand. Disrupting this unified motion is not only inefficient but also harmful since it affects general motor function. Furthermore, this technique causes the palm to undesirably contract, which is uncomfortable and affects intonation. Finally, when this supportive movement in the thumb occurs when shifting from middle to high positions, it is often accompanied by the wrist curving in the opposite direction and creates serious obstacles, especially in quick tempos.

Sometimes the thumb does not move together with the wrist but remains on the same spot, serving as a kind of pivot point. When executing the passage in Example 2.21, the thumb is placed as if it is in second position, and the actual shift to first position is made only with the wrist.

Example 2.21

The following Example 2.22 illustrates an analogous function of the thumb.

Example 2.22 Ernst: *Violin Concerto.*

In this passage the thumb assumes a central point of support for the entire duration of the passage. Specifically, in executing the first part of the passage, the hand remains closer to the thumb and then continues its movement in the opposite direction. Thus the thumb maintains an immobile point of support for the displacement of the wrist for the duration of the entire passage. Realizing this technique naturally depends on the violinist's individual adaptation, which is why the movements may slightly differ and be more personalized. However, we find the described form of movement to be the most efficient.

When playing in very high positions it is normal to bring the thumb out onto the bout of the violin. This is unavoidable when the player has small hands or short fingers (especially in the case of a short little finger). But even when the player's hands are big enough, it is still common to transfer the thumb to the bout since this eliminates excessive tension in the wrist, frees vibrato, and leads to a better tone quality.

There is significant disagreement in pedagogical practice and in the methodological literature regarding the necessity of transferring the thumb to the violin bout. For example, some methods, including those of Campagnoli and Spohr, recommend this technique.[70] Campagnoli explicitly states that it is necessary to bring the thumb from underneath the neck to the bout of the violin (which should be held firmer with the chin, to prevent the instrument from dropping as the balance shifts with a new point of support). In other treatises, predominantly German ones, this technique is categorically prohibited. This is stated very clearly in Reinhold Jockisch's *Katechismus Der Violine und Des Violinspiels*, where he writes that the thumb should never leave the neck of the violin.

Let us examine this matter more closely. The primary reason for forbidding the thumb to transfer to the bout is the fear of losing a point of support. As already noted, even Campagnoli, who recommended the technique, took this into consideration. Indeed, an element of the technique is associated with a very common risk of losing support when the thumb needs to return to its normal position in descending sequences. However, the impression of losing support in this case occurs only when there is no coordination between the fingers and the movement of the thumb as it returns to its normal position.

For example, some players instinctively delay the thumb's return until that moment when the rest of the fingers descending on the fingerboard attain that position in which the thumb would normally find itself on the neck of the violin. That moment at which the thumb delays its return indeed creates a sensation of losing support. And conversely, it is common to encounter the thumb returning to the regular position at the exact same moment the fingers shift positions on the fingerboard. This similarly creates a feeling of losing support that naturally has an adverse effect.

However, if the fingers are coordinated correctly, there should be no risk of losing the point of support. The thumb should return to its normal position only when all the fingers are in one position or, in descending movement, before they have reached the thumb's position. This allows the player to anticipate the thumb's return to its regular position on the violin neck. These moments naturally depend on the individual particularities of the player and may be easily developed with specific exercises.

Consequently, the idea of transferring the thumb to the violin bout should not be rejected in principle, since the difficulties that ensue are readily overcome. Indeed, rejecting this technique would make playing in high positions impossible for many violinists. It should be noted that sometimes violinists with very small hands are unable to play in high positions even with the thumb on the violin bout, and they are forced to transfer the thumb to the side of the fingerboard.

In cases of an immediate shift from a very high to a very low position, the thumb is released and returns to its normal position without touching the violin neck. The technique is useful in situations similar to Example 2.23.

Example 2.23 Wieniawski: *Violin Concerto No. 1, mvt. 1.*

Sometimes we may observe the thumb released in a similar manner in other parts of the fingerboard. However, since this is clearly the result of an individual adaptation, it should not be recommended as a general rule.

As we have seen, the functions of the thumb are quite diverse and often complex, and they require a lot of flexibility and agility. There is no doubt that they closely depend on the general condition of the entire left hand and, conversely, the latter in its turn is affected by the position and functions of the thumb.

Maximum freedom of movement in the left hand is ensured not only by correctly positioning the thumb but also by the positioning and character of movement in the other fingers. The angle at which the fingers touch the fingerboard is of primary importance. Naturally, to a certain extent this depends on the individual particularities of the player. However, in all cases it is more efficient to place the fingers at a slight angle in relation to the string. The angle should only be slight, but the fingers should never be perpendicular to the string. This ensures both free movement in the left hand and better tone quality.

The slight angle helps the quality of sound by providing more contact between the cushion of the fingertip and the string, and it also creates more favorable conditions for vibrato. Furthermore, the angle facilitates the process of sliding and extending the fingers and transferring the fingers to different strings. Finally, an inclined position of the fingers provides one consolidated positioning for playing both technical passages and cantilena (i.e., playing with and without vibrato). We will also note that an inclined position of the fingers is justified by corresponding more closely to their natural position. The so-called steep position of the fingers is therefore not rational.

It is most efficient to place the fingers so that they touch the string at the middle of the fingertip. In practice, we may sometimes find the fingers positioned on the side of the fingertip. This leads to a series of undesirable consequences, including poor tone quality and problems with vibrato; it may also cause the fingers to slide off the string when shifting.

Another equally important factor in assuring free movement in the left hand is the angle at which the fingers fall to the fingerboard, in respect to the curvature of the latter. Mikhailovsky correctly analyzed this matter in his method, noting that in all parts of the fingerboard the fingers should press the string perpendicular to the tangent of the fingerboard.[71] Effectively, in this position the entire cushion of the fingertip, and not just one side, presses the string. This helps the sound and also allows the finger to be more stable on the string during shifts. If the fingers do not fall at an angle perpendicular to the string, another common problem is that the fingers may pull the string sidewise, in the direction of the E string.

The correct angle for the fingers to drop to the string depends on the corresponding turn of the hand, which is connected to the corresponding position of the elbow underneath the violin. The angle of the fingers on different strings changes depending on the curvature of the fingerboard, and consequently the corresponding positioning of the elbow also changes. The elbow moves slightly to the left when playing on the higher strings, and draws inward to the right when playing on the lower strings. The position of the elbow also depends on the way the instrument is held; if the violin is held flat, then the elbow moves further under the instrument to the right, and vice versa. In the higher positions the elbow is required to move further under the violin than in the lower positions. Consequently, the maximum degree that the elbow draws inward to the right occurs when playing on the G string in the higher positions, and the elbow moves furthest to the left when playing on the E string in the lower positions.

Thus, it becomes clear that it is impossible to speak of a single fixed position of the elbow. Moving the elbow is a necessary component of moving the left hand. Voiku called these elbow movements, which allow a comfortable positioning of the fingers on each string, "steering movements"; this term became widespread and is still used in pedagogical practice today.[72] A correct understanding of this "steering movement" is also found in other methodological works, including Nemirovsky's treatise (that appeared in 1915, ten years before Voiku's) and publications by Lesman and others.[73]

We have now analyzed the components of left-hand activity that are necessary to ensure complete freedom of movement along the fingerboard. This analysis has attempted both to determine the particular positioning that allows free movement in the left hand and to uncover those "inhibitory" elements that could restrict it. On this basis we proceed in the following section to analyze the actual character of left-hand movement along the fingerboard, which is essential to mastering the technical and artistic sides of violin playing.

6. PARTICULARITIES OF DESCENDING SHIFTS. COORDINATING THE PRINCIPAL MOVEMENTS OF THE LEFT HAND WHILE SHIFTING.

The flawless mastery of shifts is one of the fundamental conditions of excellent left-hand technique. This section focuses on general shifting techniques, and is followed by a detailed analysis of executing various types of shifts.

When we analyze the movement of the left hand along the fingerboard, we readily discover that changing positions while moving up the fingerboard is, as a rule, easier than changing positions when moving down. This is explained firstly by the fact that ascending movement toward the player naturally helps support the instrument, while moving down requires extra measures to secure the instrument (specifically, the chin plays an important role as previously noted). Furthermore, ascending shifts are made with a naturally uninterrupted movement of the hand, while descending shifts are more complicated because of the supportive thumb movements (for those who use them) that anticipate the movement of the entire hand. In leading the hand, the thumb is able to better stabilize the instrument, and as already noted this technique requires considerable agility in the thumb and good coordination with the other fingers.

Both Auer and Flesch considered the technique of using supportive thumb movements to be the only possibility in descending shifts.[74] However, they also noted the complications that arise. Auer writes that the relative facility of ascending shifts is explained by the simultaneous movement of the thumb and hand, while in descending shifts the thumb must transfer to the lower position ahead of the sliding finger (while that finger is still in the higher position) to provide the necessary counterbalance.[75]

When the violin is not held securely with the chin, the beginner's initial attempts to shift down often create an unpleasant feeling of instability. As practice shows, this can develop into a subconscious fear of shifting downward that later restricts the development of this skill. Specifically, these students are unable to master a descending chromatic glissando with one finger on one string. When they start this movement the students fear the instrument will drop, and they tend to press the palm toward themselves and the body of the violin. Consequently, they create a movement in the opposite direction from the sliding finger, and this naturally prevents them from realizing this technique.

Another significant difference between ascending and descending movements along the fingerboard is the particular means of intonation required in descending sequences. If in ascending sequences notes are produced by fingers dropping onto the string, then in descending sequences notes are produced by the fingers lifting from the string. This creates the additional problem of having to prepare the fingers in advance and explains why the scale's ascending fingering usually differs from the descending fingering. In an ascending scale, it is most common to alternate the first and second fingers (Example 2.24), while in a descending scale shifts are made to the third or fourth finger, which allows the other fingers to prepare to play two or three notes (Example 2.25). If we try to play the scale with the opposite fingering, that is, alternating two fingers going down and shifting to the first finger after the third of fourth when going up, we immediately find this much less comfortable.

Example 2.24

Example 2.25

In a descending scale the necessity to constantly prepare the following notes requires the first finger to remain on the string to connect the movements. In addition, we are also obliged to use the fourth finger, whose relative weakness creates even further instability in these types of sequences. The instability increases if the fourth finger is much weaker and shorter than the rest. It is possible to use the more secure third finger as a replacement only in certain cases, and completely impossible in sequential double stops such as thirds. All these examples clearly demonstrate the relative complexity of descending motion on the fingerboard.

As we examine the characteristics of the left hand's horizontal movement along the fingerboard, we need to emphasize once again that all these procedures are only a means of connecting sounds that occupy a specific place in a musical phrase—be it a cantilena or a virtuoso passage. Consequently, complete mastery of shifting is essential to provide flexible, diverse, and expressive portamento in cantilena; light, quick, and unnoticeable shifting in passagework; and so on. Shifting turns out to be one of the most important tasks in mastering the instrument.

The main criterion for determining the correct movements must be the resulting sound that they produce. Therefore, movements and sound become two inseparable components of the same process. Any attempt to separate these elements and to examine a movement on its own should be considered a manifestation of formalism in violin pedagogy.

And yet, when working on movements, attention is often turned toward the external appearance, and the association between the movement and the corresponding sound is ignored. This occurs for both the right and left hands. A clear example is when work on bowings does not fully take into account the resulting sound, and the bowing exercises turn into gymnastics for either the entire right arm or separate parts of it. For the left hand, this problem is usually observed when working on shifts. Let us examine this in greater detail.

Since all professional skills must be developed only in conjunction with the corresponding sounds they are designed for, it is necessary to establish a system that assures the development of reliable aural-motor connections. Only this type of system can fully resolve the fingering problems posed by sight-reading, a matter that has recently been getting special attention. Today, there is no doubt that one of the primary solutions to this problem is the creation of conditioned reflexes so that the visual perception of the score immediately induces the corresponding aural perception and motor reactions. It is these connections that need to form the basis for developing all motor skills, including those that involve shifting.

There are two aspects to studying left-hand activity in violin pedagogy. These correspond to the two fundamental elements of left-hand movement: the vertical movement of the fingers dropping to the string; and the horizontal movement of the arm, or parts of the arm, transferring the fingers to various parts of the fingerboard. Needless to say, left-hand activity is not limited to these two elements, and other techniques are also commonly used. These include sliding the fingers along the string (such as when playing chromatic scales), transferring the fingers across the strings, playing pizzicato, and so on. Developing the correct skills necessary to make all these movements, and being able to coordinate them with the appropriate sounds is essential to mastering left-hand technique.

Coordinating vertical movement in the fingers with horizontal movement of the hand and arm along the fingerboard is one of the fundamental problems of violin playing. Simultaneously combining these movements that are so different in nature creates significant difficulties (even when the movements are not so difficult on their own), and this restricts movement throughout the left arm. Only methodical nurturing of correct coordination between these movements assures their unity and guarantees unrestricted activity in the left hand.

In order to develop this coordination, it is important for the student to understand that violin playing is constantly associated with changing positions, and that movement of the hand along the fingerboard is integrally connected to movement of the fingers. Nonetheless, as already noted, left-hand technique is often taught by spending an excessive amount of time in only one position. While at a certain stage it is indeed necessary to maintain relative stability while positioning the hand and fingers, it is important to never remain in one position longer than necessary to accomplish this goal. On the contrary, the horizontal movements associated with shifting or preparing to shift should be covered as early as possible. Only then can the student perceive the coordination, unity, and inseparability of these movements. Otherwise two separate skills are developed: the vertical movement of the fingers and the horizontal movement of the hand. If these techniques are initially developed on their own and only later combined, then the new technique of uniting the movements is only possible by effectively overriding the initial techniques, which have already turned into habits. This not only results in a loss of time but also hinders the creation of a new integrated technique.

Some teachers recommend a system of exercises for the fingers of the left hand based on "hammering" each note. This creates excessive finger pressure on the string that, as already noted, restricts free movement in the left hand. It is perfectly obvious that such exercises restrict the development of unified movement in the hand and arm. The "inverse" procedure (i.e., shifting very abruptly) has an equally negative effect on unified movement.

The complexity of left-hand movement requires all the components to be perfectly coordinated. Ivan Nazarov suggests an excellent set of exercises to accomplish this.[76] His system is based on the progressive development of coordination between the different types of movement. He starts with trills and shifts with one finger, followed by scales with two fingers where both types of movement occur in equal proportions, eventually leading to the regular scale that incorporates all the different movements. Nazarov illustrates the necessity of developing an integrated movement in which the separate elements are coordinated as they interact with each other. This coordinated interaction is extremely important since it helps make the left-hand movement light and swift, thereby ensuring a good tone (as much as it depends on the left hand) and solving the problem of finger agility.

Poor coordination between movements in the left hand is frequently encountered in practice, which makes this issue very relevant. We should note that the primary cause is insufficient command of the horizontal movements while shifting. In these cases the change of position, which requires the separate movements of the fingers to be integrated into a unified movement, ends up disrupting the unified movement.

The methods of the leading Russian pedagogues for working on passages were based on finding an integrated movement. Thus, for example, Mostras and Yampolsky proceeded from the principle of transferring the left hand by position and recommended the following technique. When first working on a passage, all the intermediary movements of the fingers in one position are eliminated and only the outer borders remain (i.e., the first and last notes in the position). This technique focuses the student's attention on unifying the horizontal movement and helps to establish the necessary degree of muscular tension in the fingers that this horizontal movement requires. Once the framework of the passage is mastered, it is not difficult to add the vertical movement of the fingers. It goes without saying that separating the elements of the movement is only a temporary tool to be used for a short period of time, since a feeling for the complete movement can only be developed by understanding the entire melodic line.

The following examples clearly illustrate this technique (Example 2.26 is from Yampolsky and Examples 2.27–2.28 from Mostras).

Example 2.26a

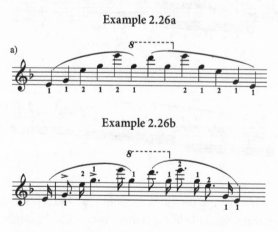

Example 2.26b

Example 2.26c Lalo: *Symphonie Espagnole, mvt. 1.*

Example 2.27a

Example 2.27b

Example 2.27c Rimsky-Korsakov (Zimbalist): *The Golden Cockerel Fantasy.*

Example 2.28a

Example 2.28b

David Oistrakh's playing provides an example of exceptional coordination between the separate elements of movement that occur lightly, accurately, and with virtuoso technical agility. When he played sequential passages, his left hand moved extremely smoothly in one unified motion, almost not stopping between positions.

In developing smooth left-hand movement during shifts, the teacher should constantly turn the student's attention to the nature of the movement in relation to the quality of the corresponding sound. Only this constant correlation develops those sensations and skills that provide the required fluidity, facility, and elasticity of horizontal movements of the left hand along the fingerboard. The creation and retention of these types of skills determines to a significant extent (if not entirely) the quality of movements that the violinist needs to produce diverse and expressive portamento in cantilena or to make light and imperceptible shifts in passagework. These skills need to be nurtured from the very beginning stages of learning the instrument, and they should be the result of a correct and systematic course of study.

Aside from the causes of tension that restrict free movement (gripping the violin neck, excessive finger pressure, etc.), tension can also occur because of habitual reactions to these same causes. Thus, even if one succeeds in getting the student to correctly hold the violin, release the fingers on the string, and so on, the fingers might still remain tense in themselves. This type of tension is commonly retained in the joints of the wrist and elbow and in the shoulder. These cases make it difficult to count on those subtle sensations that violin playing requires, such as feeling the string, perceiving distances, making supple movements, and so forth.

These bad habits can appear both in the beginning stages of studying as well as later on when the student encounters new difficulties. Late detection and inadequate attention from the teacher cause the bad habits to become entrenched, which naturally prevents the development of free movements (significantly affecting shifting) and generally makes the entire pedagogical process more difficult.

When making a shift, the fingers, thumb, and entire wrist need to be able to change shape at any moment, depending on the technique required. Thus it often happens that the second finger in passing from third to first position entirely changes its shape, especially in cantilena that requires a very expressive portamento. The finger straightens at the joint of the third phalange as it slides, then assumes its regular naturally curved shape only after ceding its place to the third finger.

Another similar example is the flexing and straightening movement of the wrist. The following may be observed in many violinists as they shift from third to first position: the hand, which is being led by the forearm, anticipates the movement of the finger by slightly bending in the direction of the scroll. As the wrist straightens, it draws the first finger sliding on the string toward it, and finally assumes its normal shape the moment the second finger lands on the string. The described movement is especially obvious in a slow tempo. As the tempo increases, the scope of the wrist movement decreases, and at a certain tempo (depending on the violinist) the movement entirely disappears.

Naturally, it is difficult to foresee all the possibilities of similar changes in the shape of the hand, since there are not only a variety of tasks but also a great number of individual ways of adapting to them. David Oistrakh's playing is an excellent example of how different parts of the hand adapt to the character and particularities of the movement. The freedom and flexibility in his hand movements allowed him to solve these tasks with remarkable ease.

It should be emphasized that these changes in shape of different parts of the hand and the additional movements that arise (such as the bending and straightening described above) should never assume an independent character. They should appear only as a result of the principal movements, reflecting the freedom and elasticity of these movements and the absence of any kind of tension in the hand and arm. These additional movements should not be developed in isolation from their cause. Rather, the initial development of free and supple movement should in itself lead to the appearance of these additional movements that conform in each case to the violinist's personal adaptation.

This is why the requirement found in many treatises—to keep one fixed shape of the hand, irrespective of what is performed—should be considered inadvisable. It is therefore also difficult to agree with Joachim, who believed that a good shift requires the hand to always retain the same shape as in first position.[77] According to Joachim, the back of the palm should naturally extend from the forearm, the wrist should not bend in either direction, and the finger on the string must retain the same hammer-like shape both in a fixed position and while shifting. Mikhailovsky's treatise contains a similar recommendation.[78] Attempting to retain a consistent shape while shifting necessarily creates tension, deprives the movement of its necessary freedom and flexibility, and also excludes the possibility of individual adaptation.

Not realizing that a relaxed hand is the fundamental prerequisite for correct left-hand movement creates many problems. One of the most widespread and problematic mistakes is an abrupt, jerky movement that is closer to a jump than a smooth slide. One reason is excessive finger pressure on the string, for if the finger presses too hard during the shift, the finger abruptly leaves the position and abruptly stops in the new position. This abrupt movement often leads to inaccurate intonation and makes the shift audible and jerky in quick tempos, especially when playing legato. In some cases this is even reflected in the smoothness of the bow movement.

Another reason that causes this undesirable phenomenon is the tendency of some teachers to require shifts to be imperceptible too early on in the process. For example, Kayser's method not only makes no mention of smooth shifting, but even states before each shifting exercise that the student should focus on shifting quickly and vigorously.[79] It is no surprise then that Kayser recommends learning to shift with a martelé stroke. Valter's treatise also requires that the shifts be made as fast as possible.[80]

These erroneous approaches can cause significant harm and lead to the creation and reinforcement of bad habits that are extremely difficult to get rid of. This is why it is especially important that the correct skills and habits are cultivated from the very beginning stages of study. At the same time it is important to remember that the nature of the verbal explanation of the movement is particularly important. Thus, if one states that the shift should be quick, then, as a rule, the student generates an image of a sudden jerky movement instead of a smooth and supple one. If the essence of shifting is described as being smooth, then the idea of a jump disappears and it is easy to establish the necessary sensory-motor connections that ensure seamless movement. This is thoroughly illustrated in Pavlov's physiological studies on the second signaling system.[81] The teacher should always be aware of how to correctly utilize this powerful means of educating the student.

In light of the above, we find it best to explain shifting to the student as a sliding motion, in spite of the fact that the sound of a glissando is not always desirable while shifting and may even be detrimental in many cases. Explaining the shift using this kind of imagery makes the movement smooth and flexible, and eventually the sound of the shift gradually disappears. Furthermore, a glissando in the beginning stages of learning to shift helps establish more precise coordination between the movement and the ear, which establishes the fundamental condition for clean intonation. Conversely, in exercises that shift by "leaps" there is less development of the essential aural-motor connections and consequently less accuracy in sensing distances on the fingerboard. Moreover, the suggested way of learning to shift is a good preparation for shifting in cantilena passages where the musical context requires the connection to be deliberately slowed down.

Thus the correct approach to learning to shift is not to eliminate the glissando (which, as noted, produces the opposite effect) but rather to slide smoothly, with a relaxed hand, gradually accelerating (while maintaining the quality) and releasing the pressure. It goes without saying that one must be careful that the glissando does not turn into a goal itself and become a bad habit. The indicated method for developing the correct character of shifting movements and their accompanying sensations turns out to be one of the essential elements of left-hand technique.

We already mentioned that the development of any skill is accompanied by the emergence and solidification of sensations associated with the nature of the movements—their smoothness, form, swiftness, and so on. Working on the appropriate exercises helps to establish the accompanying sensations. Eventually these sensations appear not only when the movements occur but also when the movements are only perceived or, as a rule, a split second before they are carried out. It is precisely these sensations that allow the movements to be made correctly and to be fully mastered. In performance and pedagogical practice we call this "pre-feeling." Without going into the accuracy of this terminology, it is only necessary to emphasize that a movement cannot be considered completely mastered without the emergence of such a pre-feeling.

An analogous phenomenon is "pre-hearing," which, just like pre-feeling, is developed with practice. Mostras discusses this in his work, where he claims that aural preparation preceding a movement is an essential prerequisite for clean intonation.[82] It should also be noted that pre-feeling and pre-hearing are connected and interdependent since they belong to the same set of skills.

7. GENERAL PRINCIPLES OF SHIFTING IN CANTILENA AND TECHNICAL PASSAGES. THE ROLE OF OBJECTIVE METHODOLOGY IN ANALYZING SHIFTING. A CLASSIFICATION OF SHIFTS.

On all bowed instruments, the horizontal movement of the left hand along the fingerboard is almost always made by sliding a finger along the string (exceptions are certain types of shifts examined in section 9). This slide provides an uninterrupted connection to the instrument, helping the player perceive distances on the fingerboard.

In the pedagogical literature we encounter the opinion proposed by Flesch—that all shifts be divided into two categories, with some considered "technical" and others considered "expressive" (Flesch's terminology).[83] And these shifts should be played differently, with the term *glissando* referring only to the "technical" shifts, and the term *portamento* referring to the "expressive" shifts.

However, glissando is determined by musical context. While in some cases it should be inaudible, in others it serves as a tool for special expression. For this reason we consider it incorrect to principally divide shifts into being either "expressive" or "purely technical." While the character of sound in what seems to be a purely "technical" passage may strive to be inaudible, it should only be determined by how the passage needs to sound within the musical context of the entire piece.

It is also necessary to note the similar methods of studying portamento and glissando; both are based on mastering smooth and elastic movements while shifting. By adhering to the principle that "shifts must be inaudible," many pedagogues prohibit students from smoothly connecting notes in the early stages of study. This has the opposite effect, since students develop the habit of moving suddenly and abruptly and end up making the shifts even more obvious.

In analyzing portamento as an expressive device and attempting to determine its principles, some violinists have attempted to systemize it. Alard, for example, believed that shifts should be light and quick when playing allegro and slower when playing adagio, thereby associating the character of the shift with the length of the note.[84] However, when playing cantilena there are many examples of using both fast and slow shifts in the same tempo, depending on the musical context.

Bekker makes a similar attempt by classifying portamento into three categories depending on how audible it is: nonexistent, slight, and strong.[85] He also distinguishes the styles of portamento ("lyrical" or "heroic"), depending on the fingering that is used. This is discussed in more detail below. It is perfectly clear that classifying portamento in this way, taking into consideration only how audible it is and ignoring the quality and character of its sound, is purely mechanical. It similarly does not make sense to connect the sonic character of the portamento to the fingering used in the shift. There are many examples where a shift that Becker labels as "lyrical" can sound energetic or passionate, such as in Lev Tseitlin's interpretation of a Bach aria. Or a "heroic" shift might sound lyrical when played gently *piano*.

The problem in trying to establish such rules is that it is impossible to systemize the diversity of artistic processes in general and portamento in particular. The diversity is explained by the multitude of artistic problems; the varying musical content; the style of the piece; and the performer's understanding of the character and nuances of sound, phrasing, the correlation of various elements in the musical fabric, and so on.

Naturally, only a performer technically in command of shifting can produce the subtlety that different portamenti require. And although the ear is the determining factor in evaluating the quality of the connecting notes, auditory perception on its own cannot always tell what purely technical process of connecting the notes will work best in each case.

To determine general guidelines for shifting, we conducted a study of the connections between notes in both the context of a musical composition and randomly sampled, in addition to a comparison of both categories. The study was made with the help of an oscillograph, and the results are presented in the following section.[86]

In presenting this material, we divided shifts according to how they are executed. This subdivision is based on the classification presented in Davidov's cello treatise in which the principal types of shifts are categorized as follows:[87] (1) shifts with the same finger; (2) shifts where an open string separates the positions; (3) shifts where the first note in the new position is played with a higher finger than the last note of the former position; and (4) shifts where the first note in the new position is played with a lower finger than the last note of the old position.[88] Davidov not only categorizes the shifts but also provides examples of each type of shift, including those between notes lying on different strings and shifts that incorporate harmonics.

Consequently, we propose the following classification of shifts on the violin:

Type 1: shifts with one sliding finger.
Type 2: shifts from a lower to a higher finger while moving up, and from a
    higher to a lower finger when moving down the fingerboard.
Type 3: shifts from a lower to a higher finger moving up the fingerboard,
    made by sliding the higher finger.
Type 4: shifts from a higher to a lower finger moving up the fingerboard
    and from a lower to a higher finger moving down the fingerboard.

Besides these types of shifts, there are also shifts made without a connecting slide (e.g., shifts via an open string, shifts accomplished by extending or
contracting the fingers, and shifts that incorporate harmonics). Furthermore,
there is also a special kind of shifting made with a glissando in scalar (usually
chromatic) passages.

The first four types of shifts were analyzed in detail with the help of an oscillograph. This study produced a large and interesting amount of material that
clarifies the way shifts are executed. The diagrams in the following section are
based on a transcription of the oscillograph readings.

8. DETAILS OF EXECUTING DIFFERENT TYPES OF SHIFTS. HOW SHIFTING TECHNIQUES DEPEND ON MUSICAL CONTEXT.

Each type of shift has its own specific characteristics. In order to determine these
characteristics in the most detailed and objective manner possible, we made a
series of oscillographic recordings of Type 1, 2, 3, and 4 shifts played by the emi-
nent violinists David Oistrakh, Yakov Rabinovich, and Dmitri Tsyganov. The
results are presented below in the form of graphs for easier analysis.

In all graphs, the vertical axis represents the pitch (with each division corresponding to a semitone) and the horizontal axis delineates time (with each
division corresponding to a determined fraction of a second, varying according to each graph). Each graph also shows the overall time it took to produce
the given shift, which is especially important in determining its character.

Type 1 Shifts

For these types of shifts, the oscillograph study first analyzed the shift from E^1
to G^1 without any musical context. As the graph illustrates, the shift played by

Tsyganov begins slowly and ends with significant acceleration in the sliding finger (Graph 2.1). An analogous phenomenon is observed in the return shift from G¹ to E¹ as the hand moves back down the fingerboard. Both the shifts played by Oistrakh (Graph 2.2) and Tsyganov (Graph 2.3) are distinguished by the same characteristic—a slow beginning followed by a slide that accelerates to a greater or lesser extent.

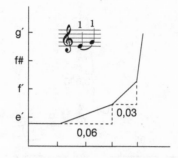

Graph 2.1 I division = 0.03 seconds. Total duration of the shift = 0.09 seconds.

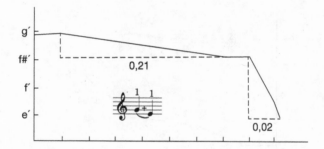

Graph 2.2 1 division = 0.01 seconds. Total duration of the shift = 0.23 seconds.

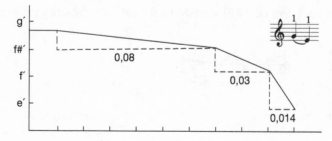

Graph 2.3 1 division = 0.014 seconds. Total duration of the shift = 0.124 seconds.

Subsequently these types of shifts were analyzed in a specific musical context. We examined the opening to Tchaikovsky's violin concerto played by Oistrakh (Graph 2.4), Rabinovich (Graph 2.5), and Tsyganov (Graph 2.6).

Even though the individual interpretations differed, the main characteristic of the connection remained the same (i.e., the finger began to slide slowly and then subsequently accelerated). The individual characteristics of the shift were reflected in the length of the entire process and the exact moment and intensity of acceleration.

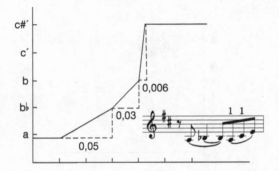

Graph 2.4 1 division = 0.03 seconds. Total duration of the shift = 0.086 seconds.

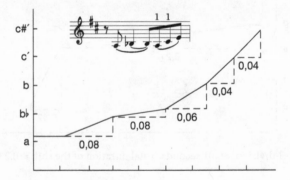

Graph 2.5 1 division = 0.04 seconds. Total duration of the shift = 0.3 seconds.

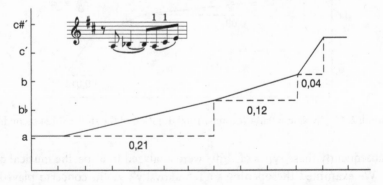

Graph 2.6 1 division = 0.04 seconds. Total duration of the shift = 0.37 seconds.

The notes were connected in a similar fashion (this time at the interval of a fifth) in the following shift from Tchaikovsky's *Serenade Melancolique* (Graph 2.7 = Tsyganov, Graph 2.8 = Rabinovich, Graph 2.9 = Oistrakh).

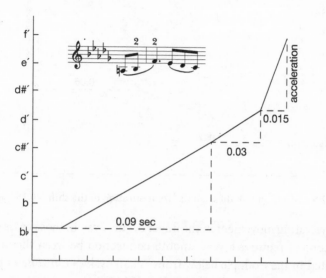

Graph 2.7 1 division = 0.015 seconds. Total duration of the shift = 0.135 seconds.

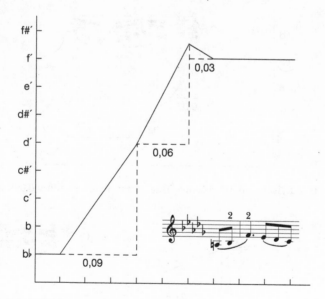

Graph 2.8 1 division = 0.03 seconds. Total duration of the shift = 0.18 seconds.

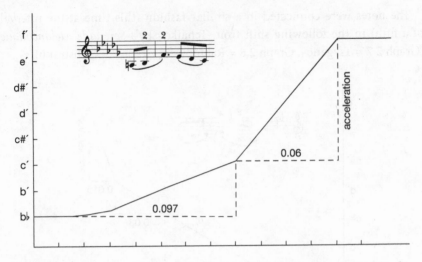

Graph 2.9 1 division = 0.014 seconds. Total duration of the shift = 0.157 seconds.

An accelerating movement in the finger occurs even in those cases when the musical context requires a very smooth connection between the notes. This is illustrated in the example below from Tchaikovsky's *Canzonetta* played by Oistrakh (Graph 2.10) and Tsyganov (Graph 2.11).

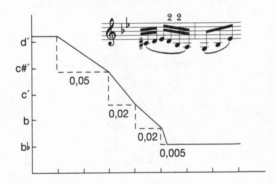

Graph 2.10 1 division = 0.023 seconds. Total duration of the shift = 0.095 seconds.

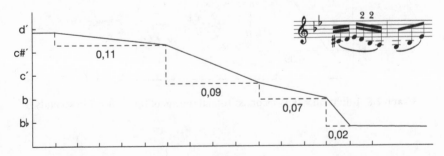

Graph 2.11 1 division = 0.02 seconds. Total duration of the shift = 0.29 seconds.

Thus, we find that Type 1 shifts are characterized by acceleration toward the end of the shift. This acceleration occurs primarily because of aesthetic considerations having to do with the sound. This is easy to observe, for if the shift is played without acceleration it loses its definition, and the glissando that connects the notes predominates. (In Type 2 shifts the second note is produced by dropping the next finger, thus there is less need for acceleration.) Although Type 1 shifts appear to be the simplest, practice shows that executing them correctly entails certain difficulties. One of the most widespread problems observed in students making Type 1 shifts is the absence of a smooth beginning or, conversely, the absence of the subsequent accelerando. In the first case the shift sounds jerky, and in the second it sounds sluggish and unpleasant. Uncovering the principles of how these shifts are made can help teachers concretize the way in which they teach them. In fast passages, the slow beginning and subsequent acceleration may be less obvious because of the quicker tempo. However, the indicated method of working on shifts by developing a smooth and calm beginning also affects shifts in a fast tempo and gives them the necessary smoothness and elasticity.

The ease of making Type 1 shifts directly depends on the pressure of the finger on the string. Thus, at the moment of shifting it is necessary to release the finger pressure, especially as the distance of the shift increases and the tempo increases (e.g., in fast passages). However, it should be noted that if students have insufficiently mastered this technique the opposite result may occur, and excessively releasing the finger will actually restrict movement. The problem lies in the fact that after lifting from the string during the shift, the finger presses again onto the fingerboard as it arrives at the new note. Rather than moving along the fingerboard, it moves "into the fingerboard" (using Yampolsky's expression), thereby restricting the movement. This is commonly observed in the movement of the fourth finger when playing octaves.

When shifting to a harmonic (Example 2.29), the finger pressure is rather particular.

Example 2.29 Taneyev: *Theme and Variations.*

In these cases it is inadvisable to gradually release the finger pressure as recommended in certain methodological texts. The finger should press the string normally for the entire duration of the slide and release only at the last moment. This allows accurate arrival on the harmonic with a flawless sound.

Type 1 shifts to a harmonic are associated with various types of portamento and are a widely used expressive device. In the following Example 2.30, the glissando to the harmonic (emphasized by the bow arm) gives the passage a brilliant bravura character.

Example 2.30 Glazunov: *Violin Concerto.*

A similar shift, but this time with a slightly different portamento and smoother movement in the bow arm, makes the sound slightly coquettish and more grazioso (see Example 2.31).

Example 2.31 Rimsky-Korsakov: *Mazurka.*

It is rare to find Type 1 shifts that also involve transferring the finger to another string, for usually in these cases another fingering is used to ensure a better sound. When these shifts do occur, Lesman indicated that the moving finger should transfer to the new string at the same time as the bow.[89] However, Tseitlin's technique may be considered more appropriate. Tseitlin suggested preemptively preparing the fifth, that is, placing the finger immediately on two strings. When the change to a new string coincides with a change in bow, then another method is also possible. If the glissando occurs on the initial bow stroke, then the finger slides along the string of the first note; whereas if the glissando occurs on the subsequent bow stroke, then the finger slides along the string of the second note. If the shift requires the finger to transfer to a new string in conjunction with activity in the other fingers (e.g., in double stops or chords), then the only possibility is to slide the finger along the initial string and then make the transfer.

The special lyrical quality of shifts made with one finger is explained by the close resemblance to vocal portamento (something to also strive for in other shifts where possible). This also explains why Type 1 shifts are widely used to give additional expression to the sound. Similar to any other technique, the manner in which these types of shifts are used largely depends on the individual style of the player. Thus Tseitlin, whose playing was broad, powerful, and full, tended to employ a slower portamento, making the shifts sound rich and deep as in Example 2.32.

Example 2.32 Beethoven: *Violin Concerto, mvt. 2.*

When Kreisler plays his *Caprice Viennoise*, he gives this type of shift a slightly tremulous and sensuous quality that intrinsically reflects his interpretation (see Example 2.33).

Example 2.33 Kreisler: *Caprice Viennoise.*

Oistrakh often used this type of shift and would give it a completely different, lyrical color. It was characteristic for Oistrakh to make a descending glissando with the first finger (Examples 2.34 and 2.35).

Example 2.34 Rakov: *Violin Concerto, mvt. 1.*

Example 2.35 Kabalevsky: *Violin Concerto, mvt. 3.*

Type 2 Shifts

Before moving to an analysis of Type 2 shifts, we should note that the vast majority of specialized texts, such as those by Alard, Voldan, Voiku, Jockisch, Koeckert, Mikhailovsky, Radmall, Flesch, and many others, confirm the necessity of using so-called auxiliary or intermediary notes in these types of shifts.[90] "Intermediary notes" refer to those notes that correspond to where the initial finger (i.e., the finger making the slide) would lie in the new position (see Examples 2.36a–d).

Example 2.36a

Example 2.36b

Example 2.36c

Example 2.36d

The oscillographic analysis of these types of shifts clearly shows the actual borders of the finger movement and the degree to which they correspond to the intermediary notes. Graph 2.12 represents the shift E^1–B^1 played by Oistrakh. As the curve indicates, the connecting finger only arrives at the note $F_\sharp$, whereas the corresponding intermediary note for this type of shift is supposed to be G^1. Consequently, in this example the sliding finger falls a half-step short of the intermediary note.

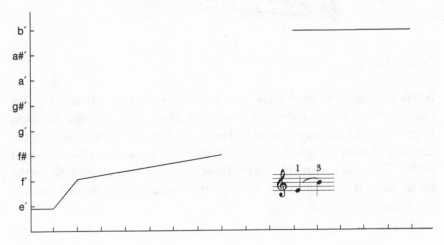

Graph 2.12 1 division = 0.013 seconds. Total duration of the shift = 0.142 seconds.

A slightly larger gap in this respect is observed when Tsyganov plays the same shift (Graph 2.13).

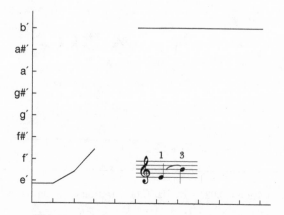

Graph 2.13 1 division = 0.02 seconds. Total duration of the shift = 0.089 seconds.

A similar break occurs when Tsyganov plays another shift of the same interval C^2–G^2 (Graph 2.14). As the curve indicates, the connecting finger only makes it to the note D^2 (indeed even a quarter-tone below), even though the intermediary note should theoretically be E^2. In this example the gap is wider than a whole step.

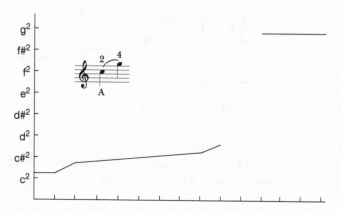

Graph 2.14 1 division = 0.013 seconds. Total duration of the shift = 0.13 seconds.

At the same time we should note that in other shifts of the same distance, the sliding finger does indeed reach the corresponding intermediate note. This can be seen in Graphs 2.15 (Oistrakh) and 2.16 (Rabinovich), which represent the shift F^1–B♭ from Tchaikovsky's *Serenade Melancolique*.

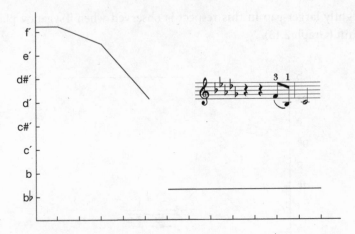

Graph 2.15 1 division = 0.023 seconds. Total duration of the shift = 0.0117 seconds.

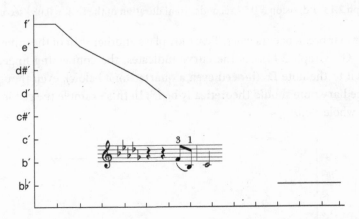

Graph 2.16 1 division = 0.042 seconds. Total duration of the shift = 0.42 seconds.

In another example, looking at the shift $G\sharp^1$–$D\sharp^2$ in Rakov's violin concerto, we see that Oistrakh (Graph 2.17) does not reach the intermediary note (missing it by a whole step), while Tsyganov does reach the intermediary note (Graph 2.18).

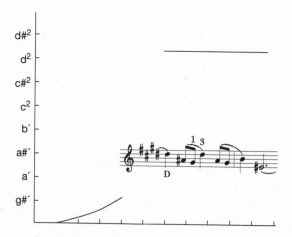

Graph 2.17 1 division = 0.016 seconds. Total duration of the shift = 0.096 seconds.

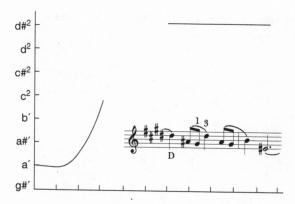

Graph 2.18 1 division = 0.026 seconds. Total duration of the shift = 0.133 seconds.

If the disparity is not always observed in small shifts (though most often it is) it becomes perfectly obvious when the distance of the shifts increases, as shown in the following examples. Thus, in shifts at the interval of a seventh, the discrepancy is the equivalent of a whole tone, and sometimes it is even larger, as seen in Graphs 2.19, 2.20, and 2.21.

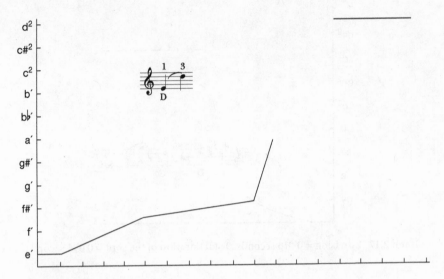

Graph 2.19 1 division = 0,013 seconds. Total duration of the shift = 0.173 seconds.

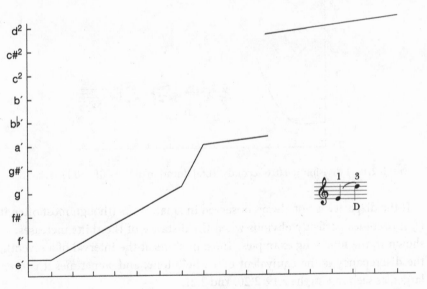

Graph 2.20 1 division = 0.025 seconds. Total duration of the shift = 0.3 seconds.

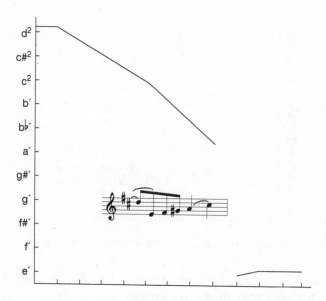

Graph 2.21 1 division = 0.013 seconds. Total duration of the shift = 0.106 seconds.

An even larger discrepancy is observed in shifts of a tenth. When playing the shift E–G from Vieuxtemps' Violin Concerto No. 5, both Rabinovich (Graph 2.22) and Tsyganov (Graph 2.23) miss the intermediary note by more than one-and-a-half whole tones.

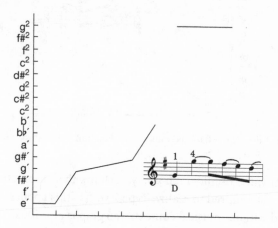

Graph 2.22 1 division = 0.03 seconds. Total duration of the shift = 0.17 seconds.

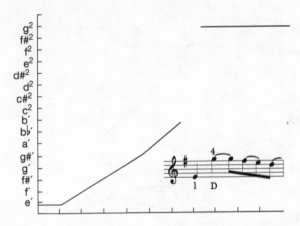

Graph 2.23 1 division = 0.013 seconds. Total duration of the shift = 0.187 seconds.

In the shift of a tenth between F#^{1} and A^2 in Wieniawski's *Tarantella* (Rabinovich, Graph 2.24), the gap is even four-and-a-half tones.

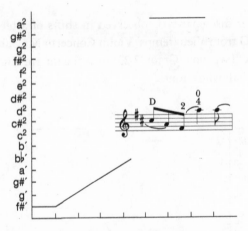

Graph 2.24 1 division = 0.03 seconds. Total duration of the shift = 0.13 seconds.

Consequently, the oscillograph analysis shows that in practice intermediary notes are not required to realize Type 2 shifts. This applies to shifts made both with and without musical context. The graphs also illustrate that in the majority of Type 2 shifts, the shift begins slowly and then the sliding finger accelerates. Although this is less clearly articulated than in Type 1 shifts, it nonetheless turns out to be a necessary condition for making the shift freely and smoothly.

A specific characteristic of Type 2 shifts, associated with their particular sound quality, is that the pressure of the sliding finger gradually releases, often to the point of lifting from the string until the moment the new finger drops. However, in some cases when the subsequent note needs to be prepared (for example, when making a shift with a glissando), the finger may release without lifting from the string.

If the shift is made with the help of an intermediary note, then the finger must press the string and slide precisely to the intermediary note before the new finger drops. With this method, even if the intermediary note is inaudible because of the well-timed placement of the subsequent finger, one still hears the end of the connecting slide and the consequent break between the notes.

The reason intermediary notes are recommended by many teachers (particularly Lesman) and supported in the literature is because they seem to simplify all types of shifts, in essence consolidating them into shifts made with one finger. We find it extremely helpful to compare Type 1 and Type 2 shifts, but it is necessary to turn the student's attention not so much to similarities in the movement of the sliding finger (in this case, the index finger) as to differences.

When Type 2 shifts occur between different strings (Example 2.37), they are played the same way (i.e., the finger connecting the notes has the same character as described earlier, and the only difference is that the new finger drops onto a different string). The same is true for ascending Type 2 shifts that arrive at a harmonic (Example 2.38). The difference in Type 2 shifts that descend from a harmonic (Example 2.39) is that the connecting finger presses the string the moment it begins to slide (not earlier). Afterward, the regular character of the slide is retained and the finger pressure gradually releases.

Example 2.37

Example 2.38

Example 2.39

Type 3 Shifts

In a whole series of violin treatises, especially in the classical nineteenth-century methods, Type 3 shifts were not only not recommended but even considered "anti-artistic and a sign of poor taste."[91] Spohr, for example came to the categorical conclusion that slides with the new finger must always be rejected since they always create an unpleasant sound.[92] David, Alard, and others reject in principle the use of Type 3 shifts for expressive purposes, and only acknowledge their use in certain cases as a technical device to facilitate specific difficulties. Thus, David notes that it is possible to slide the finger that plays the second note only in exceptional cases and when making a very large leap going up the fingerboard. Alard also writes that these types of shifts should be only an exception (replacing Type 2 shifts) and used only when one or more strings separate the connected notes. In these cases a new finger replaces the initial finger that would usually make the slide.

In our opinion, Type 3 shifts turn out to constitute some of the most unique expressive devices. The particular characteristic of this shift is that the beginning of the second note is not clear but rather soft, and it is arrived at gradually. Different ways of playing Type 3 shifts can create different nuances in the sound (i.e., making it suave, intimate, more expressive, passionate, etc.). This is why these shifts are often irreplaceable and why they are widely used by many outstanding violinists. However, we should note that these shifts should be used only when moving up, since they produce unfavorable results when shifting down. We will also add that in large leaps (especially to harmonics), or when the left hand needs to jump between one or two strings, this type of shift often provides more secure intonation than sliding with the initial finger.

Nonetheless, Type 3 shifts are generally limited to the aforementioned examples. They are mostly used as a special expressive device in cantilena, depending on the musical context. This type of shift is impossible in fast sequential passages since the arrival note is not distinct and thus the alternating notes are not precise. Thus this shift should not be used in the early stages of study—it is a special expressive device that requires a developed musical taste and high level of mastery.

In his analysis of Type 3 shifts, Carl Flesch proceeded from the necessity of using intermediary notes, as seen in Example 2.40.[93]

Example 2.40

(incorrect)   (correct)

However, the oscillograph studies show that this shift never begins on an "intermediary" note. This is seen in an excerpt from the Glazunov concerto (performed by Rabinovich, Oistrakh, and Tsyganov) and in an excerpt from Concerto No. 5 by Vieuxtemps (performed by the same violinists). In all cases without exception, this slide began to a greater or lesser extent near the second note, becoming, as Mostras would say, a kind of "ramp" leading into the note. Thus, for example, in Rabinovich's version the slide begins only at a half-tone from the second note, and not at the distance of a major third that would correspond to the intermediary note (Graph 2.25).

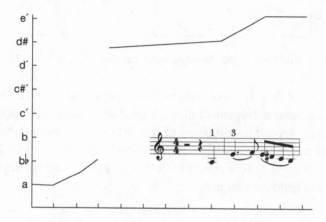

Graph 2.25 1 division = 0.04 seconds. Total duration of the shift = 0.38 seconds.

The same is observed when Oistrakh (Graph 2.26) and Tsyganov (Graph 2.27) play this shift.

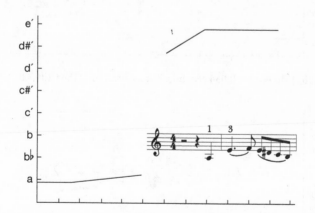

Graph 2.26 1 division = 0.02 seconds. Total duration of the shift = 0.15 seconds.

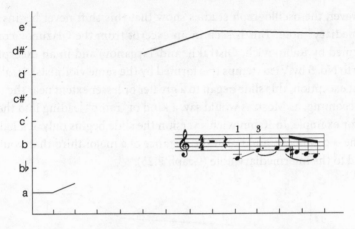

Graph 2.27 1 division = 0.034 seconds. Total duration of the shift = 0.25 seconds.

An analysis of these types of shifts in Vieuxtemps' Concerto No. 5 produced the following results: Tsyganov's slide (Graph 2.28) started at the distance of a third from the second note (instead of at a distance of a fourth, which would correspond to the intermediary note); and both Oistrakh (Graph 2.29) and Rabinovich (Graph 2.30) started the slide at a distance slightly larger than a major second from the new note.

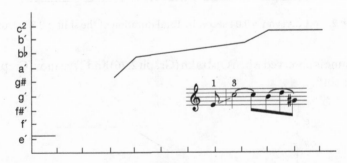

Graph 2.28 1 division = 0.034 seconds. Total duration of the shift = 0.29 seconds.

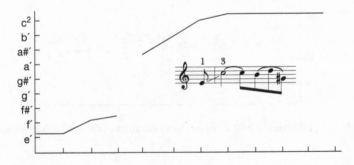

Graph 2.29 1 division = 0.02 seconds. Total duration of the shift = 0.133 seconds.

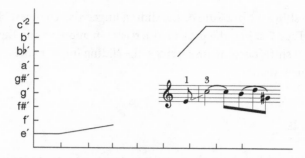

Graph 2.30 1 division = 0.03 seconds. Total duration of the shift = 0.17 seconds.

Flesch did note the possibility of making Type 3 shifts without auxiliary notes, although he referred to them as "free portamento-fantasies" representing a "purely individual means of expression." For example, Flesch considered a slide that started as close as possible to the second note to be a personal trait of the violinist Jacques Thibaud. Yet, as the examples above show, the discrepancy between the intermediary note and the actual start of the portamento is not just a characteristic of one performer.

In other cases, the finger may even begin sliding before the intermediary note. For instance, let us examine Example 2.41.

Example 2.41 Wieniawski: *Violin Concerto No. 2, mvt. 3.*

For this shift, Tseitlin recommends bringing the third finger closer to the first, and letting the third finger make the slide along the entire fingerboard from start to finish. In this type of shift, the accelerating speed and increase of pressure in the bow plays an important role. The use of this technique depends on the musical context, which in Example 2.41 requires a lot of brilliance and emotional excitement to emphasize the transition to the new theme.

Comparing the previous examples of the Glazunov and Vieuxtemps concerti, it is easy to see that all performers make the portamento longer in the Vieuxtemps than in the Glazunov. This again proves that the fundamental factor that determines the difference is the different character of the music—more expressive and sentimental in the Vieuxtemps and more strict and noble in the Glazunov. On this basis we may conclude that the nature of movement in Type 3 shifts should not be determined by intermediary notes, but by the specific sound required by the character of the music.

In Type 3 shifts the pressure of the sliding finger also changes. However, in contrast to Type 2 shifts, the pressure increases in approaching the new note. When Type 3 shifts occur across strings, the sliding finger makes the connection on the new string.

Type 4 Shifts

In the specialized literature there are two points of view regarding ascending Type 4 shifts. Both of these opinions involve intermediary notes, but they differ in how they are used. According to the first point of view, which dates back to the classical German treatises of David, Joachim, and others, the shift is made using a so-called upper intermediary note (Example 2.42). As Joachim notes in his treatise, in these cases the last finger on the string before the shift slides to the position in which the second note lies.

Example 2.42

The other point of view is based on the so-called lower intermediary note (Example 2.43). This idea was developed by Flesch and was propagated in the later methods of Ševčík, Voldan, and others.

Example 2.43

Although both of these points of view attempt to assure a smooth connection between notes, neither opinion is really justified. For the musical and expressive purpose of this shift is to make the connection between notes as uninterrupted as possible. Therefore any glissando that occurs outside the framework of these notes, as occurs with both upper and lower intermediary notes, is inappropriate.

An oscillographic analysis of Type 4 shifts shows that in practice neither upper nor lower intermediary notes are used. An analysis was made of two separate shifts: F^1–C^2 (Graphs 2.31 and 2.32; performers Tsyganov and Rabinovich) and D^2–A^2 (Graph 2.33; Oistrakh). As the graphs illustrate, neither the upper nor the lower auxiliary notes were used in any of the examples,

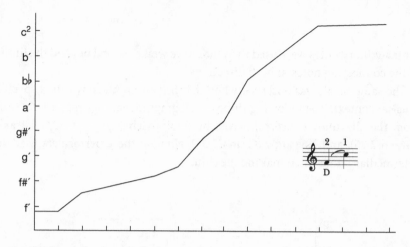

Graph 2.31 1 division = 0.023 seconds. Total duration of the shift = 0.25 seconds.

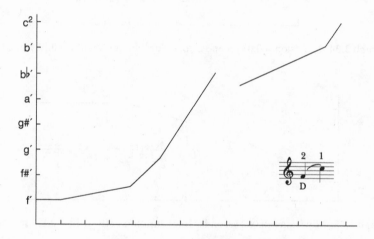

Graph 2.32 1 division = 0.019 seconds. Total duration of the shift = 0.228 seconds.

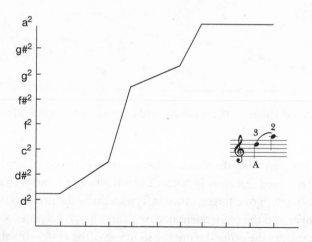

Graph 2.33 1 division = 0.025 seconds. Total duration of the shift = 0.15 seconds.

for if auxiliary notes were used then the curve would extend beyond the limits of the connecting notes in both directions.

The same result was observed when the shifts were made within a specific musical context. The following three oscillographic readings represent a shift from the Glazunov concerto, played by Rabinovich (Graph 2.34), Oistrakh (Graph 2.35), and Tsyganov (Graph 2.36). None of these performers used an intermediary note when making the shift.

Graph 2.34 1 division = 0.03 seconds. Total duration of the shift = 0.12 seconds.

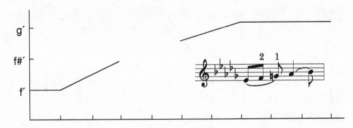

Graph 2.35 1 division = 0.022 seconds. Total duration of the shift = 0.132 seconds.

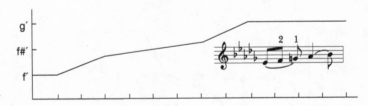

Graph 2.36 1 division = 0.022 seconds. Total duration of the shift = 0.198 seconds.

The curve representing the slide is either completely uninterrupted or close to being uninterrupted. As already noted, an uninterrupted line is characteristic of Type 1 shifts with one finger. Since in Type 4 shifts the initial note is played with one finger and the consequent note with another, it becomes obvious that one finger replaces the other during the slide itself. The closer this substitution coincides with the general movement of the hand, the closer does the curve resemble an uninterrupted line. Thus, looking at Graph 2.32 one can conclude that in this case the general hand movement was slightly slower, and the new finger repeated some of the path covered by the initial finger (albeit only fractionally by a quarter-tone). In Graph 2.35 the opposite is observed: the movement of the hand is slightly accelerated, causing the new finger (the first) to be carried further along, instead of capturing the glissando right where the old finger (the second) ended. This explains the slight break in the graph. However, we should remember that these kinds of breaks are so short and insignificant that they are only noticeable on such a sensitive instrument as the oscillograph.

One might suppose that in more difficult circumstances, when the shift is made not with adjacent but with outer fingers (such as the first and fourth), auxiliary notes are indeed necessary. This matter was also subjected to an oscillographic analysis (Graphs 2.37–2.43). No intermediary notes were used in the shifts G^1–B^1 (Graph 2.37; Rabinovich) and D^2–A^2 (Graph 2.38; Oistrakh) made with the third and first fingers. The same result was observed when Rabinovich played the shift A^1–D^2 (Graph 2.39) with the outer fingers

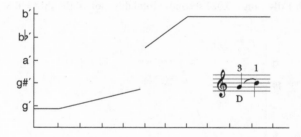

Graph 2.37 1 division = 0.016 seconds. Total duration of the shift = 0.096 seconds.

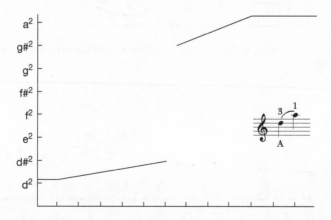

Graph 2.38 1 division = 0.017 seconds. Total duration of the shift = 0.153 seconds.

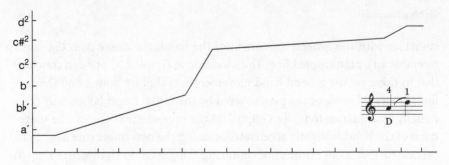

Graph 2.39 1 division = 0.017 seconds. Total duration of the shift = 0.229 seconds.

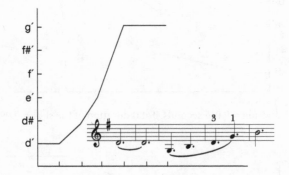

Graph 2.40 1 division = 0.022 seconds. Total duration of the shift = 0.37 seconds.

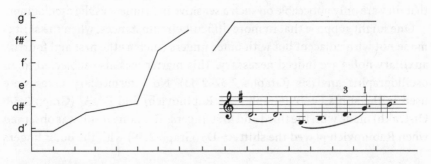

Graph 2.41 1 division = 0.03 seconds. Total duration of the shift = 0.09 seconds.

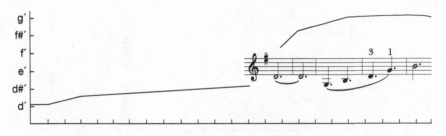

Graph 2.42 1 division = 0.019 seconds. Total duration of the shift = 0.28 seconds.

Graph 2.43 1 division = 0.03 seconds. Total duration of the shift = 0.21 seconds.

(i.e., shifting from the fourth to the first). Moreover, as the graphs indicate, the connecting slide did not go higher or lower than the indicated notes.

Therefore, it is clear that in practice intermediary notes are not used to play these types of shifts, no matter what fingers are used.

This is entirely confirmed by oscillographs that represent shifts taken in musical context. The following graphs represent a shift from Wieniawski's *Scherzo Tarantella* played by Tsyganov (Graph 2.40), Rabinovich (Graph 2.41), and Oistrakh (Graph 2.42) as well as a shift from Sarasate's *Introduction and Tarantella* played by Rabinovich (Graph 2.43).

We notice that the curve shows a break in certain shifts that are not played with adjacent fingers (Graphs 2.37, 2.38, 2.40, 2.42). As already noted for shifts with adjacent fingers, this break is a result of the coordination between the hand movement and the simultaneous finger substitution.

Thus in the shifts in Graphs 2.37, 2.38, and 2.42, the hand moved faster, which caused the new finger to drop to the fingerboard beyond where the initial finger finished its slide. Graph 2.40 illustrates the opposite, where the slow movement of the hand caused the new finger to repeat the path already made by the previous one. Graphs 2.39 and 2.43 are interesting examples of an in-between kind of coordination. They show the hand moving progressively, with the new finger neither repeating the path of the first finger nor carried further. Instead, the new finger lands precisely where the previous finger finished its slide. This causes the note at this point on the fingerboard to lengthen, making the curve on the graph not only uninterrupted but also slightly more horizontal in some segments. However, the more typical examples are Graphs 2.31, 2.33, 2.34, 2.36, and 2.41, which represent a gradual, uninterrupted line.

The particular characteristic of Type 4 shifts turns out to be the substitution of one finger by another as the hand is moving. The indicated method of shifting always ensures a connection in which the slide does not exceed the limits of the connected notes, and this is justified from a musical and aesthetic point of view. It is necessary to again emphasize that attempting to simplify this technique by using intermediary notes (i.e., reducing all shifts to Type 1 shifts) distorts the musical essence of this type of connection.

Although learning Type 4 shifts is more difficult than other types, once they are assimilated they do not pose any additional problems. It helps to begin learning these shifts with adjacent fingers. The "mechanism" of substituting one finger with another can be studied with the help of the following exercises in Example 2.44. These exercises help clarify the essence of this technique, which is also important when correcting previously developed bad habits.

Example 2.44

The principles of making Type 4 shifts remain the same even when adjacent fingers are not used. Generally only the movement of the hand accelerates, since the new finger must be transferred further because of the greater distance between the fingers. It should be remembered that, in these shifts the pressure of the new finger increases while the pressure of the previous finger releases. In this respect the movement of the initial finger is similar to the movement it makes sliding to a harmonic (see Example 2.45).

Example 2.45

In practice, when Type 4 shifts are played with nonadjacent fingers, the outer fingers often draw close together before the shift as the inner fingers slightly lift. This technique is recommended in some specialized methods including Lesman's work and Davidov's treatise for cellists.[94] However, we find this technique should be considered more of an individual adaptation. Also, as the tempo increases, the degree to which the fingers draw together decreases. S. Kozolupov and L. Ginsberg make a similar point when analyzing this technique for cellists.[95] In a fast tempo this technique inevitably restricts movement in the hand and can make the position unstable, thereby causing problems in intonation.

In descending shifts, the initial finger makes the slide, and the subsequent finger immediately drops to the necessary spot on the fingerboard. Using an intermediary note in this case means the connecting glissando must go beyond the limits of the connected notes, as in Example 2.46.

Example 2.46

Moving to an analysis of descending Type 4 shifts, we must emphasize that it is essential to correctly master these shifts since they are in constant use, especially in descending sequences. By contrast, Type 4 shifts are not typical in cantilena; if used at all they are made with adjacent fingers, but usually they are replaced with other types of shifts.

The oscillographic studies represented in Graphs 2.44 (Oistrakh), 2.45 (Rabinovich), and 2.46 (Tsyganov) show that none of these shifts made use of intermediary notes. In all three cases the initial finger slid no more than a whole tone, whereas if an intermediary note were used the slide would have extended down a fifth.

Graph 2.44 1 division = 0.025 seconds. Total duration of the shift = 0.1 seconds.

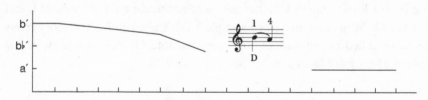

Graph 2.45 1 division = 0.016 seconds. Total duration of the shift = 0.16 seconds.

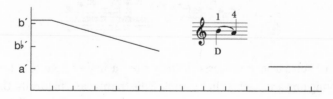

Graph 2.46 1 division = 0.025 seconds. Total duration of the shift = 0.3 seconds.

The character of the slide is determined by the particular movement of the initial finger. Here, the finger does not press the string for the duration of the slide as would happen if intermediary notes were used. Instead, the finger releases its pressure and even lifts off the string as it assumes its appropriate placement in the new position. In fast sequential passages, the initial finger may not lift as much because of the necessity to prepare the following notes. In extremely fast sequences the finger may not even lift at all, although it will still significantly release its pressure from the string. For instance, this is clear when playing the passage in Example 2.47.

Example 2.47

In most cases an oscillographic analysis of Type 4 shifts illustrates the same principles as oscillographic analyses for Type 1 and Type 2 shifts (i.e., a slow beginning followed by an acceleration that depends on both the musical content and the individual player). This characteristic is clearly represented in Graphs 2.31, 2.33, 2.36, 2.37, 2.38, 2.41, 2.42, and 2.43.

Type 4 shifts can be divided into the following subcategories, depending on the interval between the connected notes. The first subcategory involves shifting from a lower note to a higher note when ascending the fingerboard, and has already been examined (see Example 2.44). The second subcategory refers to the so-called substitution of fingers on one note. Or more precisely, in this case one finger displaces another (see Example 2.48).

Example 2.48 Goedicke: *Etude.*

The third subcategory involves shifting from a higher note to a lower note while moving upward, such as in Example 2.49. In this case, naturally, there is no finger substitution and the notes are connected by a glissando made by either the initial or the subsequent finger, depending on the technical and musical context.

Example 2.49 Goedicke: Etude.

The last two subcategories of Type 4 shifts refer to descending shifts. Example 2.50 illustrates the variety of ways of shifting to an identical note when moving down.

Example 2.50 Goldmark: *Violin Concerto, mvt. 1.*

The final subcategory involves shifting from a lower note to a higher note when moving down (Example 2.51).

Example 2.51 Brahms: *Violin Concerto, mvt. 1.*

Both Spohr and Alard already noted that the Type 4 shifts involving finger substitution are widely used in cantilena, and are a particularly expressive device comparable to vocal techniques.[96] These shifts are used not only as a means of separating notes played in one bow but also when the bow changes, as in Example 2.52.

Example 2.52 Glazunov: *Violin Concerto.*

So far we have examined Type 4 shifts where both notes lie on one string. However, Type 4 shifts often occur between different strings. In these cases four variations are possible: in Examples 2.53a–d, versions *a* and *b* illustrate movement up the fingerboard; and versions *c* and *d* illustrate movement down the fingerboard.

Example 2.53a–d

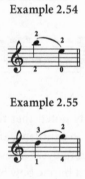

Naturally, these examples may also be played differently (see Examples 2.54 and 2.55).

Example 2.54

Example 2.55

Yet, although these shifts may be avoided by using an alternate fingering, an analysis of the literature shows that these shifts are still nonetheless sometimes indicated.

Thus, Examples 2.56 and 2.57 illustrate shifts that correspond to Example 2.53a.

Example 2.56 Bach: *Sonata No. 3, Largo.*

Example 2.57 Goedicke: *Etude.*

Examples 2.58 and 2.59 illustrate shifts similar to Example 2.53b.

Example 2.58 Glazunov: *Adagio from the ballet "Raymonda"*

Example 2.59 Glazunov: *Meditation.*

Examples 2.60 and 2.61 illustrate shifts similar to Example 53c.

Example 2.60 Taneyev: *Tarantella.*

Example 2.61 Khachaturian: *Song-Poem.*

And finally, Example 2.62 illustrates shifts similar to Example 2.53d.

Example 2.62 Khachaturian: *Violin Concerto, mvt. 1.*

Many treatises indicate the benefits of using either upper or lower inter-mediary notes for these shifts (analogous to the use of intermediary notes for Type 4 shifts on one string). When changing strings, the intermediary note occurs on the string of the connecting slide (Examples 2.63a–d).

Example 2.63

This method of incorporating intermediary notes retains all the associated problems that we have already noted.

In Examples 2.63a and 2.63c, it is not difficult to notice that even though the intermediary note lies within the framework of the connected notes, it still disrupts the continuity between the notes by emphasizing the break in the connection. This becomes immediately obvious when attempting to play the *Largo* by Bach (Example 2.56) with either upper or lower intermediary notes. The use of intermediary notes in Examples 2.63b and 2.63d is further complicated by the fact that the slide occurs in the opposite direction from the connecting notes, separating them even further.

A similar rift occurs with Type 2 shifts (Examples 2.64 and 2.65), and for this reason we consider it more appropriate to discuss these shifts here in this section.

Example 2.64 Taneyev: *Theme and Variations.*

Example 2.65 Conus: *Violin Concerto.*

In all such cases, where the glissando cannot entirely connect the notes, it is impossible to find a technique that completely eliminates the problem. Therefore, the shifting technique in each case must stem from the particularities of the musical excerpt and conform to the specific sound that is required. Once again, using intermediary notes only accentuates the rupture. In some Type 2 shifts it may be entirely logical to slide with the subsequent finger. This gives the sound a certain depth and lyricism, comparable to the human voice (Example 2.66).

Example 2.66 Taneyev: *Theme and Variations.*

In other cases, where the character of the music requires something different, a slide with the initial finger may be recommended (Example 2.67).

Example 2.67 Taneyev: *Theme and Variations.*

In order to avoid undesirable additional sounds, the glissando in this shift must be as unnoticeable as possible. This is achieved by significantly releasing the pressure of the sliding finger, changing the bow at the same time, and making the shift quickly. This is the only method possible in fast sequences, since if executed properly it best conceals the problematic sounds associated with this type of shift (Example 2.68).

Example 2.68 Paganini: *Caprice No. 17.*

Sometimes, the undesirable glissando may be avoided by making a barely noticeable pause. If perfectly executed, this technique may indeed be useful.

For Type 4 shifts in Example 2.53a, one finger replaces the other in the course of the movement (i.e., the initial finger starts the slide, and then the next finger takes over and continues on the new string). However, for shifts in

Example 2.53b, we recommend sliding with the subsequent finger in cantilena (similar to what was described for Type 3 shifts). In fast sequences the same technique may be used, but it is made less noticeable by shortening the slide and changing the bow at the same time.

For the descending shifts in Example 2.53c, the slide is made solely with the initial finger, and the new finger falls immediately to the note in the new position on the new string. And finally, the shifts in Example 2.53d are the most awkward in regards to their sound, which is why they are not used in cantilena. They must be made quite discreetly, with the help of all the methods already indicated.

All the types of shifts we examined may be further complicated under certain conditions. One example is when the shifts cover a great distance (i.e., so-called leaps that create well-known problems in intonation). Two other reasons, common in pedagogical practice, often make the problems in leaps even worse. The first reason is when the student constantly fears playing out of tune. This creates a lack of confidence in moving the left hand, and consequently the student flattens or "falls short" of the arrival note. The second reason is tied to the fear of playing out of rhythm. This causes the shift to be made too quickly, almost convulsively, and this also creates problems for intonation.

In these cases we recommend focusing special attention on the fluidity and tranquility of the actual movement. This helps to make the shift properly, thereby improving the intonation and quality of sound. When working on making a shift smooth, it is important to keep in mind the principle of beginning the shift slowly and then accelerating. Pedagogical practice has shown this method helps overcome the difficulties associated with large leaps. The player perceives the beginning of the leap to be associated not with the initial note, but with the moment the movement accelerates. Thus, the distance between the notes appears to diminish, providing greater confidence in accomplishing this kind of shift. Moreover, the smooth movement of the left hand then does not disrupt the smooth movement of the bow, which is especially important when making the leap in legato.

There are many different opinions on how best to execute large leaps. For example, some believe that in making a leap from a lower finger to a higher finger, the higher finger should help by also sliding (as in a Type 3 shift). On the other hand, others believe that only the initial finger should be used. We find the answer to depend on the player's individual adaption. However, in all cases, the solution must proceed from the degree to which either method produces the sound closest to that required in the musical excerpt.

We should also emphasize that the use of intermediary notes when making large leaps to the high positions creates excess tension in the hand and is consequently inadvisable. This is clear in Example 2.69.

Example 2.69 Paganini: *Witches's Dance.*

When making leaps to the high positions, it is important to note that the shape of the instrument requires the hand to be prepared in advance in order to make a unified movement. The feeling of this unified movement should be so thoroughly assimilated that it is able to almost anticipate the movement itself. As Tseitlin notes, this makes it much easier to execute the leap accurately. According to Mostras, one reason for problematic intonation in large leaps is when vibrato is used during the shift, since this obscures a clear perception of distance.[97]

To insure accurate intonation in large leaps, we recommend special exercises that involve leaps of varying distances and their subsequent comparison (the latter is particularly important). These exercises enable the correct calculation of distance on the fingerboard (developing a "good eye," as Yampolsky would say), and they also develop confidence in making large leaps. The exercises may be structured according to the following principles.

1. Leaps from the same note to different positions. There are two versions of this exercise that may also be combined.
   (a) Shifts with the same finger, but to different notes separated by various intervals all the way down to a half-step (these exercises especially help sharpen the sense of distance on the fingerboard).
   (b) Shifts with different fingers, but to the same note.
2. Leaps from different positions to the same note (for example, to a harmonic).
3. Leaps from different notes to different notes.

Even before making the leap one must clearly imagine the sound of the desired note and pre-hear it. This way, the movement of the hand realizes a sonic relationship that has already been perceived. Only in this manner, and not through mechanical repetition, can the necessary aural-motor connections be created that allow command of the fingerboard ("knowing the fingerboard," as Oistrakh would say).

Shifts that involve notes separated by rests are a special case. These shifts often make it difficult to play the new note in tune since sometimes it is played as if it were an independent note instead of being associated with the previous one. This happens when contact is lost with the fingerboard during the rest. For example, this is a common problem in the following excerpt from the Tchaikovsky concerto, where the difficulty lies in playing the note E^3 in tune (see Example 2.70).

Example 2.70 Tchaikovsky: *Violin Concerto, mvt. 3.*

Another example is found in Ernst's *Othello* where many performers do not always accurately land on the natural harmonic E (in this case the rest is not indicated, although the nature of the variation requires it) (see Example 2.71).

Example 2.71 Ernst: *Othello Fantasy.*

To avoid these types of difficulties it is necessary to retain uninterrupted contact with the fingerboard during the pauses. This is why Yampolsky recommended the following method of playing in Example 2.70: the first finger, on the note F^3, does not leave the string, and during the rest shifts one step lower to E^3 (see Example 2.72).

Example 2.72

In Example 2.71, one may recommend not playing the harmonic randomly from above but instead making a Type 2 or Type 3 shift during the rest. The choice of shift can be left to the player.

This analysis of different methods of shifting allows us to critically evaluate their main elements and also determine the correct ways they should be studied. Returning again to the use of intermediary notes, we should note that this method could be useful in the very early stages of study. It allows the student to develop a sense of distances on the fingerboard and helps to organize the correct placement of the fingers in the new position. However, it is important to remember that the use of intermediary notes should be as short-lived as possible so that the conditioned reflexes are not fixed. Otherwise, this turns into a bad habit that restricts further development.

9. SHIFTS MADE WITH THE HELP OF AN OPEN STRING OR NATURAL HARMONIC. SHIFTS THAT INCORPORATE A CHROMATIC GLISSANDO.

Shifts Via an Open String

It is useful to begin studying these types of shifts first. In the early stages of study, shifts via an open string are the easiest since the fingers are not involved, and only the hand needs to move along the fingerboard. However, there are other hidden dangers in these types of shifts. Specifically, these shifts often cause the player to lose the perception of distance on the fingerboard. To remedy this, the open string may be temporarily eliminated, reestablishing the uninterrupted connection of the fingers with the string and thereby helping to develop and reinforce the correct perception of distance. For example, the exercise in Examples 2.74a–b may be helpful in studying the excerpt in Example 2.73.

Example 2.73 Tchaikovsky: *Valse-Scherzo.*

Example 2.74a

Example 2.74b

As Mostras notes, an open string may often cause technical difficulties by disrupting finger coordination in sequential passagework. For example, in the following passage from *The Golden Cockerel Fantasy* (concert fantasia by Zimbalist on themes from Rimsky-Korsakov's opera), the problems usually occur not in the most difficult part of the passage (in the high octave) but right after the open string (see Example 2.75).

Example 2.75 Rimsky-Korsakov (Zimbalist): *The Golden Cockerel Fantasy.*

The matter of shifting via an open string and also using expressive portamento (either sliding down to the open string or up from the open string) requires special attention. The descending portamento, which links the higher-sounding note to the open string, encounters a lot of criticism in the specialized pedagogical literature. In our opinion, the answer to this matter entirely depends on the character of the music. In some cases this kind of shift may indeed be entirely inappropriate, while in other cases the music will call for it. For example, it is difficult to imagine playing the following excerpt from Tchaikovsky's *Canzonetta* expressively without making a portamento gently connecting the note D^2 to the open string (Example 2.76).

Example 2.76 Tchaikovsky: *Violin Concerto, mvt. 2.*

Clearly, in this instance there is no foundation for criticism, for if the excerpt were written in another key, the lower note would not be an open string and the portamento would not be questioned. Sometimes, when the music requires particularly expressive connections between notes, portamento may even be required between two notes in the same position.

When shifting via an open string, it is entirely inappropriate to slide to the corresponding intermediary note, even though this is occasionally recommended in the specialized literature. The portamento should happen as the finger gradually releases its pressure until it completely lifts from the string. This is analogous to the movement of the upper finger when playing descending Type 2 shifts.

When the open string is connected to a higher note, it is perfectly acceptable to slide with the finger playing the subsequent note (analogous to Type 3 shifts) if the character of the music justifies it. It is interesting to note that these shifts may also occur by sliding from the initial note (analogous to Type 2 shifts) using the following technique recommended by David: the first finger is placed on the string behind the nut and begins sliding from this position.[98] This kind of shift may be entirely appropriate at times and helps to extend the expressive possibilities of portamento.

Shifts Made without Sliding

Sometimes musical and aesthetic considerations require the sound of portamento in a shift to be avoided. Israel Yampolsky recommended two methods to accomplish this.[99] The first method consists of stretching the hand until the necessary note is reached, then bringing the rest of the hand into the new position. (A "hidden form" of this kind of shift is found in the movement of the left hand when playing a whole-tone scale as in Example 2.77).

Example 2.77

This method is illustrated in Example 2.78 and this type of shift may be used when performing the following excerpt from the Khachaturian concerto (see Example 2.79).

Example 2.78

Example 2.79 Khachaturian: *Violin Concerto, mvt. 1.*

The second method is based on contracting, rather than extending, the fingers. In a similar way the finger reaches the required note, then the hand follows and assumes a normal position. The type of shift is illustrated in Example 2.80.

Example 2.80

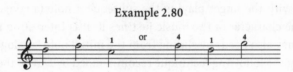

This is also a way to make a Type 4 shift when moving to a lower note when the hand is ascending, or to a higher note when the hand is descending (see Example 2.81).

Example 2.81 Goedicke: *Etude.*

Since these types of shifts serve a particular aesthetic purpose and are consequently limited in use, teachers usually do not spend a lot of time on them. However, exercises for developing an extended, normal, and contracted position of the hand are helpful for developing general elasticity and flexibility in the hand. An example of such a useful exercise is to play a descending scale in broken thirds using Baillot's fingering (Example 2.82).[100]

Example 2.82

However, one should not consider this fingering to be used in performance practice as Emil Kross recommends.[101]

Shifts from Natural Harmonics

The decision on whether or not to use portamento when shifting from a harmonic should depend solely on the musical context. Thus, sometimes a shift without portamento may sound too dry, while in other cases the portamento may be clearly inappropriate. The particular characteristic of the harmonic's sound is that it remains audible for some time after the finger has left the string. Here, the duration of the sound depends on the right hand; the closer the bow is to the bridge, the longer the sound of the harmonic (naturally, the distance between bow and bridge is relative since one still needs to produce a proper sound) (see Example 2.83).

Example 2.83

The following exercises may be used in working on these kinds of shifts, with the length of the lower note A^1 gradually shortened until it ceases to be heard (see Example 2.84).

Example 2.84

This exercise is fundamentally different from Flesch's exercises, which involve intermediary notes. Exercises with intermediary notes develop habitual movements that differ from those used in practice, whereas this exercise develops precisely the movement that is required in this situation. Shifting from a harmonic as illustrated above is most common when the hand descends, although in some instances this may occur when ascending.

Another version of this type of shift is when it is necessary to shift from one harmonic to another. The character of how these shifts are made depends on the musical context. In Example 2.85, the necessity of connecting the two harmonics obliges the player to make a portamento as follows: as the hand begins moving, the third finger presses to the string and makes the connecting slide, and the fourth finger plays the harmonic by lightly touching the string.

Example 2.85 Paganini: *Violin Concerto No. 1.*

In Example 2.86, the fourth finger does not press the string at all, and moves directly from one harmonic to another, only gently touching the string.

Example 2.86 Wieniawski: *Scherzo Tarantella.*

Chromatic Glissando

The chromatic glissando, produced by sliding one finger, is a special kind of shift. As we are aware, this shift involves the complicated task of both gradually moving the entire arm and making a pulsating movement in the sliding finger. Comparing it to the right hand, Lesman aptly describes this movement as "left-hand staccato."[102] The progressive general movement is made with the whole arm, while the pulsating movement of the sliding finger is made by either moving the wrist (similar to vibrato) or by tensing the forearm and the shoulder. We should emphasize that the tension in the forearm should not be excessive so that the necessary feeling of elasticity is still maintained. The optimal conditions for a chromatic glissando are when these movements are perfectly coordinated.

The essential element in achieving this coordination is the aural regulation of the glissando that controls intonation and the general quality of sound. Thus, when the coordination is disrupted because the general movement of the arm is too active, the sliding finger moves at intervals greater than a half-step. If the pulsating movement in the finger is too active, then the general movement of the arm slows down and the sliding finger moves at intervals smaller than a half-step.

Consequently, when the chromatic glissando occurs in a musical context and is tied to a specific rhythm, the player must pay attention to the following two points: if the movement in the arm starts too quickly it will inevitably slow down unnaturally later; and, conversely, if the movement begins too slowly it will have to unnaturally accelerate. Clearly, in both instances the intonation of the chromatic progression will suffer.

Flesch correctly noted that the most common reason for poor coordination is that the general arm movement is too slow.[103] He recommends the following method to correct this: The student should first play the chromatic scale as an uninterrupted glissando, around twelve times in a row, keeping it rhythmical. After this movement of the forearm is assimilated, a "vibrato-like" movement in the wrist is added. This creates an even vertical movement in half-steps and, after sufficient practice, leads to mastery of a clean chromatic glissando. Although this exercise seems to be structured correctly, it contains a serious flaw. In attempting to initially establish an even, rhythmical arm movement, this method does not take into consideration the fact that the distances between adjacent intervals are different in the lower and upper regions of the fingerboard. Therefore, the descending movement of the arm cannot be even, but should constantly accelerate (naturally, this accelerando movement must always be developed in conjunction with the ear). Consequently, it isn't possible to use Flesch's recommended preparatory exercise of making an uninterrupted glissando since it does not allow one to establish the required degree of acceleration.

In this respect, Abraham Yampolsky's method of mastering the chromatic glissando may be considered more efficient. For example, when working on a passage from Wieniawski's *Violin Concerto No. 2* (Example 2.87), Yampolsky recommends the following exercises. The first exercise (Example 2.88) sketches out the general movement of the arm, taking into account the acceleration as it approaches the lower positions. The second exercise (Example 2.89) retains the main elements of the general arm movement and fills in the intervals with a pulsating finger movement in half-steps.

Example 2.87

Example 2.88

Example 2.89

If the student has difficulties making the pulsating half-steps with the finger, or when the chromatic glissando is first introduced, the student may be advised to practice small sections of the scale (staying within the intervals of a fourth, fifth, or octave). These can be played in different rhythms (triplets, quadruplets, etc.) in both ascending and descending directions. These exercises are especially useful when working on glissandi in diatonic sequences, which are encountered less frequently. Diatonic sequences are more difficult because of the need to move the hand at irregular intervals, but in all other respects they follow the same principles laid out for chromatic sequences.

It is important to note the specific role the thumb plays in descending chromatic glissandi over large distances. The thumb may be involved in two ways. Firstly, the thumb can be a point of support for the wrist as the latter moves from the higher positions to where the thumb is positioned, and then the thumb continues to move in tandem with the whole arm. Alternately, the thumb can move together with the arm from the very beginning, sometimes even losing contact with the violin neck. The choice of method usually depends on individual adaptations, although we find the second method to be more efficient.

In most cases the descending chromatic glissando is made with the third finger. However, it is also a useful exercise to play it with other fingers. For example, playing it with the first and fourth fingers helps develop this technique for octaves, and using the second and third fingers helps prepare the chromatic scale in sixths.

While usually the chromatic scale is played in a descending direction, it should also be studied ascending. This helps in preparing the chromatic glissando in double stops, which, as we know, occurs in both directions. We should also add that the glissando in sixths is usually played with the second and third fingers, the glissando in thirds with the first and third fingers, and the glissando in octaves with both the first and fourth fingers and the first and third fingers.

When playing the chromatic glissando legato, it is important to pay special attention to even and smooth movement in the right arm. When the chromatic glissando is played with different bowings (such as détaché, spiccato, staccato, or ricochet), the nature of the left-hand movement changes completely. In these cases, there is no need for a gradual, interrupted movement in the left hand; it simply makes a continuous smooth movement while the right hand provides the necessary pulsation. In these cases coordination is especially important between the progressive accelerating movement in the left hand (or decelerating movement when ascending) and the bow changes that determine the steps of the chromatic scale.

The chromatic glissando is a special expressive device that demonstrates virtuosity, allowing the passage to be played in a tempo and with such brilliance that would be impossible with alternating fingers. Sometimes it may even be preferable to use a chromatic glissando in cases where the passage may easily be played with alternating fingers, especially when the character of the music requires a soft and lyrical sound, as in Example 2.90.

Example 2.90 Chopin (Burmester): *Etude.*

10. SHIFTING IN DOUBLE STOPS: OCTAVES AND TENTHS, THIRDS AND FINGERED OCTAVES, SIXTHS AND FOURTHS.

Shifts made with double stops are based on the types of shifts we have already examined. The difference here is that two shifts take place on two strings. To systemize our analysis, we find it convenient to group the double stops in the following categories: (1) octaves and tenths; (2) thirds and fingered octaves; and (3) sixths and fourths.

Octaves and Tenths

OCTAVES

Movement in octaves consists of two Type 1 shifts made simultaneously on two strings. The main problem of octaves is the difficulty in connecting the shifts smoothly, which causes the shifts to be sudden and abrupt. This jerky quality arises from the desire to give the sound more definition. However, usually it only creates a harsh tone, leads to poor intonation, and makes the octaves sound heavy and stiff. Unfortunately, many treatises even recommend playing octaves by "jumping." In reality, the only efficient way to play octaves is to move the hand as lightly and smoothly as possible, in the same way described earlier for Type 1 shifts. Starting the shift gently ensures a smooth general movement in the arm, while the direction toward the end of each shift gives the sound the required definition. At the same time it is important to make sure the fingers do not excessively press the string so that the general progression of the hand is not restricted.

Since octaves are usually played with the first and fourth fingers, the question often arises of what to do with the second and third fingers. Many methods recommend keeping the second and third fingers on the string, since this seemingly makes the first and fourth fingers more secure, and therefore helps intonation. Other treatises recommend that only the third finger remain on the string, and other methods recommend taking off both the second and third fingers. In our opinion the latter is the more rational. Leaving all the fingers on the string (even just the third finger) binds the entire hand. This makes vibrato impossible in cantilena, reduces agility in faster tempos, and complicates playing in the higher positions because of the smaller distances.

According to Mostras, the fourth finger becomes the point of support when octaves ascend, and the first finger is the point of support when the octaves descend. Because the distances diminish in the upper part of the fingerboard, it is very important to note that the first and fourth fingers must draw considerably closer when playing octaves. This complicates the general progression of the hand and requires additional coordination. How, then, should we study octaves to most efficiently develop these coordinated elements? The specialized literature offers two different points of view.

The first suggests starting to learn octaves by connecting two or three notes of the scale, and then gradually increasing the range to an octave. Sometimes it may be recommended to begin with the chromatic scale, since this keeps the intervals consistent and seemingly facilitates shifting. In this method, the main focus is on learning the gradual progression of octaves.

The second, more efficient point of view is based on studying the change in distance between the first and fourth fingers in different parts of the fingerboard. Flesch, for example, recommends the exercise in Example 2.91.

Example 2.91

In this exercise, the process of diminishing and augmenting the distance between the first and fourth fingers is made very clear, both in ascending and descending directions. Tseitlin used a different exercise involving shifts over a large distance (both ascending and descending), in which the two octaves are connected by a slow glissando with the intonation controlled for the entire duration of the slide (see Example 2.92).

Example 2.92

It is important to keep in mind that the process of diminishing and augmenting the distance between the fingers occurs primarily by drawing in or drawing out the first finger, which slightly changes its shape (becoming flatter as the fingers draw closer and vice versa). This is explained by the fact that the first finger is located in a lower position than the fourth finger, where the distances between intervals are naturally wider.

In our opinion, the best results are obtained through exercises that allow both elements of movement to be developed simultaneously, ensuring coordination of the gradual arm movement with the contraction (or extension) between the first and fourth fingers. We find the exercise by Sibor in Example 2.93 to provide the correct solution to the problem.

Example 2.93 Sibor: *Technique of Double Stops.*

The principle here is that the exercises are based on initially establishing the general borders that determine the distance between the first and the fourth fingers, and then the incremental shifts in octaves are added. Structuring the exercise this way makes it possible to focus on separate elements of the movement, while simultaneously retaining their unity. If for any reason one of the elements poses difficulties, it can be developed separately using exercises similar to those in Examples 2.91 or 2.92.

It is also necessary to examine shifts in octaves that move from one pair of strings to another. These shifts are possible either with or without the use of an open string. In these cases it makes sense to slide one finger along the common string, especially since for a split second the bow inevitably remains on one string due to the curvature of the bridge.

The following example shows both versions of this method: Example 2.94a illustrates the fourth finger making a Type 2 shift; and in Example 2.94b the shift is made through the open string.

Example 2.94

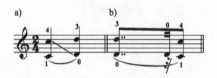

Shifting in octaves from one pair of strings to another without using the open strings is especially difficult, since both fingers need to simultaneously move to a new position and change strings. The specialized literature provides almost no advice on how to make these shifts, leading Flesch to dub them "leaps into the unknown." However, Voiku does provide the following suggestion for making these types of shifts (see Example 2.95).[104]

Example 2.95

According to Voiku, for the shift to sound even and clear, the fingers should transfer to the first position and subsequently slide to the E♭ (i.e., to the D and A strings), without losing contact with the strings. However, this method is not very efficient since it based on simultaneously sliding both fingers, which tenses the hand and affects the sound. This method only brings the hand to the new position without being able to avoid the simultaneous transfer of two fingers to different strings, which creates extraneous sounds.

We consider Abraham Yampolsky's method to be more successful. His technique is based on the fact that at some point in shifting from one pair of strings to another, the bow lies only on the common (middle) string (Example 2.96).

Example 2.96

This is the precise moment when the connecting Type 2 shift is made to the new position, which is immediately followed by a transfer of the initial finger (Example 2.97).

Example 2.97

Tseitlin recommends a slightly different method for descending shifts (when the hand is moving up the fingerboard). He suggests placing the first finger on two strings and having it slide simultaneously along two strings. However, this method is not very practical for players with very thin fingers.

When playing scales in octaves in tonalities that don't include open strings, the shift from one pair of strings to another should occur at the interval of a major second, since the distance of the shift will be smaller. This is illustrated in Examples 2.98a–b, where version *a* is preferable to version *b*.

Example 2.98a

Example 2.98b

A particularly useful exercise for mastering these types of shifts is to play arpeggios in octaves. The many shifts from one pair of strings to another help develop clean intonation as the distances between fingers constantly changes in various parts of the fingerboard.

Octaves are often played with the first and third fingers rather than with the first and fourth fingers, especially in the higher positions. This is explained by the smaller distances between the fingers and also because in some cases this improves the quality of the sound.

Playing octaves in cantilena involves many specific qualities that need to be taken into consideration, since all the notes of the melody are connected by shifts and this can negatively impact the sound. Attempting to shift unnoticeably in cantilena can cause the phrase to lose its melodic character; but at the same time, if all the octaves are connected with portamento, then the cantilena sounds aesthetically wrong. This is why it becomes necessary to diversify the different connections between the octaves in conjunction with the musical meaning of the phrase. When octaves are played with separate bows and not legato, different types of portamento may be used that will be examined later.

Tenths

The main difficulty of tenths is created by the extension in the fingers, especially in the lower part of the fingerboard. Just like octaves, tenths are connected with Type 1 shifts made simultaneously on two strings. The jerky, abrupt shifts that are intrinsically problematic to octaves become even more common and significantly accentuated when playing tenths. This is due to both the large stretch in the fingers and the excessive pressure of the fingers on the fingerboard caused by the desire to keep the fingers in their extended state. In this case (just as in octaves), the hand should try to remain free and relaxed, which also facilitates vibrato in phrases where the tenths need to sound more melodious and expressive. Meanwhile, it is especially important to note that the correct shape of the hand may significantly relieve excessive pressure and tension. Effectively, in extending the fingers, it is much easier to draw the first finger back than it is to stretch the fourth finger forward.[105] This is because of both the anatomical structure of the hand and the relative weakness of the little finger. Therefore, the hand should be positioned primarily by adjusting to the position of the little finger, taking into account the placement of the thumb. And yet, we often find the opposite occurs; when starting to learn tenths, students reach up with the fourth finger instead of drawing back the first finger. If this is not corrected in due time, the student will usually always be afraid of playing tenths.

The exercise in Example 2.99 facilitates the study of tenths.

Example 2.99

This exercise starts in the upper positions, where the distance between the intervals is smaller. This relieves excessive tension and makes the extension easier. As the hand moves to the lower positions, the distance between the intervals is increased gradually, making it easier to make the subsequent extensions without extra tension. At the same time, the progression in the lower voice helps the ear to hear the interval correctly and play it in tune. This is an important point, since students often begin learning tenths without a clear perception of how they should sound. And finally, this exercise correctly positions the hand, since it requires the first finger to extend down instead of stretching the fourth finger up.

Another significant difficulty that is specific to tenths and not encountered in octaves is that the fingers often need to move to different intervals in diatonic sequences. And this is made even more difficult by the fact that even if both fingers move the same interval, the distances they cover are not the same. This is especially obvious when both voices move a whole step and is explained by the great distance between the fingers.

The student must be entirely aware of all these factors when playing diatonic sequences and never lose sight of the varying distances between the fingers in the upper and lower positions. With this in mind, we recommend the exercises in Example 2.100 for work on intonation, which start by connecting any two degrees of the scale and then subsequently widening the interval.

Example 2.100

Auer suggested working on intonation in tenths by playing with the bow alternatively only on the upper or lower string.[106] Mostras presents an interesting opinion by suggesting that, in connecting tenths, the guiding finger should be the one that covers the greater distance.[107] Thus, in example Example 2.101a, the fourth finger leads; and in Example 2.101b, the first finger leads.

Example 2.101a

Example 2.101b

When playing in a key without open strings, it is possible to shift in tenths from one pair of strings to using Abraham Yampolsky's method for similar situations in octaves (see Example 2.96). For shifts that use an open string, Voiku suggests the method in Example 2.102, which we cannot agree with.

Example 2.102

We find this method entirely irrational because it "fixes" a position that consequently restricts movement. Also, the temporary change in the hand's position (extended—normal—extended again) can cause problems in intonation.

It is interesting that, according to Carl Guhr, Paganini played tenths in the upper positions with the first and third fingers instead of the customary first and fourth fingers.[108] However, this fingering is naturally only possible for players with extremely long fingers.

The shifts in octaves and tenths we have analyzed are related to sequential passages in unisons, seconds, and artificial harmonics. However, we will note that passages in unisons and seconds are rarely encountered in the current repertoire.

Thirds and Fingered Octaves

THIRDS

It is possible to use all the main types of shifts when playing in thirds. Shifts that retain the same pair of fingers (Type 1 shifts) may be subdivided into two subcategories. In the first subcategory the fingers practically do not change shape as they move from one major third to another major third, or from a minor third to another minor third (Examples 2.103a and 2.103b). In the second subcategory, the fingers significantly change their placement as they shift from a major third to a minor third or vice versa (see Examples 2.104a–d).

Example 2.103a Rachmaninov: *Romance.*

Example 2.103b Tchaikovsky: *Violin Concerto, mvt. 1.*

Example 2.104a Khachaturian: *Violin Concerto, mvt. 1.*

Example 2.104b Tchaikovsky: *Violin Concerto, mvt. 1.*

Example 2.104c Dvarionas: *Violin Concerto, mvt. 1.*

Example 2.104d Rachmaninov: *Romance.*

It is important that the player is aware of the different placement of the fingers in shifts in the second subcategory (when the fingers draw closer or further apart) since this helps with intonation. Because the first subcategory of shifts is slightly easier, it is logical to begin with them when studying shifts in thirds. Type 1 shifts in thirds (just like the octaves examined earlier) adhere to the same principles already established for shifts with one finger (i.e., a gentle start followed by an acceleration toward the end of the movement).

Ascending shifts from a lower pair of fingers to a higher pair may be made using a Type 2 shift (Example 2.105) or a Type 3 shift (Example 2.106). The character of the music determines which type of shift to use.

Example 2.105 Glazunov: *Violin Concerto.*

Example 2.106 Dvořák (Kreisler): *Slavonic Dance.*

Descending shifts from an upper pair of fingers to a lower pair of fingers adhere to the guidelines for descending Type 2 shifts (see Example 2.107).

Example 2.107 Chopin: *Nocturne.*

Ascending shifts in thirds from an upper pair of fingers to a lower pair (Example 2.108), and also descending shifts from a lower pair of fingers to an upper pair (Example 2.109), follow the principles of Type 4 shifts.

Example 2.108 Glazunov: *Violin Concerto.*

Example 2.109 Dvarionas: *Violin Concerto, mvt. 3.*

Shifting in thirds while changing pairs of strings requires special attention. Many treatises, including those by Voiku and Koeckert, indicate that these shifts be made by sliding both fingers to the corresponding intermediary notes (see Examples 2.110 and 2.111).[109]

Example 2.110 Voiku: from *Formation of a Natural System of Violin Playing.*

Example 2.111 Koeckert: from *Rationelle Violintechnik.*

Koeckert notes that it is even better to make this shift with "two intermediary double-stop notes" (Example 2.112).

Example 2.112

We already noted the nonutility of this method of sliding both fingers in our previous analysis of octaves.

Shifts across strings in thirds with the same pair of fingers (similar to Type 1 shifts) are rarely employed. However, we still find it necessary to indicate the best way of playing them, which corresponds to the method of shifting in octaves without using the open string. In Examples 2.113a–b, the shift starts at the moment the bow is only on the A string and continues with the first finger transferring to the note A^2.

Example 2.113a

Example 2.113b

The method of shifting in thirds from one pair of strings to another is based on utilizing the common string (analogous to shifting in octaves as already described). The shift is made with the finger that lies on the common string precisely when the bow is solely on that string. These shifts usually resemble Type 2 or Type 4 shifts. This method is illustrated in Example 2.114a, where the second finger makes the slide while the bow is on the D string. Similar shifts are illustrated in Examples 2.114b and 2.114c.

Example 2.114a

Example 2.114b

Example 2.114c

The expressive quality of Type 3 shifts in thirds requires both fingers to slide, as Example 2.115.

Example 2.115 Rakov: *Violin Concerto, mvt. 2.*

It is evident that the slide should not use intermediary notes, and generally it should follow the principles we described for this type of shift in one voice.

The right hand plays an important role when shifting from one pair of strings to another. The moment when the bow lies solely on the common string should not disrupt the impression of two uninterrupted voices. Therefore, the bow needs to remain for as little time as possible on the one string and transfer softly and smoothly, avoiding any kind of emphasis.

In those cases when there is no common string, the principle of shifting remains the same. The main difference is that the slide is made with the finger that is closest to the two arrival strings.

Thirds are among the most commonly used double stops. Often employed in cantilena, they are, together with sixths, the most rewardingly expressive intervals for violinists. This is because the fingers lie closer together than in other intervals (such as octaves and tenths), and this significantly facilitates the vibrato that is so important in cantilena. Also, of all double stops, thirds are the easiest to use to demonstrate brilliant virtuosity. This is evident in the numerous virtuosic passages, and even entire pieces, written only in thirds. Therefore, mastering thirds is essential to violin playing.

The most common problem in playing thirds is excessive pressure of the fingers on the string. This causes abrupt shifts that lack the necessary flexibility and disrupt the flow of one unified movement. We have already noted how this affects violin playing in general, but when playing double stops, and thirds in particular, these problems are even more pronounced.

Mastering shifts in thirds (or any other double stops) should be based on properly mastering simple shifts, since the same principles generally apply to double stops. For example, preliminary exercises in playing scales with two fingers (with the first and second and with the third and fourth) are very useful. Once regular shifts have been mastered, the more difficult conditions of double stops (i.e., moving both pairs of fingers), which require better coordination and more exertion in the muscles, should not affect the skills that are already in place. This should be always taken into account in pedagogical practice so that exercises for shifting in thirds are structured correctly.

Unfortunately, many irrational suggestions in the specialized literature essentially block the development of the basic elements of shifting. For example, in David's *Violinschule* it is suggested to play the preparatory exercises for scales in thirds with a martelé stroke (probably because the rest is supposed to facilitate the preparation of the following fingers).[110] However, this exercise prohibits the possibility of controlling the actual quality of the shift itself, which then naturally blocks the development of the necessary skills.

Flesch breaks down playing in thirds into the following three elements: (1) dropping the fingers in one position; (2) shifting between positions on the same pair of strings; and (3) shifting from one pair of strings to another.[111] He recommends studying each of these elements separately, spending one month on each type of movement. This creates a standardized system that doesn't take into consideration the individual particularities or the prior preparation of each student, and can lead to undesirable results. In separating the elements of playing thirds, Flesch's system directs the student's attention away from developing one unified movement, for even ideal mastery of separate elements does not necessary result in ideal mastery of the combined elements. Also, it is not necessary to apply the preparatory exercises equally to all three elements, but only to the weaker components. Thus, if for any reason one of the components in the movement is problematic, it should be corrected with the corresponding exercise. But even then, the exercise needs to be integrated into the unified movement so that the player realizes how this element fits into the entire process.

The choice of the correct fingering is very important in ensuring free and swift sequences in thirds, especially when the thirds are played in the lower registers and involve shifting between different pairs of strings. In the higher registers, where the shifts usually occur on the same pair of strings, the problem generally lies in making the shift coincide with the strong rhythmic pulse.

Some violinists are able to play thirds very freely and lightly in fast tempos in the upper positions. This is largely explained by the possibility of not having to lift the first and third fingers from the string, especially when ascending. However, this is impossible in the lower positions where the alternating up and down hand movements are in themselves quite difficult. To further complicate matters, these shifts from one pair of strings to another create difficulties for the right hand that affect the sound quality.

Many violin methods suggest fingerings based on contrasting tonalities that may or may not make use of open strings. When open strings are used, two types of fingerings are recommended: shifting through third position (Example 2.116) or shifting through second position (Example 2.117)

Example 2.116

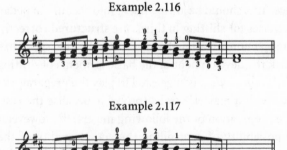

Example 2.117

In our opinion the first fingering is not rational, especially when ascending. Shifting the relatively large distance to third position, just for the sake of one note, inevitably restricts mobility in the passage. Even when perfectly executed, this method still seems busy. This fingering is possible when descending, but only when making one shift and not a series of shifts, which are especially awkward when playing staccato. We should also add that this fingering disrupts correct voice leading, which, as Flesch notes, becomes especially obvious in cantilena (see Example 2.118).[112]

Example 2.118

The other suggested fingering that moves through second position (Example 2.117) is more rational. The shorter distance between shifts allows the passage to be played smoothly and lightly in quick tempos, especially when the shifts coincide with the strong beats.

However, we do not always find it necessary to use open strings when tonalities allow it. In some cases it can be better to use a fingering that avoids the open string, even if the distance of the shift is increased (see Example 2.119). [113]

Example 2.119

It would be awkward to play this scale using open strings, since the shifts would coincide with weak beats rather than strong beats and also occur from a major third to a minor third and vice versa.

When tonalities don't permit the use of open strings, two fingerings are possible: moving through the even-numbered positions (i.e., half position to second position, second position to fourth position) or moving through the odd-numbered positions (first to third, third to fifth).[114] At the same time the following must be taken into consideration: On the one hand in the higher positions (e.g., from third to fifth), the hand needs to travel less distance, but at the same time the higher positions on the A and D strings sound less brilliant. However, the choice of fingering should still be based on whether the shifts coincide with the strong rhythmic beats. Both these types of fingerings may also be used in progressions in thirds when the tonalities do permit open strings.

In certain cases when thirds are played in the lower positions, a fingering may be used that incorporates extensions and eliminates the need to shift. This fingering is very useful as an exercise to strengthen the fingers and develop dexterity and agility. This is how Sergei Korguyev presents it in his work *Exercises in Double Stops.*[115] However, the practical uses of this fingering are limited.

FINGERED OCTAVES

Fingered octaves are used for more clarity and brilliance in octave passages. It is also clear that many figurations such as trills, mordents, and so on can only be played with the help of fingered octaves (see Example 2.120).

Example 2.120 Khachaturian: *Violin Concerto, mvt. 1.*

Fingered octaves are also used when octaves are played in cantilena and a glissando must be entirely avoided.

The technique of fingered octaves is very similar to that used in playing thirds, with the only difference being the reverse placement of the fingers (i.e., in fingered octaves the first and second fingers move along the lower string, and the third and fourth fingers move along the higher string). Therefore all shifts in fingered octaves on the same pair of strings adhere to the principles for Type 1, Type 2, Type 3, and Type 4 shifts in thirds.

Some methods, including Voiku's, recommend sliding two fingers on two strings, as in Example 2.121.

Example 2.121

However, this technique that we already noted to be ineffective for thirds is even less advisable for fingered octaves, since it is particularly difficult to slide the fingers on two strings while they are extended.

The extension of the fingers in fingered octaves makes all the difficulties of mastering this technique even more complicated. The stretch, the tension it creates, and the instinctive desire to maintain the extended position of the fingers by pressing harder on the string all contribute to limiting the free movement of the hand between positions. The stretch also affects the smoothness of the shift. Therefore, when working on fingered octaves it is absolutely necessary to make sure that the effort in stretching the hand does not create extra finger pressure on the string and that all the conditions for ensuring smooth shifts are respected.

It is logical to begin studying fingered octaves in the higher positions where the distances are smaller and the difficulties reduced. Many players in possession of a virtuoso technique in playing fingered octaves are able to achieve an almost keyboard-like precision and lightness, especially when ascending—often their first and third fingers will barely come off the string.

Let us examine some aspects of the fingering for this technique in more detail. We consider Joachim's fingering for scales that start from open string to be illogical (see Example 2.122).

Example 2.122

The problem with this fingering is that it requires the hand to change from a fourth-wide to fifth-wide position in the course of the passage. Moreover, the two fingers have to cover different distances simultaneously (i.e., the first finger needs to move a major second and the third finger a major third). Clearly this creates additional difficulties, especially in a fast tempo. Instead, the following fingering is usually used, which eliminates these problems (see Example 2.123).

Example 2.123

Flesch believes that the open string (with the second finger) can only be used at the beginning, not in the middle, of a sequence.[116] However, he contradicts his own point of view when he suggests fingering for Paganini's Caprice No. 17 that incorporates the open string in the middle of the passage (see Example 2.124).

Example 2.124

The most common fingering for scale passages in fingered octaves can be seen in Example 2.125.

Example 2.125

We should note that in some cases it is also possible to play fingered octaves using the open string and shift through second position, similar to what was already described for thirds. This is the fingering Georgy Dulov recommends for playing ascending scales (Example 2.126).[117]

Example 2.126

At first this seems to be more difficult, primarily because of the need to transfer the second finger across the string. But there is enough time to do this, since the transfer happens when the bow lies only on the common string (although it is very important to correctly determine the moment the finger transfers). The more serious problem with this fingering is that the half-steps often occur between adjacent fingers (i.e., between the first and second or third and fourth). This creates significant difficulties, which is why this technique is usually avoided in practice.

Kayum Baiburov has an interesting suggestion of shifting at the half-step in such cases. This is possible not only with the first and third fingers but also with the second and fourth fingers (see Example 2.127). The advantage of this fingering, which becomes evident after a certain amount of practice, is that the distance of the shift is smaller and this allows greater smoothness and mobility.

Example 2.127

This fingering may be used both in ascending and descending. The fingering for the descending scales suggested by Auer and Dulov, which uses open strings and shifts through third position, is considerably less efficient. It doesn't diminish the distance of the shift, and disrupts the smoothness of the passage since the shift to third position is only made for the sake of one note (see Example 2.128).

Example 2.128

Sixths and Fourths

Sixths

The special characteristic of these double stops is that the fingers have to transfer from one string to another. However, it is also possible to shift in sixths without transferring the fingers. Let us first examine Type 1 shifts. These may be divided into two subcategories, similar to the analogous shifts in thirds. In the first subcategory the fingers maintain the same placement (for example, shifting from a minor sixth to another minor sixth, or a major sixth to a major sixth). In the second subcategory the fingers change their placement (from a minor sixth to a major sixth and vice versa). Since Type 2 shifts in sixths are more difficult for intonation, we find it logical to begin studying shifts in sixths using Type 1 shifts (just as we did with thirds). This way the fingers do not change, and it is possible to start by connecting those degrees of the scale that retain the same interval.

Another example of when the fingers don't need to cross strings while shifting is when one pair of fingers replaces another, such as when shifting from the first and second fingers to the third and fourth (or vice versa) or shifting from the first finger and open string to another pair of fingers. Those shifts in sixths that don't involve transferring the fingers across the strings may be made using Type 1, Type 2, or Type 3 shifts and they follow the same principles established for these shifts in one voice.

Transferring the fingers across the strings creates significant technical difficulties that affect the sound (by creating extraneous noises). For this reason, in both the pedagogical literature and in practice, we encounter many attempts to avoid this transfer by using alternate fingerings. The first option is to play all the shifts in sixths, as well as sixths in one position, by sliding the same pair of fingers (Type 1 shifts). Another option that avoids transferring the fingers is to always alternate the first and second fingers with the third and fourth fingers.[118] And finally, by combining these two fingerings it becomes possible to play long melodic excerpts in sixths almost without transferring the fingers across strings (see Example 2.129).

Example 2.129 Glazunov: *Violin Concerto.*

When playing scale passages in sixths that are similar to those shown in Example 2.130, it is preferable to use the first fingering that is based on sliding the same pair of fingers.

Example 2.130 Chopin: *Nocturne.*

In this case it is not effective to use a combined fingering (as in Example 2.129) because the numerous alternating movements of the hand up and down the fingerboard will disrupt the fluidity and cause insecure intonation.

Aside from the two fingerings already indicated, there is also a third fingering in which the sixths are not played with adjacent fingers, more reminiscent of fingered octaves (see Example 2.131).

Example 2.131

A similar fingering may be used in chromatic sequences consisting of major sixths. In these cases, the shifts adhere to the same principles that apply to fingered octaves (see Example 2.132). However, this fingering is not justified in diatonic sequences, since it creates a variety of difficulties that affect intonation, even in slower tempos. These include an extremely cramped position of the fingers in minor sixths and the consequent unnatural position of adjacent fingers that have to create a fifth, or even a diminished fifth, across the strings (see Example 2.133).

Example 2.132 Rachmaninov: *Romance.*

Example 2.133

This is why in practice this fingering is usually used in conjunction with the standard fingering.

Since the alternate fingerings presented above are not always able to avoid transferring the fingers across strings, and also because many other situations (combinations of double stops, chords, etc.) make transferring the fingers inevitable, we find it nonetheless necessary to still work on shifts with the standard fingering that includes the transfer. We should also keep in mind that these kind of exercises help develop dexterity and agility in the fingers. For this reason we cannot agree with Flesch's recommendation to eliminate transferring the fingers above third position when playing scales in sixths, and only make a glissando with two fingers instead.

Preparatory exercises of transferring the fingers in one position are required before mastering shifts in sixths that transfer the fingers. Here too, it is important to remember that excessive finger pressure can cause problems. Such exercises are found in the methods of Boris Sibor and Sergei Korguyev.[119] Pedagogical experience shows us that sufficient practice of this technique provides players with great agility and dexterity and also a good sound in progressions in sixths. It is easy to make a shift that incorporates the transfer of the fingers if it is based on the correct principles of making a simple shift (see Examples 2.134a–b).

Example 2.134a

Example 2.134b

When we analyze the function of the second finger in this case, we find it consists of two elements: the second finger begins the shift, but then it also needs to transfer to the lower note (A^1) in the second sixth. Therefore, the movement of the second finger needs to correctly coordinate both these elements. The first part of the shift follows the principles of a Type 2 shift, with the finger gradually releasing until it completely lifts away from the string. This is precisely the moment when the finger can easily transfer to the adjacent string. Sometimes, to avoid extraneous sounds, the bow may momentarily rest on one string.

Type 3 shifts that transfer the fingers are made the same way, respecting the general principles for these types of shifts. However, in this case the finger transfer occurs slightly earlier than in Type 2 shifts (see Example 2.135).

Example 2.135

In Type 4 shifts, such as in Examples 2.136a–b, the second finger that starts to slide on the D string is pushed out by the first finger that follows. The moment the second finger cedes its place to the first finger, instead of lifting it transfers to the adjacent string and continues its movement by pushing the third finger out. Thus, this shift really consists of two simultaneous Type 4 shifts, which is evident not only in the fingering but also in the manner of shifting. This is easily illustrated by drawing the bow only on the upper or lower strings.

Example 2.136a

Example 2.136b

Shifts in sixths from one pair of strings to another make use of the instant when the bow lies only on the common string. When the shift occurs precisely at this moment, there is no need to cross-transfer the fingers. The method of sliding both fingers in these cases on two strings is entirely illogical.

Shifts can be avoided in the lower registers by using open strings when the tonality permits (see Example 2.137).

Example 2.137

In tonalities that don't permit the open string, and in the upper registers, the fingering can be structured as in Example 2.138.

Example 2.138

In these cases Korguyev also presents a fingering that merits attention (see Example 2.139).[120]

Example 2.139 Korguyev: *Exercises in Double Stops.*

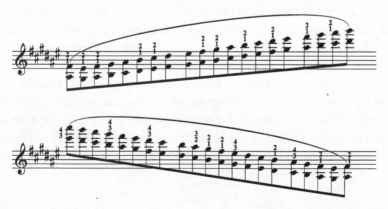

This fingering manages to reduce the general number of shifts and finger transfers because of the descending shifts to the third and fourth fingers. Using the half and second positions in the lower register creates the same advantages as for thirds in analogous conditions, and likewise reduces the number of shifts.

FOURTHS

In terms of execution, these double stops are related to sixths in all respects. Fourths differ from sixths by the reverse placement of the fingers in the same way fingered octaves differ from thirds (see Example 2.140).

Example 2.140

This difference determines some aspects of how they are played, similar to the relationship already described between thirds and fingered octaves. However, fourths are closer to sixths than fingered octaves are to thirds, since fingered octaves also involve extensions that affect how they are played. We should note that it is very rare to encounter progressions in fourths in their pure form in the violin literature. However, from a pedagogical point of view these double stops are useful for developing good intonation as well as agile and supple fingers.

11. THE INTERDEPENDENCE OF THE LEFT AND RIGHT HANDS WHILE SHIFTING. METHODS OF SHIFTING WHILE CHANGING BOWS. SHIFTS AND VARIOUS BOW STROKES.

When analyzing the activity of the left hand, we must always consider its role in the general process of violin playing. In this respect, an important element is coordination between the left and right hands, which requires special attention in our study.

As practice shows, shifts are often accompanied by a change in the intensity of the bow pressure or a disruption of the bow's steady movement along the string. It is very common for both beginners and those violinists with entrenched bad habits to release the bow pressure as they shift. This is particularly noticeable in long-distance shifts in which the bow almost seems entirely to lift away from the strings. This phenomenon is also observed in smaller shifts that follow each other in immediate succession (e.g., in scale passages) and is the most common problem for the right hand while shifting. The opposite problem is also encountered—when shifts are accompanied by extra pressure that causes an unintentional crescendo. Naturally, we are not speaking of those cases where a portamento is specifically hidden or emphasized by the right hand for musical purposes.

Other problems that affect the right hand while shifting include slowing down the bow (which usually coincides with releasing the pressure) or speeding up the bow (which is less common). Additionally, other complications present themselves that illustrate the interdependence of both hands. For example, when shifting from the higher to lower positions, sometimes the right hand begins to follow the movement of the left hand and draws the bow away from the bridge toward the fingerboard. Although to a certain extent this movement is natural to help the tone quality, it is often so excessive that the bow seems to slide onto the fingerboard, as Mostras notes in his work *Intonation on the Violin*.[121]

A good example of the interdependence of the hands is when most students first attempt to play a chromatic glissando with one finger. Their right hand often imitates the pulsating movement of the left hand and plays something similar to *staccato*. We should also note that the right hand might have an equally disruptive effect on the left hand. For example, changing the bow pressure on the string usually immediately affects the pressure of the fingers in the left hand. This often makes fixing this widespread problem even more difficult. The danger here is that releasing the finger pressure then causes a release in bow pressure, which naturally affects the sound. But when the teacher asks the student to play with a fuller bow stroke, the fingers again may press too hard on the string.

The influence of the right hand is similarly evident when the same passage is played first with one bowing and then with another. The different movements in the right hand, as a rule, alter the movements in the left hand and affect the execution of the passage. For instance, in Example 2.141, the passage from

Example 2.141 Saint-Saëns: *Introduction and Rondo Capriccioso.*

Saint-Saens' *Rondo Capriccioso* may come out perfectly when played détaché but not work at all in spiccato, because of problems in shifting.

Flesch gives an interesting example of how the right hand influences the left. He notes that when a passage ends with a harmonic, the last note often doesn't sound because the fourth finger reflexively copies the movement of the bow (which lifts from the string at the end) and thereby does not quite reach the final note (see Example 2.142).[122]

Example 2.142

We also need to emphasize that problems in coordination depend not only on the difficulty of the movements themselves but also on the degree to which the student is prepared for these movements. Expecting the student to prematurely execute a technique that he or she is not prepared for usually leads to poor results. For example, asking the student to make the shift inaudible before he or she is prepared usually causes the student to release the bow from the string or slow it down. Consequently the student will always associate the shift with a disrupted movement in the right hand, creating a bad habit (which can be very dangerous if the teacher does not observe it in time). It is therefore important to strictly follow a sequential method that progresses from simpler to more complicated tasks, gradually adding movements that are more and more difficult. In this respect it is important to note the order in which different shifts are studied. For example, it would be wrong to begin by learning Type 4 shifts, which are technically more difficult. And yet, this mistake is made all too often, especially in the older treatises.

An extremely important pedagogical task is to develop good coordination between the hands. Unfortunately, all too often the teacher is confronted with another, rather thankless task of correcting problems in coordination that developed because the first stages of study were structured incorrectly. For this reason it is essential to prevent the possibility of developing bad habits. However, it is also important to remember that in the pedagogical process it is not enough to just develop a certain number of coordinated relationships, for it is impossible to foresee all the coordinated interactions that might be encountered in the student's musical future. The teacher must work on developing the student's facility for quickly assimilating new tasks, which allows any type of coordination to be integrated with ease. For this reason it is necessary to focus on developing quick reactions in the nervous processes right from the beginning, especially if these reactions appear to be slow.

With this in mind, we first recommend very carefully observing every element in a movement that may create a problem for coordination. For example, if a new, slightly more complex movement is introduced in the left hand, the right hand may also experience some changes, such as an increase or decrease of intensity. Although the new movement in the left hand may not be easy in itself at first, it must never disrupt the activity of the right hand. Whenever such a disruption is observed, the element that is responsible must be temporarily removed since the student has not been sufficiently prepared. Instead, in these cases it is best to use various preparatory exercises that can help make the student make the movement later on without any problems.

Right from the beginning stages we recommend introducing special exercises to help establish coordination between the hands (any of the exercises widespread in pedagogical practice may also be adapted for this purpose). For example, a popular exercise is to use multiple bow strokes for each finger in the left hand (détaché exercises on one note). Without taking away the importance of this exercise for beginners, we suggest structuring it based on varying rhythmical patterns, using any appropriate etude or scale (see Examples 2.143a–e).

Example 2.143a-e Komarovsky: *Etude No. 8.*

The main purpose of the exercise is the following. The first variation (Example 2.143a) develops coordination between the fingers of the left hand and the corresponding movement (up or down) in the bow. The other variations (*b–e*) make the coordination more difficult as the frequency increases. Later, the use of quintuplets, sextuplets, and septuplets is also beneficial because of the difficulties associated with the more complex rhythmical figures. All these variations provide excellent preparation for accurately coordinating the fingers and bow in fast sequences. These exercises are useful not only at the beginning stages of studying but also when working on accurate coordination in specific bow strokes.

As we already mentioned, the development of the required coordination depends on the rapidity of the nervous processes, which should naturally be taken into consideration in any pedagogical process. However, there are often indications in violin methods that completely contradict this idea. For example, Flesch recommends studying each scale with only one specific fingering, believing that this facilitates sight-reading. Indeed, this does enable the violinist to easily develop and secure the corresponding conditioned reflexes so they only need to glance at such a sequence for the fingers to quickly and easily execute the memorized movements. By recommending the scale be studied with only one fingering, Flesch attempts to eliminate the difficulty of having to make a choice in the moment of performing.

However, Flesch's mistake is that, in working on prepared movements in advance, it is impossible to foresee all the possible sequences in the literature. And moreover, even a movement that has been prepared may require a completely different means of execution, including a different fingering, if the context changes. Thus, as often happens, the player may be forced to override the movements that were already established. This is naturally much more difficult and affects quick orientation while sight-reading.

The solution to the problem should be approached differently by developing the quickest motor reaction to visual and subsequent aural perceptions. Therefore, studying scales with various fingerings, that is, creating different conditioned motor reflexes in response to specific, consciously created tasks, can only generate flexibility in these processes. Abraham Yampolsky recommends an interesting exercise in this regard.[123] He suggests the violinist start from any note (for example, from A) and play descending scales in different keys (for example, B♭ major, D major, D minor, G major, etc.). In contrast to Flesch's method, this helps to activate the player's quick reflexes, which are indispensable when sight-reading.

Lesman does somewhat address the coordination between the left and the right hands in his work *Paths of the Violinist's Development*.[124] But although his suggested exercises may be used to develop the corresponding conditioned reflexes, their main purpose is to correct problems that have resulted from incorrect prior studies rather than ensuring that the correct reflexes be developed from the very beginning. And yet, each teacher must primarily concentrate on developing the correct skills from the beginning in order to anticipate any problems with coordination that may arise.

These kinds of problems usually manifest as follows. Firstly, as we already noted, problems in the right hand can occur because of shifts in the left hand. Another problem is poor coordination between fingers in the left hand and corresponding movements in the bow (for which we have already recommended special exercises). Generally, a great number of problems in coordination happen precisely when intensifying the movement in one hand impacts the activity of the other.

Thus, for example, a trill is often accompanied by either an increase in or significant release of pressure. This usually happens when a fast trill is attempted prematurely and the inadequate preparation causes tension. This in turn reflects not only on the trill itself but also on the right hand. To correctly develop the trill, it is necessary to start by calmly and rhythmically dropping the fingers while maintaining a completely relaxed hand. These exercises allow a natural preparation for a fast trill in the future.

Intensified movement in the left hand associated with vibrato, accelerated finger movement (in fast passages), and so forth may also affect the right hand, which can in turn then also disrupt the left hand. For example, increasing the bow pressure when moving from *piano* to *forte* will often cause a passage to accelerate or it may cause extra vibrato in cantilena.

The process of shifting while making a bow change is one of the most fundamental problems of coordination. Unfortunately, this matter is either entirely omitted in the specialized literature or approached incorrectly. For example, Joachim simply writes that if the shift coincides with a bow change, then the shift should be made particularly quickly, deftly, and inaudibly for the connection to be smooth.[125] Yet he does not provide any details on how to accomplish this. Ševčík, Voldan, and Lesman believed that in these cases the beginning of the shift should apply to the new stroke.[126] Nemirovsky believes the opposite— that the beginning of the shift belongs to the first and not the second stroke. Attempting to bypass the entire matter, Mikhailovsky recommends the following: "make a rest after having finished playing in one position, change to the new position during the rest, and only then start the new stroke."[127]

The main mistake of these violinists is that they generalize their recommendations for all types of shifts that involve a change in bow. However, the various types of shifts differ not only in how they are executed but also in their musical and expressive significance. In this respect, Israel Yampolsky is more correct to note the different ways of making different types of shifts.[128] For example, Israel Yampolsky links the connecting slide to the first bow stroke in Type 2 shifts and to the second bow stroke in Type 3 shifts (see Example 2.144).

Example 2.144 I. Yampolsky: from *Principles of Violin Fingering.*

We should also note that this entirely coincides with the musical and expressive qualities of these types of shifts.

Because Type 2 and Type 3 shifts differ in their musical and expressive properties, the nature of the music determines which shift to choose. Because a Type 2 shift is characterized by a portamento that seems to naturally flow from the previous note, it would therefore be wrong to prematurely change the bow. Similarly, it is not logical to separate the portamento from the new note in a Type 3 shift, since this shift was musically chosen precisely because the portamento flows into the new note.

In this light, let us look at bow changes for other types of shifts. In Type 1 shifts, Voldan and Ševčík, among others, recommend making the slide with the new bow stroke.[129] Other violinists, such as Koeckert and Israel Yampolsky, believe the slide belongs to the first stroke and not the second.[130] In our opinion, being confined to just one of these methods limits the expressive possibilities, since modifying the moment the bow changes significantly affects the sound. One version emphasizes the beginning of the slide (because the portamento is linked to the first note) and the other emphasizes the end of the shift (because the portamento is linked to the second note) (see Example 2.145).

Example 2.145

The appropriate use of both these methods broadens the expressive possibilities open to the performer, similar to choosing between a Type 2 or Type 3 shift.

The question of what to do in a Type 4 shift should be resolved the same way (see Example 2.146).

Example 2.146

In the first measure of Example 2.146, the portamento is tied to the first bow stroke, emphasizing the beginning of the shift and the slide of the initial finger. In the second measure of Example 2.146, the portamento is tied to the second bow stroke, emphasizing the end of the shift and the slide of the subsequent finger. Thus the expressive potential of this shift becomes greater than using a single method, as some treatises recommend. The choice of method must always stem from which expressive quality the particular shift requires.

The above mostly concerns ascending shifts. When descending, only portamento from the initial note is acceptable because of musical and aesthetic considerations. This is the reason Type 3 shifts are not used when descending. This is also the principle that determines when to change the bow in descending Type 1 and Type 4 shifts when the portamento should be tied to the first bow stroke (see Examples 2.147a and 2.147b).

Example 2.147a

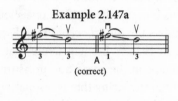

(correct)

Example 2.147b

(incorrect)

There are exceptional situations when certain players will do the opposite, but this should be considered an exception determined by their particular mastery.

All that applies to shifts in descending progressions is equally applicable to descending shifts where one finger substitutes another on the same note. See, for instance, Example 2.148.

Example 2.148

So far we have examined shifts in cantilena, where it is necessary to emphasize or give character to the portamento for musical reasons. Matters are different in fast passages that require the portamento to be inaudible. Type 3 shifts are not used at all in quick progressions, and in Type 2 shifts the slide is tied to the first bow stroke. In ascending Type 1 and Type 4 shifts, the portamento is tied to the second bow stroke, since this makes the shift less noticeable. Doing the opposite causes the left hand to slow down on the fingerboard, making the movement uneven. In descending Type 4 shifts in a quick tempo, the shift is tied to the first bow stroke, since in this case it is only possible to slide with the initial finger.

The problem of coordinating the right and left hands is closely tied to problems of tone quality (i.e., fullness, richness, clarity, timbre, etc.). It is important to remember that notwithstanding other conditions, the tone quality depends on the point of contact between the bow and the string. Flesch even wrote specifically on this subject.[131] He reaches the conclusion that the point of contact between the string and bow depends on the following factors (in order to achieve the best tone quality): (1) the height of the position in which the note occurs; (2) the dynamic (*forte* or *piano*); and (3) the speed of the bow. After the appearance of Flesch's work, the idea that the point of contact between the string and bow determines the sound always came to be associated with Flesch's name. While this is certainly justified, one should also not forget that Lesman discussed this subject in his *School of Violin Playing* seven years before Flesch's work appeared in 1924.[132] Lesman wrote that the optimal sounding point on the string depends on the speed and pressure of the bow, as well as the length of the segment of the string that is resonating.

With that, Lesman developed a special chart that we find useful to reproduce here (see Table 2.2).

Table 2.2 OPTIMAL SOUNDING POINT UNDER
SPECIFIC CONDITIONS

Playing Conditions		Optimal Sounding Point
Faster bow stroke	} (under specified pressure)	Further from the bridge
Slower bow stroke		Closer to the bridge
"Lighter" bow stroke	} (with specified speed)	Closer to the bridge
"Heavier" bow stroke		Further from the bridge
Shorter string segment		Closer to the bridge
Longer string segment		Further from the bridge

All the above shows how important it is (depending on good coordination between the hands) to find the spot on the string that will sound the best in each particular case. Clearly, the player's ear must evaluate the sound and its appropriate character, similar to what was discussed regarding intonation. This is an essential prerequisite to developing any professional skills.

An important element of coordination between the hands is developing the required skills in respect to different bow strokes. For example, in a slurred passage with a series of shifts, the bow should move away from the bridge to the fingerboard as the passage descends, or from the fingerboard to the bridge when the passage ascends.

A specific type of coordination is required when playing broken octaves in legato. In this case, the decisive moment is when the bow changes between strings, which often causes problems. In practice, changing the fingering often solves this problem. For example, instead of using the fingering in Example 2.149, it is customary to use the fingering in Example 2.150.

Example 2.149 Brahms: *Violin Concerto, mvt. 2.*

Example 2.150 Brahms: *Violin Concerto, mvt. 2.*

However, it is important to keep in mind the following. Although the alternate fingering does indeed eliminate unpleasant extraneous sounds, it also makes the sound more pianistic. On the other hand, the first fingering has the advantage of making the sound more lyrical. Therefore, the deciding factor on when to transfer the bow from one string to another must stem from aesthetic musical considerations.

The solution to the problem depends on whether the sequence of broken octaves begins from the upper or lower note.

In Example 2.151a, the bow should remain on the lower string until the left hand has shifted to the new position, which perfectly corresponds to earlier analysis of these kinds of shifts. If the bow transfers prematurely to the higher string, an aesthetically unpleasant glissando occurs. In Example 2.151b, the bow should remain on the upper string until the left hand has shifted to the new position. This also corresponds to our previous analysis for these types

Example 2.151a

Example 2.151b Brahms: *Violin Concerto, mvt. 2.*

of shifts. In both cases, prematurely transferring the bow to the next string changes the actual type of shift; that is, a shift that is supposed to slide with the initial finger turns into a shift that slides with the new finger (and naturally this is supposed to be avoided when descending).

However, even transferring the bow at the right time in these examples does not completely guarantee a good sound. For the sound also depends on the nature of the finger movement in the course of the shift. Here the first finger cannot be released as usual since it must always remain on the string. The correct procedure is to release the finger without letting it lift from the string. Thus the finger remains in contact with the string, and the harsh aspect of the slide that causes an unpleasant sound is eliminated. When broken octaves are played quickly it seems as though the bow transfer almost naturally coincides with shifts in the left hand. But nonetheless, even in a fast tempo, the broken octaves should be correctly prepared by first mastering the indicated technique. Broken octaves in an ascending direction are played in the same manner.

When shifts are played détaché, the most common problems of coordination include a release in bow pressure, a smaller amount of bow, tense fingers in the right hand, and so on. These problems are more marked when the shift has not been properly prepared or the student has not sufficiently assimilated the technique in the right hand.

In a punctuated bowing (i.e., when the notes are separated by rests as in martelé, spiccato, etc.), the shifts should happen precisely when there are breaks in sound. Because the rests in these cases are created by shortening the notes, the shift should always occur before the start of the new stroke. Otherwise the glissando will be audible and interfere with the purpose of the bowing, which is defined by a clear attack at the start of every note. Similarly, shifts take place during the rests in staccato when the separate notes are connected in one bow.

When strokes such as détaché and spiccato occur in a fast tempo, coordination between the hands becomes especially difficult. One of the main problems is having the movements in the left hand accurately coincide with the change of bow, and this difficulty only increases when the bow changes strings or the left hand changes positions.

The main element that coordinates the hands in this case is, of course, the rhythm, which becomes especially important. Therefore, primary attention should be turned to those key moments that can contribute to rhythmic stability. At the same time it is important to remember that inadequate command of shifting can easily disrupt the rhythm and consequently cause problems in coordination.

If off-the-string strokes, such as spiccato and ricochet, are to be played rhythmically, the movement of the bow must be consistent as it leaves the string. Otherwise, when the bow rises to varying heights it takes a different amount of time for the bow to return to the string, which naturally disrupts the rhythm. Similar problems in rhythm occur while shifting, especially when the shifts are abrupt, since this affects the right hand and causes the bow to lift unevenly. It is significantly more difficult to coordinate shifts with off-the-string bowings in fast tempi. The difficulty lies in making the shift coincide with the precise moment the bow leaves the string and having the new note coincide with the bow's return to the string. This explains the difficulty of playing scales and arpeggio-like passages that involve a lot of shifts with off-the-string bowings. Having the student focus on making sure the bow leaves the string as little as possible can significantly help in these cases.

The coordination between the hands that the music requires is established through the interrelation and interdependence of the chosen bowings and fingerings. This relationship is primarily determined by what most accurately conveys the character of the music, which is why this relationship is dynamic and constantly changing. For this reason, we cannot speak of a permanent relationship between certain bowings and fingerings. And this is why we cannot entirely agree with Moser's opinion regarding the fingering for the following excerpt from the finale of Viotti's Violin Concerto No. 23 (see Example 2.152).[133]

Example 2.152

Moser provides two possible fingerings and writes that if the passage were to be played with a different bowing (all détaché or all legato in one bow), then there would be no problem with the upper fingering. But the indicated bowings cause the shifts to fall awkwardly (creating acoustic-aesthetic problems), which is why Moser suggests using the lower fingering where the change of position coincides with a change in bow. Thus Moser seems to canonize a very specific relationship between bowings and fingerings. Yet, such a permanent relationship may in other cases completely contradict the musical essence of what is being played. In Moser's example, the relationship is based on the principle of shifting while changing the bow. This largely helps to cover up the sound of the shift itself. Unquestionably, this principle has positive attributes, but only when the passage needs to sound very clear and brilliant in a quick tempo. Applying this to other musical material that is more lyrical would have an adverse effect. Thus, there is a good reason that Abraham Yampolsky suggests the opposite fingering in an analogous passage in Bach's *Chaconne*. This creates a more expressive and lyrical sound in this particular case (see Example 2.153).

Example 2.153

Because shifts occur at the expense of the length of the previous note, in sequences that contain notes of different lengths, it is logical to choose a fingering in which the shift takes place after the long note rather than after the shorter note (see Examples 2.154 and 2.155).

Example 2.154 Taneyev: *Tarantella*.

Example 2.155

The opposite scenario causes the shift to be made hastily and tensely, thereby affecting the sound and depriving the music of the required lightness and elegance.

All the above clearly confirms the importance of developing good coordination between both hands in order to establish unity and correctly convey the musical character of the piece. This places an important responsibility on the teacher, whose challenge is to create the best conditions for developing these kinds of coordination.

This study has examined different aspects of the problem of shifting in the context of musical interpretation. Our analysis allows us to establish a series of general principles that can be used in performance and pedagogical practice. For clarity and convenience, we will list them here as separate points.

1. Work on clean intonation while shifting should be based on developing skills that cultivate a feeling for distance.
2. A shift is made with a unified movement in the arm and hand, not with the isolated movement of just one component such as the wrist,

forearm, or shoulder. However, depending on the circumstances, the leading element may be either the forearm or the wrist, with the other parts of the arm following or making auxiliary movements.

3. In the beginning stages of study, horizontal movements of the hand used in shifting or preparation for shifting should be studied as early as possible. This method aims to overcome the inborn grasping reflex that may otherwise restrict free movement in the left hand while shifting. This method also allows the early development of coordination between the main movements of the left hand, that is, the vertical movement in the fingers and the horizontal movements of the hand and arm.

4. Every technique and procedure turns out to be dynamic and modifiable, depending on the musical context. This includes how the violin is held (with one or two points of support), the position of the left elbow, the position of the thumb, and the pressure of the fingers on the string.

5. The development of any playing movement should be based on perceiving and consolidating a feeling for the character of the movement in association with the corresponding auditory perception.

6. Most shifts are characterized by a relatively slow beginning with a subsequent acceleration. Both the individual particularities of the performer and the musical context may, to a certain degree, alter the moment when the acceleration starts and how it develops, although they essentially do not change the nature of the movement itself. This method of shifting establishes smoothness, flexibility, facility in changing positions, a lyrical sound, and a light and agile technique.

7. It is not necessary to use so-called intermediary notes while shifting. Instead of following a prescribed method of utilizing intermediary notes, the procedures for shifting should be determined by the specific musical context. However, we should point out that intermediary notes may be helpful for learning to shift in the very early stages.

8. Shifts in double stops generally adhere to the same principles established for simple shifts.

9. A good setup for the violinist should be determined by its organic relationship to the movements required while playing. If this relationship is disrupted, the setup becomes dogmatic and removed from the active processes of playing. This kind of incorrect positioning can restrict the player's subsequent development.

10. The creation and development of playing movements must occur in constant relation to auditory perceptions, instead of being based on abstract "correct" systems that have no relation to sound.

11. The character of the sound, and consequently the character of the movements, must always be determined by the character of the music.

In this way a unified, inseparable chain is created between the aural perception of a sound, the playing movements, and the setup. Breaking this connection at any of its links causes errors of a formalistic nature. The pedagogical process must assure that the student harmoniously develops both the artistic and technical aspects of playing.

NOTES

1. Carlo Tessarini, *Nouvelle methode pour apprendre par theorie dans un mois de tems à jouer du violon divisée en trois classes, avec des leçons à deux violons par gradation* (Paris: n.p., 1750). The following references and notes, unless otherwise mentioned, are those supplied by Yuri Yankelevich in the original text; English titles for Russian texts are supplied by the translator.
2. Lionel de la Laurenci, *L'école francaise de violon de Lulli à Viotti. v. III* (Paris: n.p., 1909).
3. Leopold Mozart, *Osnovatel'noe skripichnoe uchilishche/perevod s nem* (Fundamental Violin Treatise, translated from German) (St. Petersburg: n.p., 1804).
4. Bartolomeo Campagnoli, *Neue Methode der fortschreitenden Fingerfertigkeit* (Leipzig: Breitkopf und Härtel, 1797).
5. Louis Spohr, *Violinschule* (Wien: T. Haslinger, 1832).
6. Joseph Joachim and Andreas Moser, *Violinschule* (Berlin: N. Simrock, 1905).
7. Leopold Auer, *Moia shkola igry na skripke* (Violin Playing as I Teach It) (Moscow: Muzyka, 1965).
8. Karl Davidov, *Shkola dlia violoncheli. Ridaktsia i dopolneniia S. M. Kozolupova i L. S. Ginzburga* (School of Cello Playing), ed. and rev. S.M. Kozolupov and L. S. Ginzburg (Moscow: n.p., 1947).
9. Carl Flesch, *Iskusstvo skripichnoi igry* (The Art of Violin Playing) (Moscow: n.p., 1964).
10. Israel Yampolsky, *Osnovy skripchnoi applikatury* (Principles of Violin Fingering) (Moscow: Gosudarstvenoye muzykal'noe izdatelstvo, 1955).
11. Ibid., 54—55.
12. In the old schools of Beriot and Spohr, it was likewise assumed that each position corresponded to its own tonality; the tonality was based on the second rather than the first finger on the G string.
13. Flesch, *Iskusstvo skripichnoi igry.*
14. Otakar Ševčík, *Shkola skripichnoi tekhniki/perevod s cheshskogo* (School of Violin Technique, translated from Czech) (Moscow: n.p., 1929).
15. Jean Delphin Alard, *Polnaia shkola dlia skripki, priniataia dlia rukovodstva v parizhskoi konservatorii* (Complete Violin Method in Use at the Paris Conservatory, translated from French to Russian by A. Sokolova) (Moscow: n.p., 1909).

16. Nikolai Garbuzov (1880–1955) was a Russian musical acoustician and theoretician who proposed a theory of hearing centered around "zones," which takes into account the influence of such factors as pitch, loudness, timbre, and rhythmic relations. —*Translator's note.*

17. Flesch, *Iskusstvo skripichnoi igry.*

18. Konstantin Mostras, *Intonatsiia na skripke* (Intonation on the Violin), 2nd ed. (Moscow: Gosudarstvenoe muzykalnoe izdatelstvo, 1968).

19. Leopold August Sass, *Neue Schule für Geiger* (Leipzig: Steingräber Verlag, 1920).

20. Campagnoli, *Neue Methode der fortschreitenden Fingerfertigkeit.*

21. Siegfried Eberhardt, *Absolute Treffsicherheit auf der Violine* (Berlin: Fürstner, 1912).

22. Gustave Koeckert, *Rationelle Violintechnik* (Leipzig: Breitkopf & Härtel, 1909).

23. P. Radmall, "Change of Position," *The Strad* 689 (1947).

24. L. Nemirovsky, *Mekhanicheskie i psikhologicheskie momenty v osnovnykh priemakh skripichnoi tekhniki* (Mechanical and Psychological Moments in the Fundamental Skills of Violin Technique) (Moscow: n.p., 1915).

25. Leopold Auer, *Graded Course of Violin Playing: A Complete Outline of Violin Study for Individual and Class Instruction* (New York: Carl Fischer, 1926).

26. Bedřich Voldan, *Nová škola poloh: (analogická soustava skupinová)* (Praha: Neubert, 1924); Jan Mařák and Viktor Nopp, *Housle, dějiny výroje houslí, houslařstvi a hry houslove. Methodika. 3. vydáni, dopiněné až do doby přitomné, upravil Viktor Nopp* (Praha: Hudební matice umělecké besedy, 1944).

27. It should be noted that by *free* movement, we mean a minimal expenditure of neuromuscular energy (with no restrictive elements) that the given task requires.

28. Voldan, *Nová škola poloh.*

29. Ion Voiku, *Postroenie estestvennoi sistemy skripichnoi igry (tekhnika levoi ruki). Perevod s Nem. V. N. Rimskogo-Korsakova* (The Formation of a Natural System of Violin Playing [Left-Hand Technique], translated from the German by V. N. Rimsky-Korsakov) (Moscow: n.p., 1930). Further information on the author of this work is unknown and the text appears not related to the recognized Romanian violinist of the same name Ion Voicu (1923 – 1997) —*Translator's note.*

30. Iosef Lesman, *Shkola igry na skripke* (School of Violin Playing) (Leningrad: n.p., 1924).

31. This is readily seen with beginners, who become tired and need a rest even when holding the violin only for five minutes.

32. B. Mikhailovsky, *Novii put' skripacha* (New Direction for the Violinist) (Moscow: n.p., 1934).

33. In this treatise the term "first" joint refers not to the bottom, as is customary today, but to the top joint; Rode-Baillot-Kreutzer, *Skripichnaia shkola* (Violin School), 2nd ed. (St. Petersburg: n.p., 1829).

34. Pierre Marie François de Sales Baillot, *L'art du violon: nouvelle méthode* (Mayence: n.p., 1834).

35. Alard, *Polnaia shkola dlia skripki*; Hubert Leonard, *Ecole Leonard pour le violon* (Paris: Richault et Cie, 1877); Jules Charles Pennequin, *Nouvelle méthode de violon, théorique et pratique: en deux parties* (Paris: Enoch, 1900).

36. Campagnoli, *Neue Methode der fortschreitenden Fingerfertigkeit*; Auer, *Moia shkola igry na skripke*; Joachim and Moser, *Violinschule*; Edmund Singer and Max Seifriz, *Grosse theoretisch-praktische Violinschule* (Berlin: Cottaschen Buchhandlung, 1887); Heinrich Ernst Kayser, *Neueste Methode des Violinspiels, op. 32 Th. 3* (Leipzig: Cranz, 1900); R. Gofman, *Bol'shaia i podrobnaia shkola tekhniki igry na skripke, v progressivnom sistematicheskom raspolozhenii ot pervyh shagov obucheniia do visshego ssovershenstvovania. Perevod s Fr.* (Large and Detailed School of Violin Technique, in Progressive Systematic Format from the First Steps to the Highest Mastery, translated from French) (Moscow: n.p., 1959).

37. Andreas Moser, *Methodik des Violinspiels* (Leipzig: Breitkopf & Härtel, 1920).

38. Ivan Petrovich Pavlov (1849–1936) was a renowned Russian physiologist, psychologist, and physicist largely known for his work on conditioned reflexes. —*Translator's note.*

39. Kayser, *Neueste Methode des Violinspiels, op. 32 Th. 3*; Reinhold Jockisch, *Katechismus der Violine und des Violinspiels* (Leipzig: J. J. Weber, 1900); V. Val'ter, *Kak uchit' igre na skripke* (How to Teach Violin Playing), 3rd ed. (St. Petersburg: n.p., 1910).

40. Lesman, *Shkola igry na skripke*; and Lesman, *Puti razvitiya skripacha* (Directions of the Violinist's Development) (Leningrad: n.p.,1934), 23.

41. Hugo Bekker, *Tekhnika i estetika igry na violoncheli (perevod s nem.)* (Technique and Aesthetics of Cello Playing, translated from German)) (Moscow: n.p., 1977).

42. Konstantin Mostras, "Lektsii po metodike igry i prepodavaniia na skripke" (Lectures on Methodology of Playing and Teaching the Violin). Manuscript.

43. Jockisch, *Katechismus der Violine und des Violinspiels.*

44. As always, the sound naturally depends on simultaneous movement in the left and right arms. Isolating them in this example is only in the interest of analyzing in greater detail the particular aspects of playing that are the principal subjects of our study.

45. Koeckert, *Rationelle Violintechnik.*

46. Val'ter, *Kak uchit' igre na skripke.*

47. Mozart, *Osnovatel'noe skripichnoe uchilishche/perevod s nem.*

48. Voldan, *Nová škola poloh*; Pennequin, *Nouvelle méthode de violon.*

49. Nemirovskii, *Mekhanicheskie i psikhologicheskie momenty v osnovnykh priemakh skripichnoi tekhniki.*

50. Ibid., 97.

51. B. Struve, *Tipovye formy postanovki ruk u instrumentalistov. Smichkovaia gruppa* (Typical Forms of Positioning the Hands of Instrumentalists: Bowed Instrument Group) (Moscow: n.p., 1932).

52. A literal translation of Yankelevich's term is "cushion" but the term "pad" in this and later instances is used to refer to the variety of cushions and shoulder rests that are placed between the violin and the shoulder. —*Translator's note.*

53. Alexei Lvov, *Sovety nachinaeshemu igrat' na skripke* (Advice to a Beginner on Playing the Violin) (St. Petersburg: n.p., 1859).

54. In this case we are not speaking of the shoulder in the anatomical sense of the word (i.e., the humerus bone), but of the shoulder joint that includes the clavicle and spatula.

55. Val'ter, *Kak uchit' igre na skripke.*

56. Instead of a pad, Yankelevich's students used a metal shoulder rest covered in nylon that was slanted toward the shoulder. Unlike a cushion or pad, the shoulder rest didn't touch the back of the violin and didn't affect the sound. — *Original editor's note.*

57. Abraham Yampolsky, "O metode raboty s uchinikami" (On Methods of Working with studentS), in S. Sapozhnikov, ed., *Voprosy skripichnogo ispolnitel'stva i pedagogiki, sbornik statei* (Matters of Violin Performance and Pedagogy, a Collection of Articles) (Moscow: Muzyka, 1968).

58. Auer, *Moia shkola igry na skripke.*

59. Mozart, *Osnovatel'noe skripichnoe uchilishche/perevod s nem.*

60. Campagnoli, *Neue Methode der fortschreitenden Fingerfertigkeit.*

61. Auer, *Moia shkola igry na skripke.*

62. Singer and Seifriz, *Grosse theoretisch-praktische Violinschule.*

63. Joachim and Moser, *Violinschule.*

64. In this respect we agree with Struve's view of the role that the saddle joint plays in positioning the thumb in relation to the other fingers of the right hand on the bow; Struve, *Tipovye formy postanovki ruk u instrumentalistov.*

65. Flesch, *Iskusstvo skripichnoi igry.*

66. Goby Eberhardt and Gustav Saenger, *My System for Practising the Violin and Piano Based upon Psycho-Physiological Principles* (New York: Fischer, 1906).

67. Flesch, *Iskusstvo skripichnoi igry.*

68. Nemirovskii, *Mekhanicheskie i psikhologicheskie momenty v osnovnykh priemakh skripichnoi tekhniki.*

69. Narcisse Augustin Lefort, *Méthode complète de violon* (Paris: E. Leduc, P. Bertrand et Cie, 1910).

70. Campagnoli, *Neue Methode der fortschreitenden Fingerfertigkeit*; Spohr, *Violinschule.*

71. Mikhailovsky, *Novii put' skripacha.*

72. Voiku, *Postroenie estestvennoi sistemy skripichnoi igry.*

73. Nemirovsky, *Mekhanicheskie i psikhologicheskie momenty v osnovnykh priemakh skripichnoi tekhniki.*

74. Auer, *Moia shkola igry na skripke*; Flesch, *Iskusstvo skripichnoi igry.*

75. Auer, *Moia shkola igry na skripke*, 5:15.

76. Ivan Nazarov, "Psikhofizicheskii metod dostizheniia i sovershenstvovaniia muzykal'noi tekhniki," (Psychophysical Method of Attaining and Perfecting Musical Technique), diss., Leningrad, 1946.

77. Joachim and Moser, *Violinschule.*

78. Mikhailovsky, *Novii put' skripacha.*

79. Kayser, *Neueste Methode des Violinspiels, op. 32 Th. 3.*

80. Valter, *Kak uchit' igre na skripke.*

81. See n. 38.

82. Mostras, *Intonatsiia na skripke.*

83. Flesch, *Iskusstvo skripichnoi igry.*

84. Alard, *Polnaia shkola dlia skripki.*

85. Bekker, *Tekhnika i estetika igry na violoncheli.*

86. The transcripts of the oscillographs were done by O. E. Sakhaltueva, an employee of the acoustic laboratory of the Moscow Tchaikovsky Conservatory.

87. Davidov, *Shkola dlia violoncheli*.

88. By "higher" and "lower" fingers, Davidov means their placement on the fingerboard where the second finger, for example, is higher in relation to the first finger, the third is higher than the first and second fingers, the first finger is lower than the second, third, and fourth fingers, etc.

89. Lesman, *Shkola igry na skripke*.

90. Alard, *Polnaia shkola dlia skripki*; Voiku, *Postroenie estestvennoi sistemy skripichnoi igry*; Jockisch, *Katechismus der Violine und des Violinspiels*; Koeckert, *Rationelle Violintechnik*; Mikhailovsky, *Novii put' skripacha*; Radmall, "Change of Position"; Flesch, *Iskusstvo skripichnoi igry*.

91. According to Israel Yampolsky's expression; Yampolsky, *Osnovy skripchnoi applikatury*, 108.

92. Spohr, *Violinschule*.

93. Flesch, *Iskusstvo skripichnoi igry*.

94. Lesman, *Puti razvitiya skripacha*; Lesman, *Shkola igry na skripke*; Davidov, *Shkola dlia violoncheli*.

95. Addendum to Davidov, *Shkola dlia violoncheli*, 35.

96. Spohr, *Violinschule*, 71; and Alard, *Polnaia shkola dlia skripki*.

97. Mostras, *Intonatsiia na skripke*.

98. Ferdinand David and Waldemar Meyer, *Violinschule* (Leipzig: Steingräber, 1900).

99. Yampolsky, *Osnovy skripchnoi applikatury*.

100. Baillot, *L'art du violon*.

101. Rudolph Kreutzer and Emil Kross, *42 Etüden oder Capricen* (Mainz: Schott, 1884).

102. Lesman, *Shkola igry na skripke*.

103. Flesch, *Iskusstvo skripichnoi igry*.

104. Voiku, *Postroenie estestvennoi sistemy skripichnoi igry*.

105. This applies not only to tenths, but also to all other instances when the fingers are extended (fingered octaves, etc.)

106. Auer, *Moia shkola igry na skripke*.

107. Mostras, *Intonatsiia na skripke*.

108. Carl Guhr, *Paganini's Kunst die Violine zu spielen* (Berlin: B. Schott's Söhne, 1929).

109. Voiku, *Postroenie estestvennoi sistemy skripichnoi igry*; Koeckert, *Rationelle Violintechnik*.

110. David and Meyer, *Violinschule*.

111. Flesch, *Iskusstvo skripichnoi igry*.

112. Ibid.

113. There is no indicated fingering in the previous editions, which is taken to be a typographical error. The fingering Yankelevich implies is assumed to alternate between the first and third positions when ascending without using the open strings. —*Translator's note*.

114. We should stress the necessity of studying scales (not just thirds, but also fingered octaves and sixths) in the even-numbered positions, something often overlooked in the course of study.

115. Sergei Korguev, *Uprazhneniia v dvoinykh notakh* (Exercises in Double Stops) (Moscow: n.p., 1949).

116. Flesch, *Iskusstvo skripichnoi igry.*

117. Georgy Dulov, *Sistematicheskii kurs gamm dlia skripki* (Systematic Course of Violin Scales) (Moscow: n.p., 1924).

118. We should note that when this fingering is used in scale passages, the moment the third and fourth fingers drop, they seem to push away the first and second fingers. For, as Mostras notes, it is inefficient to keep all four fingers on the string simultaneously.

119. Boris Sibor, *Skripichnaya technika dvoinih not* (Violin Technique of Double Stops) (Moscow: n.p., 1928); Korguev, *Uprazhneniia v dvoinykh notakh.*

120. Korguev, *Uprazhneniia v dvoinykh notakh.*

121. Mostras, *Intonatsiia na skripke*, 15.

122. Flesch, *Iskusstvo skripichnoi igry.*

123. Yampolsky, "O metode raboty s uchinikame."

124. Lesman, *Puti razvitiya skripacha.*

125. Joachim and Moser, *Violinschule.*

126. Ševčík, *Shkola skripichnoi tekhniki/perevod s cheshskogo*; Voldan, *Nová škola poloh*; Lesman, *Ob igre na skripke*; Lesman, *Puti razvitiya skripacha*; and Lesman, *Shkola igry na skripke.*

127. Mikhailovsky, *Novii put' skripacha*, 69.

128. Yampolsky, *Osnovy skripchnoi applikatury.*

129. Voldan, *Nová škola poloh*; Ševčík, *Shkola skripichnoi tekhniki/perevod s cheshskogo.*

130. Koeckert, *Rationelle Violintechnik*; Yampolsky, *Osnovy skripchnoi applikatury.*

131. Carl Flesch, *Etuden-Sammlung für Violine* (Copenhagen: Wilhelm Hansen, 1921).

132. Lesman, *Shkola igry na skripke.*

133. Moser, *Methodik des Violinspiels.*

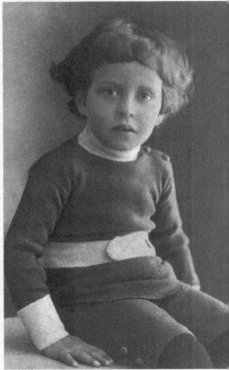

Yuri Yankelevich with his father, 1909, and as a young boy.

Yuri Yankelevich with his mother in Switzerland, 1910.

Omsk, 1923.

Poster of the first concert in Omsk.

Professor Ioannes Nalbandyan.

Professor Anisim Berlin.

Yuri Yankelevich with Abraham Yampolsky.

Concert in front of the Red Army, 1942.

Maya Glezarova.

Yuri Yankelevich with accompanist Natalia Izhevskaya.

Leonid Kogan (inscription reads: To dear Yuri Isaevich, as a token of love and respect).

Yehudi Menuhin (inscription reads: To my dear colleague Yuri Yankelevich, Yehudi Menuhin, Brussels).

Yuri Yankelevich with Isaac Stern.

With Mstistlav Rostropovich.

Yuri Yankelevich at home, at the piano.

Yankelevich's class of 1969.

Yuri Yankelevich with students: A. Futer, S. Steinberg, S. Yanovskaya, V. Slutsky.

From left to right: V. Spivakov, V. Tretyakov, V. Ivanov, N. Shkolnikova, I. Bochkova, M. Bezverkhni, L. Dubrovskaya, G. Zhislin.

3

Aspects of Yankelevich's Teaching Methods

MAYA GLEZAROVA ■

After graduating from the Moscow Conservatory in 1949, I began my pedagogical activity at one of the Moscow music schools. Approximately one year
later Yuri Yankelevich invited me to work as his assistant at the Central Music
School, the preparatory high school of the Moscow Conservatory, and at the
Moscow Conservatory itself, and I continued in this capacity until Yankelevich
passed away in 1973.

Those indispensable pedagogical qualities that struck me at the beginning
of my association with Yankelevich, and that always continued to impress
me, were largely instilled in him by nature and were refined to the point of
artistic mastery. These qualities included an exceptional pedagogical talent;
an altruistic commitment to his work; a remarkable diligence; adherence to
the highest professional standards; and honesty, experience, intuition, and
knowledge.

Observing Yankelevich in his lessons, I never ceased to be surprised by
his joyful and generous dedication, along with his irrepressible desire to
understand the student and discover his or her unique and intrinsic qualities. "In order to successfully teach and educate, one must carefully study the
subject of one's endeavors." These words of the notable Russian pedagogue
Konstantin Ushinsky perfectly characterize all of Yankelevich's pedagogical
activity.[1] Each lesson was both a continuation of the previous one and full of
new discoveries.

A very important component in the process of nurturing a violinist was
the fact that the lessons of Yankelevich and his assistants constituted a single

line of development. His lessons took as long as was required by the problems he was solving—there was never a preset structure for a lesson. Sometimes a lesson consisted of playing through a program, followed by an analysis of the performance. Sometimes he would work on the "key moments" of the piece, determining the correlation of tempi or specific culminations. At times Yankelevich was not afraid of spending the entire lesson on finding the right "color" or sonic palette of a composition.

When working on a musical composition, Yankelevich always strove for the student to make it personal, to make it "one's own." "For only then," Yankelevich said, "will the performance be convincing, powerful, and honest."[2] While always stressing that the main goal was to develop the student's creative and artistic identity, Yankelevich would work on individual elements of violin technique with remarkable patience.

> The more the violinist is in command of the instrument, the less his or her attention is diverted to the technical side and the more he or she is able to concentrate on musical content. Insufficient technical mastery limits the violinist and becomes an irrepressible obstacle in fulfilling his or her musical intentions.

It was this philosophy, illustrative of his musical-pedagogical goals, that allowed him to work with such surprising interest and persistence on etudes, exercises, and scales. Yankelevich would never appear bored, and he would never dismiss these components as something necessary but secondary in importance. On the contrary, he approached this work with such enthusiasm that he would inspire the student, assuring him or her of the necessity and importance of this kind of work in achieving long-term goals.

When working on scales, Yankelevich developed and perfected all aspects of violin technique—agility, facility, clarity, rhythmic discipline of the fingers in the left hand, and shifting—while at the same time working on a singing and even tone, perfecting bow changes and bow distribution. Scales were covered with many different variations in rhythm and fingerings.

Yankelevich attached a lot of importance to bow strokes, calling them "the most important elements of expression." Work on bowings would start from the very first stages of learning the violin. In Yankelevich's class, bowings were studied according to a specific system. The main principle of the system was to increase the difficulty gradually—starting from détaché and progressing to staccato and ricochet. One would start by working on all the elements of détaché strokes in different parts of the bow and then connecting them. This established the main movements of the right hand and arm in all parts of the bow.

Exercise 1: Long notes.

Start with 8 beats per note, then increase:

a) f

b) p

c) ⊓
   f ═══► p p ◄═══ f
   V   ⊓

d) V   V
   f ═══► p ◄═══ f p ◄═══ f ═══► p
   ⊓

Pay attention to the evenness of tone, its quality, the change of bow, and the gradation of crescendo and diminuendo.

Exercise 2: Détaché (large divisions). Using Kreutzer Etude No. 1.[3]

a) Whole bow
b) Upper half
c) Lower half
d) Combined bowing

♩ ♫
⊓ V⊓

e) Combined détaché and legato (whole bow, upper and lower halves)

Pay attention to the singing quality of the stroke and the active beginning of each note.

Exercise 3: Détaché (small divisions in six sections). Using Kreutzer Etude No. 1.

a) détaché
b) détaché + legato
c) fast détaché (duplets, triplets, quadruplets, etc.)

Exercise 4: Exercises for the wrist and fingers. Using Kreutzer Etude No. 11.[4]

a) fingers + wrist
    • Connect at the frog on different strings
    • In the middle of the bow
    • Starting alternatively V and ⊓
b) wrist
    • legato on two strings
    • détaché on two strings at the tip V and ⊓
       combination of détaché and legato at the tip

c) Détaché crossing strings. Using Kreutzer's Etude No. 1.
- spiccato at the frog in duplets or triplets
- spiccato at the frog skipping over strings (using Kreutzer No. 6).[5]

Exercise 5: Martelé. Using Kreutzer No. 1.
a) starting at different parts of the bow (both ⋁ and ⊓)
b) using the entire bow
c) upper half
d) "Viotti" stroke
e) staccato

Exercise 6: Dotted strokes

a) Whole bow
b) Upper half

c) at the tip
d) at the frog

Exercise 7: Fast spiccato (4, 3, 2 notes per bow)

Exercise 8: Slow spiccato, combined with legato

Exercise 9: Flying staccato (2, 3, 4, 5, etc. notes per bow)

Exercise 10: Ricochet ⊓ and ⋁ (2, 3, 4, 5, etc. notes per bow)

Exercise 11: Tremolo

Yankelevich was creative when taking into account a student's individuality, physical abilities, and degree and level of development. Sometimes he would change the order in which the bowings were covered, or he would regroup them. Bowings were generally studied using Kreutzer's Etudes Nos. 1 and 11. The acquired skills were then reinforced with other appropriate etudes, which helped to crystallize the skills in a musical context. Yankelevich believed that it was necessary to work on a minimum of two scales and three to four etudes every month. Etudes were studied with multiple variations, that is, different bowings, fingerings, and rhythms (using Abraham Yampolsky's edition).

Yankelevich had the remarkable ability to simplify technically difficult sections for the student. He not only simply illustrated the correct method but also provided a very clear verbal explanation. Very often just one word or one apt analogy, sometimes with humor (he liked a good joke), would be enough for the student to move forward and relieve excess tension and insecurity.

When working on scales, etudes, and bow strokes, Yankelevich strove for each technique to be relaxed and supple. He said, "the basis of playing must be naturalness," and he worked on developing virtuosity in bowings and scales.

For Yankelevich, the criterion determining good technique was the quality of the sound. A "singing tone"—this was the true credo of his teaching. Today, in spite of the enormous developments in virtuosity, the violin should foremost be understood as a melodic and lyrical instrument, in keeping with the principles of the Russian violin school. Virtuosity must never obstruct the violin's fundamental quality as an emotionally expressive, lyrical instrument.

These considerations lead to one of the most important aspects of Yankelevich's school, which was the development of the student's inner ear and auditory control. "Insistence on good intonation and tone quality should be developed from the very early stages of study," he said. He often liked to repeat Abraham Yampolsky's favorite expression in his lessons: "*Sing!*" And Yankelevich did not just want the cantilena to sing but all aspects of technique—accents, passagework, sforzandi, and so on:

> A singing tone is not just a natural gift, but is one of the most important aspects of violin technique, an intrinsic component of mastering the instrument, which requires lengthy and concentrated effort.

Yankelevich made no allowances for age or degree of talent in his demand for quality.

> That which talented students may sometimes achieve intuitively, in response to their inner ear, may also be achieved with students who are less talented. The latter simply need to be equipped with an accurate knowledge of different methods of tone production and an understanding of the timbral and dynamic possibilities of the violin.

When working with young children, Yankelevich would never talk down to them. He always spoke seriously and never lowered his standards.

In comparing the sound of the violin to the human voice, Yankelevich sought more than simply a beautiful tone—he sought a tone capable of expressing specific musical content.

How mistaken were those who referred to Yankelevich's detailed work on various skills as "overly technical." Every scale and etude studied was later put to the service of music in order to help uncover the artistic meaning of the composition.

> The highest technical mastery is when the artist can so easily overcome the difficulties that present themselves that his or her thoughts and

creativity may be entirely directed to the musical aspect of performance. Only then does the listener understand the music not by "how difficult it is" but through the essence of its content.

Because he saw the goal of his work as developing a thinking musician with a creative individual personality and excellent command of the instrument, Yankelevich spent a lot of attention on methods of practicing at home. The quality of at-home practice is closely tied to activating the student's inner ear and developing the student's attention and professional memory.

Yankelevich's lessons helped guide the student in solving musical and technical problems when practicing at home. All the necessary material was worked out during the lesson with such thoroughness that after the lesson the student understood not only the goals but also the means to achieve them. During the lesson Yankelevich would persistently work on practically securing new sensations and musical ideas. "To simply make the right observation is not enough," he said. "One needs to make sure that the student is also able to accomplish it."

Yankelevich's methods were flexible and varied. The only thing that remained consistent was his unflinching dedication to his goal. Yankelevich was generally averse to the method of demonstrating, which sometimes turns into: "Play like I do." The problem here is not just that the student copies without delving into the essence of the problem; it also interferes with the student's development of an individual personality. The essential goal is to uncover and maximize the use of the student's inner resources. Yankelevich's lessons addressed all types of problems (methods of tone production, character of the composition, individual technical problems, sound color, etc.) but the form of the lesson was never standardized, for it depended on the music itself and the student's artistic personality.

I remember Yankelevich's approach to the matter of setting up the violin and bow hold. "I never pursue one sole manner of holding the violin and bow," he said. "For me the reference point is the emergence of a supple and pure sound. If it isn't present, one must find what is blocking it." He was never interested in the external form of the positioning, but only in whether or not the playing that resulted approached the ideal of how the violin should sound. I was always impressed by his ability to give a "diagnosis," to discover the hidden defects in a setup. In these cases the setup would visually appear correct, but there was a hidden obstacle interfering with the desired result, and a specific particularity in the hands, neck, or shoulder that required individual adjustment. Yankelevich was able to accurately pinpoint the reasons for the "problem" and provide a "prescription," which invariably cured the "illness" in difficult and complicated cases.

One of the fundamental conditions of his work was the creation of individual plans for each of his students. While other teachers might consider this just a formality, Yankelevich approached this task with a considerable thoroughness. He also drew his assistants into work on creating individual plans, especially for new students. Yankelevich never presumed to have all the answers, and even at the peak of his pedagogical achievements he readily would confer with his assistants and colleagues. Yankelevich would discuss the strong and weak aspects of his students (he was able to accurately pinpoint all the problematic areas and insufficient skills). Then the paths and pace of development would be charted out, individual solutions would be constructed for each case, and corresponding musical and technical material would be assigned.

Yankelevich often noted that the standard curriculum for music schools, prep schools, and conservatories are only generally able to determine the student's path, since this program is designed for the average student. Following the same curriculum with a more talented student might slow his or her development. "Besides," he said, "there are often times in pedagogical practice when for a certain period the teacher must guide the student along a more conservative track (correcting the setup, getting rid of tension) so that the student may later be able to catch up and even make a leap forward." Even with students at the conservatory, Yankelevich was not afraid of sometimes starting "from scratch."

In these cases, the content and quality of the individual plan is especially important. I believe there are two widespread, rather debatable, approaches in guiding the choice of repertoire. The first reflects the student's external nature, that is, choosing pieces that accentuate the natural qualities of the student—pieces that are naturally suited to him or her. The second approach only takes into consideration the student's weaknesses. Here, in attempting to fix the weaknesses, the teachers dismiss all the positive qualities of the students and risk stifling each student's individuality. I believe there must be a third, truer approach: to carefully combine the individual characteristics of the student with the necessary goals for his or her future development, while at the same time also correcting any weaknesses.

Examining the individual plans that Yankelevich devised, one immediately notices how much thought went into them, the comprehensive details of every component, and how he completely unified musical and technical principles. These plans were always far-reaching, and they reflected the student's development not just for the present year but also for years to come. Because of

Yankelevich's talent, experience, and extraordinary intuition, the plans were always structured very creatively with a sense of purpose.

Upon completing and solidifying the plan, Yankelevich meticulously brought it to life, and all components were put in place. But in spite of all the care and love he put into his system, Yankelevich was never pedantic. In some cases, such as when covering the concerti of de Bériot, Spohr, Vieuxtemps, and Ernst, he could skip one or two pieces if he noticed that the prescribed goals were already achieved and the student had progressed enough to skip to the next stage. He believed that an assimilation of quality and quantity could sometimes provoke such a jump, especially with talented students. However, unless he foresaw this kind of jump, he would never make his plans excessively difficult.

Yankelevich had an interesting approach to the works of composers such as de Bériot, Spohr, Vieuxtemps, and Ernst, all whom were included in every student's lesson plan. "I know there is a tendency, especially in the West, to only incorporate the classical repertoire when teaching," he said, "but I am not sure this is always right." Yankelevich found these pieces to be excellent material for developing mastery of the instrument as well as developing the imaginative and emotional side of playing. And how much unexpected freshness and originality he brought to the concerti of Spohr and Vieuxtemps!

All the individual plans (both in the younger and older classes) included every aspect of violin technique in the appropriate quantity and level. For example, the beginning classes covered the main techniques of playing scales in one and two octaves. The goals were as follows: an even sound, good bow distribution, smooth string crossings, even rhythm in the left hand, accurate intonation, and freedom in executing all these skills. In approximately the third and fourth years, scales were studied in each position—that is, first, second, third, fourth, fifth, and so on—and three octave scales were also covered. The goals included being able to shift freely and correctly, improved tone quality, clear and precise rhythm in the left hand, and good intonation.

In the sixth, seventh, eighth, and ninth years, scales were played with many different variations: in triplets, quadruplets, and broken thirds to develop clear articulation and even movement in the fingers; chromatic scales with different fingerings, including sliding fingers; scales with two fingers (1-2, 2-3, 3-4); scales on one string; and a variety of arpeggios and double stops. As the technical skills in scales were perfected, the goals increased in difficulty. The more advanced classes required scales to be played virtuosically, with a singing tone and supple technique.

Work on bowings was included in each lesson plan from the first year. At the beginning this included familiarization with the main basic strokes, gradually increasing in difficulty; then in the more advanced classes they were polished and perfected. Bowings were studied using Kreutzer's Etudes Nos. 1 and 11. Yankelevich did not work on bowings with scales, since he found this would divert attention from the problems that scales themselves require. The gradual increase in difficulty and perfection of the technical material was made possible because of the high demands he placed on technical quality from the very beginning. About three to four etudes were covered every month. While studying at the Central Music School, students were expected to cover all the etudes of Wohlfahrt, Kreutzer, Mazas, Kayser, Rode, and Dont (books 1 and 2). The Kreutzer etudes were studied using Abraham Yampolsky's edition and were played with practically every possible variation. For additional development of left-hand technique, the exercises of Schradieck were covered, and the exercises of Ševčík (opus 9 in double stops), Conus, and Korguyev were used for double stops.

Yankelevich himself largely inspired the artistry and engagement so characteristic of his students. During the lessons he was always very active and involved. He would delve into the essence of the music with such expression and temperament, inspiring the performer to project a rich palette of emotions. One of his distinctive qualities was an aspiration to perfection in pedagogical artistry and determination in his own work. This was most likely the reason his lessons were planned so carefully. Each lesson had a clear structure, and not one minute was wasted. At times he could spend a lot of time solving one particular problem and then reject a customary solution for something new and more valuable. Almost always, he would come to the lesson with a ready solution for each student's problem.

At the beginning of his career, Yankelevich demanded that each piece attain a certain degree of perfection. At each lesson he would give numerous remarks touching on the minutest detail of phrasing, color, and dynamics. He wanted to illustrate everything, and every single accent, passage, or grace note contained a full and thorough explanation. Later on, he moved from a detailed approach to capturing the larger picture. He became much more concerned with problems of form, style, and culminations. His explanations were remarkably accurate, concise, and easy to grasp. The piece appeared to be "sculpted" before one's very eyes.

If, in his early years, Yankelevich would begin giving his remarks right away, often without hearing the piece to the end, later on it was characteristic of his method to delve into and understand the student's entire conception. He significantly increased the amount of repertoire covered from different eras and styles. Some pieces were not necessarily brought to the level of complete perfection. In this respect he seemed to adhere to the principles of Konstantin Stanislavsky, who believed, "it is better to set both the student and oneself a difficult goal and achieve only partial success, than to weigh and calculate one's strengths and thus end up lowering the bar."

It is difficult to overestimate the influence of Yankelevich's personality on his students—as both an artist and a person. He was always attentive and sympathetic, looking out for the student's future and always ready to assist. Never withdrawing into his own thoughts and concerns, Yankelevich liked people and enjoyed life. In devoting himself to pedagogy and working with students, he never stopped studying their characters, opinions, and views of the world. "The student is 'live material,'" Yankelevich said. "The student grows, changes, and takes on new qualities. This requires flexibility and a variable methodology, without ever losing sight of the final goal. The teacher can achieve this only by completely understanding the student in a manner that is flexible and creative, enlightened by intellect and warmed by the heart."

Yankelevich's planned repertoire was always created for the upcoming two to three years. Then every year the plan was extended, taking into account the student's progress and development. Below is an approximate repertoire plan for a student starting to study with Yankelevich in the second year of the Central Music School. This is geared for a student in possession of good technical capabilities, but an underdeveloped musical and emotional side and rather lifeless dynamics and expression.[6]

YEAR 2

O. Rieding	*Concerto*
A. Komarovsky	*La Course,* or *Racing*
N. Baklanova	*Sonatine, Concertino, and Allegro*
A. Yanshinov	*Concertino*
F. Seitz	*Concerto No. 1*
A.Vivaldi	*Concerto in A minor*
N. Rubenstein	*Spinning Wheel*
E. Jenkinson	*Dance*
L. Alard	*Nocturne and Serenade*
C. Dancla	*Variations*

YEAR 3

G. Hollender	*Concerto*
J. B. Accolay	*Concerto*
G. Viotti	*Concerto No. 23*
C. Bohm	*Perpetual Motion*
A. Yanshinov	*Spinning Wheel*
G. Pergolesi	*Aria*
A. Spendiarov	*Lullaby*

J. Aubert	*Presto*
C. de Bériot	*Variations No. 1*
F. Schubert	*The Bumblebee*
S. Prokofiev	*Gavotte*
J. Haydn	*Minuet of the Bull*
A. Khachaturian	*Andantino*

YEAR 4

J. Mazas	*Etudes*
C. de Bériot	*Concerto No. 9 (complete)*
G. F. Handel	*Sonata No. 6*
R. Glière	*Romance "By the Brook"*
J. S. Bach	*Concerto in A minor*
J. Fiocco	*Allegro*
J. S. Bach	*Sicilienne*

YEAR 5

G. Viotti	*Concerto No. 22* (complete)
D. Kabalevsky	*Concerto* (movement 1)
J. Matteson	*Aria*
F. Kreisler (Francoeur)	*Sicilienne and Rigaudon*
G. F. Handel	*Sonata No. 2*
H. Vieuxtemps	*Fantasie et Appassionata*
H. Wieniawski	*Concerto No. 2* (movement 1)
H. Vieuxtemps	*Concerto No. 2* (movement 1)
P. Sarasate	*Fantasy on themes from Gounod's "Faust"*
F. Kreisler	*Grave (in the style of Bach)*
F. Ries	*Perpetual Motion*
A. Aleksandrov	*Aria*
L. Daquin	*The Cuckoo*
F. Kreisler (Pugnani)	*Preludium and Allegro*
F. Chopin (Auer)	*Nocturne*
H. Wieniawski	*Concerto No. 2* (movements 2 and 3)
M. Bruch	*Concerto No. 1*
H. Vieuxtemps	*Concerto No. 5*
L. Boccherini	*Allegretto*
Vieuxtemps	*Rondino*

Certain pieces, such as the concerti and variations by de Bériot, the pieces and concerti of Vieuxtemps, *Moto Perpetuo* by Bohm and Ries, and Spohr's Concerto No. 9, were thoroughly polished and developed skills such as different bow strokes and command of the fingerboard to a very high technical level. At the same time these pieces helped develop the student's weaker side—stimulating panache and variety, a lyrical cantilena, exaggerated dynamics.

In more complicated pieces such as Sarasate's *Faust*, Wieniawski's 2nd concerto, and Vieuxtemps' 5th concerto, and short pieces by Tchaikovsky, Wieniawski, and others, the tasks became more difficult. Technique was perfected as a more important component of the piece; a deeper understanding of style and character was fostered, leading to mastery of vibrato and logical phrasing and dynamics. Simultaneously, slower pieces of various composers were covered in order to develop tone and cantilena.

The pieces that created difficulties for the student were polished to the highest possible level at a given stage of their development. By the ninth or tenth year the weaker musical side of this student would "catch up" to the technical side. Then such pieces as concertos by Mendelssohn, Mozart, Ernst, and Tchaikovsky, and the Sonatas and Partitas by Bach and other similar pieces, could be played convincingly in their entirety.

Another student might possess a big, bright, and beautiful sound, and play very emotionally, but also with rhythmic instability, excessive vibrato, heavy left-hand technique, and limited agility. In this case the repertoire plan may be almost exactly the same, but the goals would be different—that is, maintaining stricter and calmer execution, emphasizing rhythmic stability, and developing the virtuosic components. Thus the number of pieces covered in Yankelevich's classes remained relatively constant, but the repertoire was treated differently depending on the student's individual characteristics.

A good example is the individual plan for Victor Tretyakov. During his studies with Yankelevich, his plan was completed in its entirety. Tretyakov began studying with Yankelevich in the fifth year at the Central Music School, with the program that year approximately corresponding to what is listed in the table above for a Year 5 student. Subsequently his repertoire was planned as follows:

INDIVIDUAL REPERTOIRE PLAN FOR VICTOR TRETYAKOV

F. Kreisler	*The Hunt (in the style of Cartier)*
H. Wieniawski	*Etude in D major*
P. Tchaikovsky	*Meditation*
H. Wieniawski	*Polonaise in A major*

G. F. Handel	*Sonata No. 4*
F. Mendelssohn	*Concerto*
D. Popper/Auer	*Spinning Wheel*
H. Wieniawski	*Scherzo-Tarantella*
N. Paganini	*Cantabile*
N. Paganini	*Sonata no. 12*
P. Rode	*Etudes*
H. Wieniawski	*Etude in A minor*
H. Wieniawski	*Etude in G minor*
W. A. Mozart	*Concerto No. 1*
W. A. Mozart	*Concerto No. 4*
H. Ernst	*Concerto*
H. Ernst	*Fantasie on themes from "Othello"*
G. Tartini/Kreisler	*Variations*
N. Paganini	*Moses Variations*
N. Paganini	*Cantabile*
N. Paganini	*Moto Perpetuo*
P. Tchaikovsky	*Melody*
J. Dont	*Etudes*
H. Wieniawski	*Etude "Agilité"*
J. S.Bach	*"Gigue"* from *Partita in D minor*
A. Khachaturian	*Concerto*
N. Paganini	*Caprices Nos: 16, 23, 14, 15, 17, 24, 4*
D. Kabalevsky	*Improvisation*
P. Tchaikovsky	*Concerto*
P. Tchaikovsky	*Serenade Melancolique*
N. Paganini (Kreisler)	*I Palpiti*
N. Peiko	*Prelude and Toccata*
J. S. Bach	*"Sicilenne"* and *"Presto"* from *Sonata in G minor*
A. Eshpai	*Sonata*
W. A. Mozart	*Sonata in B-flat Major*
S. Prokofiev	*Sonata No. 1*
F. Schubert	*Fantasy*
H. Wieniawski	*Polonaise in D Major*
P. Sarasate	*Caprice Basque*
R. Wagner	*Album leaf*
M. de Falla	*Suite populaire espagnole*
A. Babadjanian	*Sonata*
J. Sibelius	*Concerto*
J. S. Bach	*Concerto in A minor*
L. Beethoven	*Sonata No. 1*
J. Brahms	*Sonata No. 3*
M. Weinberg	*Sonata No. 5*
C. Saint-Saens	*Rondo Capricioso*

R. Schedrin/Tsyganov	*Humoresque*
J. Brahms	*2 Hungarian dances*
D. Shostakovich	*Concerto No. 2*
M. Ravel	*Tzigane*
J. Brahms	*Scherzo*
T. Vitali	*Chaconne*
C. Scott/F. Kreisler	*Lotus Land*
C. Debussy	*Soirée exquise*
F. Kreisler	*Liebesleid*
D. Shostakovich	*Sonata*
F. Schubert	*Duo*
E. Chausson	*Poème*
A. Corelli	*La Folia*
F. Kreisler	*Caprice Viennois*
P. Sarasate	*Zapateado*
E. Bloch	*Improvisation*
S. Prokofiev	*Five melodies*
J. Brahms	*Sonata No. 1*
N. Paganini	*La Campanella*
S. Prokofiev	*Concerto No. 1*
C. Franck	*Sonata*
O. Messiaen	*Theme and Variations*
D. Shostakovich/Tsyganov	*Ten Preludes*
L. Beethoven	*Sonata No. 3*
J. Suk	*Four pieces*
F. Schubert	*Sonatina in A minor*
E. Grieg	*Sonata No. 3*
W. A. Mozart	*Concerto No. 3*
E. Ysaye	*Poème élégiaque*
R. Schumann	*Bird as Prophet*
E. Granados	*Danse espagnole*
Godart	*Canzonetta*
G. Tartini/Kreisler	*"Devil's Trill" sonata*
D. Shostakovich	*Five preludes*
C. Saint-Saens	*Havanaise*
A. Vivaldi	*Adagio*
F. Kreisler	*Liebesfreud*
M. Moszkowski	*Guitarre*
L. Beethoven	*Sonata No. 6*

This repertoire was typical for studying in Yankelevich's class at the Moscow Conservatory. However, being able to complete it in its entirety with the necessary quality was something only sufficiently gifted students were capable of.

NOTES

1. Konstantin Ushinsky (1824–1871) was an esteemed Russian writer and teacher who developed influential theories on pedagogy. —*Translator's note*
2. This and subsequent quotes of Yankelevich were noted by the author during lessons and conversations.
3. The numbering of the Kreutzer Etudes may vary according to the edition. In this case Kreutzer Etude No. 1 refers to the Etude in sixteenth notes in C Major, often listed as No. 2 in current editions. —*Translator's note*
4. Etude in sixteenth notes in A Major, often listed as No. 13. See n. 3.
5. Etude in eighth notes in D Major, often listed as No. 7. See n. 3.
6. Maya Glezarova does not provide more specific information on these works, and unless commonly known otherwise, the English translation of the Russian title is provided. —*Translator's note*

Yankelevich's Methodological System

VLADIMIR GRIGORYEV ∎

GENERAL MATTERS OF METHODOLOGY

The creative legacy of every great pedagogue—the talent, experience, and ideas that are passed on to students and captured in essays, lectures, master classes, editions, and transcriptions—is an incredibly valuable asset that furthers an art's development and enriches our knowledge of interpretive and educational processes. Yuri Yankelevich not only left us with fascinating theoretical material but also made a seminal contribution to the Russian and Soviet methodology of teaching the violin.

This chapter does not aim to provide an exhaustive summary of all of Yankelevich's methodological opinions. It generalizes material from his seminars for teachers and students that this author was able to record over the course of more than fifteen years. The chapter also attempts to outline the main contours of the pedagogical and methodological system that allowed Yankelevich to achieve such astonishing success.

Questions of violin methodology, and string methodology in general, were always at the center of Yankelevich's thoughts. In the 1950s, when methodological matters were being intensely discussed in the string department headed by Abraham Yampolsky, Yankelevich made a point of summarizing the pedagogical experience of the leading professors of the Moscow Conservatory (beginning with Yampolsky himself).[1] This work was also stimulated by the methodological lectures Yankelevich presented to students in their second year at the conservatory.

In his lectures Yankelevich combined general theories of methodology with the study of specific methodological texts. His commentaries were always accurate and not devoid of humor, and they arrived at profound conclusions that uncovered the essence of the topics being discussed. One was struck just as much by his erudition as a pedagogue-practitioner and theoretician as by his exceptional knowledge of the nature of the instrument, the psychology of the student, and the secrets of the pedagogical process. These lectures always radiated a spirit of creativity and were completely free of the rather formalistic methodological approach that was considerably widespread in those years. Yankelevich did not always answer questions categorically. Often he would only give a hypothetical opinion, cautioning that the given matter needed more research, although still offering his own perspective.

The assimilation of Yankelevich's ideas was always facilitated by an extremely clear, accurate, and logical presentation. Complicated problems were broken down into smaller ones, and his arguments were always concise. One felt that Yankelevich posed to himself similar, if not identical, questions in his own work and tirelessly sought the answers.

In the course of his teaching, Yankelevich's ideas underwent certain changes. He closely followed developments in both the methodological literature and the more specialized literature of psychology and physiology. Wherever possible, he attempted to apply the latest scientific achievements to his pedagogical activities. Thus, he examined Pavlov's theory of conditioned reflexes and concluded that the skills of playing the playing the violin are similar, if not identical, to these types of reflexes.[2]

In his later years, rich in experience, Yankelevich turned his attention to broader methodological and pedagogical issues and their interdependence, though without ceasing to provide concrete methodological directions with which he was literally "overflowing." He created a harmonious system of teaching the violin that naturally combined work with individual students and scientific research in the field of methodology. The latter would then lead him to modify the individual program in his lessons.

Yankelevich's teaching method was flexible, combining tact with determination. A logical beginning and planned, step-by-step progression to an eventual goal were very important. His demands were always precise and concise, and his remarks were profound and diverse in nature.

Yankelevich was one of the first to employ a "long-term perspective" individually catered to each student. He meticulously planned each stage of the student's progression, from early music school through conservatory graduate work and concertizing activity. Each stage entailed different goals, but in due time every problem confronting a young musician was covered. In Yankelevich's own words, this enabled him to "most effectively construct an edifice of instrumental mastery" for each student that guided him or her to the very top.

Yankelevich was prudent in selecting students to take part in competitions. He decided the benefits of participating in any competition on an individual basis, depending not only on how well the program was prepared but on whether the particular competition was a good match for the student's talents and style.

As already noted, Yankelevich's original views were founded on the methodological principles developed by Abraham Yampolsky. What were those elements of Yampolsky's methodology that particularly resonated with Yankelevich?

First, Yankelevich paid special attention to what he considered the fundamental methodological principles of Yampolsky. This entailed working with students on developing preliminary perceptions not only of the musical work itself but also of the sound needed to express the musical idea and the appropriate motor skills required to realize the conception. He would recall that Yampolsky "did not strive to develop the student's motions themselves, but rather to develop the nerve perceptions that would lead to quick reflexive reactions." In addition to requiring the student to consciously approach the musical material, Yankelevich required the student to be consciously aware of his or her own abilities. This is partly the origin of the phenomenal success of his teaching method.

Yankelevich's interest in the psycho-physiological aspect of teaching was not accidental. He believed that it is in precisely this field that the answers lie to help stimulate the pedagogical process. His method was characterized by the desire to consider and employ the latest scientific achievements in pedagogical practice. This is why Yankelevich's method went beyond simply collecting empirical experiences and moved into the realm of creating new methodological approaches. This was fueled by his natural interest in general synthesis and finding precise answers to practical problems.

The methodological matters Yankelevich focused on the most in his lectures may be divided into five categories:

(1) Knowing the student, along with his or her characteristics and capabilities, and finding the correct, individual approach to his or her development.

(2) Choosing musical and technical repertoire for individual work with the student.

(3) Providing a psycho-physiological basis for rational violin technique and systems that lead to professional mastery.

(4) Offering specific methodological directions for concrete problems such as various expressive devices, bowings, organization of lesson plans, and so on.

(5) Analyzing problems related to performance, along with showing the student how to prepare for performances and directing the entire pedagogical process towards this eventual goal.

Analyzing Yankelevich's observations, made at various times and in various contexts, one seeks answers to the following questions: What were the criteria that allowed Yankelevich to determine the student's talent and potential, leading to the choice of individual repertoire and the expressive devices that needed work? What was the interrelation between the psychological, musical, and technical problems that Yankelevich tried to solve? And finally, what where the main contours of Yankelevich's system in which all problems were closely integrated?

Yankelevich would say:

For some, methodological questions, such as the setup of the right and left hands, playing movements, fingerings, tone production, choice of repertoire, musical content, and individual development, are all isolated problems dissimilar in nature. For others, all these problems are links in one and the same chain and turn out to be completely interconnected. I am an advocate of this second approach.

There are general norms and laws—anatomical, physiological, psychological, physical, and acoustic—which, when broken, lead to failure. The purpose of an individual positioning is to take into consideration the general rules, and on their basis to create an individual and logical system. Meanwhile, the teacher must flexibly and intelligently help the student to form his or her own individual positioning, even if it does not always correspond to an "ideal." The criteria here must be freedom of movement rather than an abstract or formal "correctness."

Yankelevich also liked to quote Yampolsky in the following: "Unfortunately, the problem with many teachers is that they do not listen to the violinist, but only look to see whether the movements appear 'correct.' Yet what the hands actually create or 'express' completely escapes them."

According to Yankelevich, the pedagogue's activity must foremost be directed toward the student's psychological processes of adapting to musical and technical requirements and of assimilating new material. This is where the pedagogue determines "what is useful to the student, where one may push and from what one should temporarily abstain." But prior to this, the teacher should play out various possibilities. Then, using his or her experience, knowledge, and detailed study of the student, the teacher should choose the most effective and efficient path leading to the desired result. This system allows the teacher to switch to another approach kept in reserve if the chosen path turns out to be too easy or too difficult.

Thus, according to Yankelevich, in practice it may look like this: "The teacher illustrates how ideally he or she imagines something should be done (depending on the teacher's experience with the norms) and then carefully observes how the student adapts, what the student can and cannot do. This way the teacher is able to simultaneously study the student's individual personality."

This is a good illustration of the "scientific-experimental" approach mentioned earlier. Every lesson (and every lecture) for Yankelevich was not only a creative discovery but also a means of testing in practice the solutions or new ideas developed in his "theoretical laboratory." And he always maintained at the center of his attention the individual student, complete with his or her own abilities, aspirations, and potential.

Yankelevich always sought to stimulate his students and ignite them with his creative energy. He believed self-observation to be the first step along this path of developing a student's independence.

The process of practicing is the process of self-observation. In the process of practicing there should not be one movement or one note without a clear idea of why it is made, what is the goal facing the student, be it intonation, shifting, or something else.

However, Yankelevich would stress that practicing is more than simply persistence and perseverance. Foremost it is thinking, both with and without the instrument. The hands might be able to work more than the brain and the attention span, but is this really necessary?

The hands should never be driven to exhaustion. Fatigue is a sign of poor methods of working. The more natural the movements, the less tired the hands will be. But most important, one needs to constantly maintain conscious attention and control over the movements. It is the mind, rather than the hands, that must be exerted. And yet, even when the movements are very relaxed, the hands might still tire from excessive practice. This may be avoided by correctly alternating periods of work and rest.

Yankelevich considered it essential to "develop the correct sensations of movements" or, more accurately, the "correct perceptions of movements," since the sensations are created on the basis of the latter. The process of self-observation must therefore be initially focused on this aspect of playing. The slightest error must be corrected immediately.

Pain in the arms and hands is not normal. This reflects poor teaching and setup and can lead to professional problems. As soon as any pain appears one must "microscopically" examine the entire playing process. Sometimes playing while ill, especially with a high fever, may cause pain. This is very dangerous and I forbid my students to play when they are sick.

Yankelevich advocated a creative methodology that would take into account new developments in psychology and physiology.

Method is the scientific ordering of the process of playing and educating the performer. However, method, like pedagogy, is not a procedure, but a creative process. Here matters of psychology and intuition come to the forefront. The pedagogue must know more than the best performer: he or she is required to know the instrument, the psychology of the student, the ins and outs of concertizing, and much more. Transferring one's knowledge is not a simple process; it is a specific form of art. Abraham Yampolsky was a great pedagogue not only because he knew the technical side of playing, but also because he had a kind of pedagogical "sixth sense." He didn't speak a lot during the lessons, but every student understood what he meant. He thoroughly understood the psychology of the student. For example, he would describe the need to give way to a rebellious student, but within a few months that student would imperceptibly come around, without even noticing it him- or herself. This is true pedagogical mastery.

Yankelevich similarly considered the teacher's psychological skills to be especially important in being able to determine each student's individual personality. He classified students primarily according to their nervous constitution, though his classification slightly differed from Yampolsky's.

When it comes to serious pedagogical work, ask the question: Whom are you teaching? Find out who the student is, for they all have an array of different qualities—their own psychology, own hands, and so forth. There are some who are strong-willed, concentrated, well-behaved, smart, lazy. Only then is it possible to determine which student needs which method. The diversity of students excludes a single approach.

And then humorously he added, "In practice I divide students into two groups: the first I teach, and the second I expel."

Yankelevich had a special approach to each individual student. He believed that a comprehensive knowledge of psychology is essential for the modern pedagogue.

I am often asked about the function of psychology in actual practice, and I always reply that that it is indispensable. While all people differ psychologically and physiologically, there are nonetheless certain types who exhibit similar traits. For example, there are those musicians who are easily excited, but not very emotionally focused. These students readily progress "outwardly" but not so easily "inwardly." It is the teacher's task to study each student carefully, to determine all the strong and weak sides, the potential for development, as well as the limits or "obstacles" along the way. Only then is it possible to build an effective plan for educating the student. Meanwhile, it is still important to develop the student's most individual characteristics.

Yankelevich also believed the psychological component to be very important when interacting with the student during the actual lesson. Often an incorrect psychological approach may cause the student to be extremely resistant. For example:

A new student arrives, who was always used to being number one in his hometown, and is put on a diet of "bread and water" so to speak. Naturally he or she feels insulted and resists. Under these circumstances, neither months nor years are enough for the teacher to get him to move forward. Therefore, it is necessary to get to know the student from the beginning and understand the way he or she thinks and responds. In these kinds of cases Yampolsky made very few comments, trying to figure out the student's reaction and even testing the limits of his or her patience. Only then would he subtly begin to make corrections, eventually arriving at the point where the student independently desired to carry out the teacher's wishes.

Yankelevich understood the discovery of the student's personality as a result not only of the teacher's efforts but also of the student's efforts. He believed it is not enough to know one's own student but "the student must also be able to assess him- or herself objectively, both the strong and weak points, accomplishments and shortcomings." This is what makes the pedagogical process productive and provides the essential two-sided exchange.

Of the psychological traits that need to be initially determined by the teacher, Yankelevich listed the following: emotion, focus, endurance, capacity for work, and dedication. The early stages of study and choice of repertoire should be planned according to the combination of these traits. For example, an emotional student would be assigned pieces in a stricter style that encourage discipline and precision. A "cold" student would be assigned a brighter, more exciting repertoire and more romantic pieces. Following this preliminary study of the student and based on the experience of working together, the teacher can refine the student's characteristics and plan goals over a longer period. The better the teacher knows the student, the further the teacher can plan the student's progression and determine the rate of progress.

Yankelevich considered the most difficult aspect to be a thorough and profound unearthing of the student's individual personality.

In order to uncover the student's individuality, the first thing is to not suppress it. The teacher must reach the place where the student accepts instructions without resisting but by becoming sincerely and passionately involved.

This is why Yankelevich sought to develop the student's interest in the most essential problems, providing motivation in all his remarks and widening the perspective of every skill or suggestion, both technically and musically.

He believed that the more talented the student, the harder it is to work with them.

Many teachers complain that they have no talented students. But talented students require ten times more work. With the average student, one may use a standard procedure. But one cannot give orders to a talented student. Of course, the student may submit, but this is not the right way, for this is how a talented student may easily turn into an average one! The correct procedure is to convince the talented student of the benefits and necessity of the teacher's remarks, so the student understands and trusts what the teacher wants, but then gets there completely on his or her own.... But the teacher needs to develop a "sense for talent" in respect to every student. This means knowing the student's strong points and being able to envision the student's future. By paying attention to the student's particular style and accents, tone quality, phrasing, and so on the teacher needs to envision how that student may ideally play and work out a plan that will help. This is how I work, by being careful not to extinguish the student's individual spark, for a Procrustean approach only leads to uniformity and destroys talent.

After understanding the essential contours of the student's personality, the teacher is confronted with the equally complicated responsibility of developing the student's independent artistic personality, which is the main purpose of the entire pedagogical process. Yankelevich would say, "The more talented the student, the greater his or her 'fantasies.'"

Yankelevich recommended a variety of methods to nurture artistry.

If, for example, the student is working on the Beethoven concerto, he or she should not begin by listening to the concerto itself, but by carefully studying Beethoven's symphonies, string quartets, and trying to understand the composer's "spirit." After work on the concerto has begun, the student may listen to recordings of the piece, but not just one. By listening to at least three or four recordings the student should try to make a comparative analysis, determining what makes the interpretations similar and different.

He insisted that a vivid imagination, which is so essential to a performer, must be developed in childhood when the student is still playing simple repertoire in first position.

Even when assigning a simple dance, lullaby, or march it is important to always require expression and a unified style. Eventually the imagery will become more refined, more diverse, more complex, and less concrete. The Romantic compositions incorporate thousands of gradations and subtle shifts from one mood to another. Appropriate guidance and explanations from the teacher can help fuel the student's artistic initiative, for these processes are closely connected.

It is equally important to choose the right repertoire that progressively leads the student from clear and simple goals to more complicated ones.

It is not necessary to follow the chronological development of violin literature, that wouldn't be productive. Bright "theatrical" pieces, folk and popular genres, and programmatic music all help stimulate the imagination in the early stages more than the Italian classics do. Children should be assigned "genre" pieces. Later one can move on to pieces like Tchaikovsky's *Melancholy Serenade*. Smaller salon pieces are the best material for developing artistry and finesse. I also like to assign a lot of Kreisler's music. These pieces are very difficult to play since every note, every change of bow and harmony needs to be polished and sparkle like a diamond. The violinist who is able to play these pieces properly turns into a different musician and begins to experience music differently. Szymanowski's pieces are very useful for developing a sense of color. The music of Debussy and Ravel also consists of an inspired palette containing the subtlest of variations.

Yankelevich attached a lot of importance to the teacher's behavior during the lesson and the ability to make remarks in a clear and psychologically correct manner.

The teacher's language is very important. If the teacher says, "to express more energy, press harder with the finger and make an accent with the bow," this might be technically correct. But this kind of approach to a musical composition can lead to a loss of meaning and spirit, and the music is reduced to just technique. The teacher's remarks must always stem from their main purpose, which is music.

Yankelevich never believed in deceiving a student with false praise, with the idea of "stimulating the student." He maintained that the student must only be praised when worthy of it and criticized when deserved.

I am against falsely encouraging the student, since this does not give the student an objective assessment of his or her playing. Approaching the student with intelligence and tact means being able to instill confidence in the student.

When Yankelevich was preparing a student for a competition, he wouldn't let anything go unnoticed and was unforgiving down to the smallest details. But right before the competition itself, he would change tactics and mainly emphasize the student's merits. This gave the student confidence and a sense of tranquility on stage.

Yankelevich firmly dismissed the division of teachers into those who taught beginners and "master teachers" (as Carl Flesch did, for example). Yankelevich believed teachers at the "higher level" to be "disassociated from how the violinist's skills are established, from the real 'kitchen' where talent is developed. Conversely, those who only teach beginners, including some teachers at the Central Music School, do not see the long-term perspective. For example, they do not envision how the techniques, bowings, and so forth that they teach will be used in, say, the Brahms concerto. This kind of rift is detrimental to both groups."

In this regard, he also made another point. Teachers of beginners often tend to hurry, trying to do more than they can and should. They assign repertoire that is too difficult in an attempt to quickly "move" the student.

I am in favor of a rather slow pace when beginning the violin. The technical skills need to be acquired gradually, otherwise quality suffers and the hands become tense. Not everyone understands this. For example, one of my students, eleven-year-old Pavel Kogan, was performing Kreisler's *Preludium and Allegro* in Leningrad. Some reproached me that at his age he should already be playing the Mendelssohn concerto. I replied that while it would be difficult for me to argue with everyone now, let us all see what he will be playing five years down the road!

Despite his experience and vast knowledge of methodology, Yankelevich was always cautious about passing judgment on students of other teachers. He would often say:

It is precisely my pedagogical experience that makes me careful in my judgments and conclusions. One audition shows very little, for it is the student's teacher who sees the perspective and capabilities of the student far better than the outside listener. And the student cannot demonstrate everything in just one program.

He also warned against the "danger of general recommendations," saying, "They are so easy to give, but so often the same result may be achieved with different methods, while everyone knows the generalizations."

Yankelevich's modesty and the high standards he placed on himself were a result of his constant searching and his rejecting the idea of attaining an "indisputable truth." He would hold up Joseph Szigeti as an example of a musician who was always demanding of himself and never satisfied. "I never received pleasure from my own playing," Szigeti would say. "I was always dissatisfied, for nothing was comfortable—look at my hands, see how long they are. I can never find what works, what is the best fingering or bowing. The violin has been torturing me my whole life." Before the war Yankelevich heard Szigeti perform in Leningrad. After the concert he was scheduled to meet the violinist, who did not appear for a long time. Yankelevich went to his dressing room and recalls discovering the brilliant violinist practicing the Bach *Prelude* that he had just performed remarkably. Seeing the surprised look on Yankelevich's face, Szigeti said with embarrassment, "I played this piece so poorly in the concert, I must immediately learn it properly!" Examples such as these were also a part of Yankelevich's pedagogical method and had the appropriate educational effect.

POSITIONING THE HANDS

Yuri Yankelevich attached great importance to properly positioning the hands and arms. He believed that, in many respects, the violinist's future depends on how the hands are set up, and a poor positioning could be a serious obstacle in the future development of a talented musician. Yet, he also insisted that "there is no absolute criteria for positioning; the components of a setup are relative, for reasons both subjective and objective."

Yankelevich did not believe a setup should be dogmatic and follow some sort of "ideal" or abstract model. He believed the teacher's primary duty is to help the student find his or her individual and organic setup. Otherwise the student's motor sensations become an end in themselves rather than a means of individually realizing a personal musical conception. He said, "An impersonal or 'foreign' setup cannot create the foundation for acquiring all the movements the performer will need, and can be very problematic." Disagreeing with those teachers who put "comfort" first, Yankelevich would say, "In my opinion, this is not the right criteria. If 'comfort' is the reference, then any habit, even the most harmful, may become 'comfortable' by force of habit."

According to Yankelevich, the teacher should seek not just an efficient positioning but also one that has long-term potential.

The setup's potential is determined by how it can accommodate the entire range of movements a violinist will require in the future. It is very unfortunate that some teachers only work with children and do not work with more advanced violinists. These teachers may believe that they are doing everything right. Yet so much subtlety, sensitivity, and a thorough knowledge of the instrument is required to not only teach how to hold and move the bow but also foresee what the student will need later, say when playing the Brahms concerto. One must be able to see far ahead—this is the meaning of a long-term setup.

Yankelevich also clearly noted that elements of positioning are directly related to musical and aesthetic tendencies, that is, the tone, expressive devices, and style a particular epoch requires, as well as the personal style of the violinist and the magnitude of his or her playing.

Why do all my students play differently, with a different setup? Because it is not the visual or external characteristics that I care about, but the internal relationship between musical and motor perceptions.

Of the objective criteria that affect positioning, Yankelevich emphasized norms of anatomy and physiology, principles of psychology, and laws of acoustics. He believed that the teacher should begin by observing how each student adapts without prescribing a general formula. For example, it is common for the E string to whistle. He found this could be caused by two factors: the first concerns the setup (the bow is placed at an incorrect angle to the string); and the second concerns principles of acoustics (the E string requires a more solid start than the A string). In another example, one of his students had a particular hand structure that made it difficult for the end phalanges to curve. Consequently, it was necessary to find a flatter position for her fingers that would not interfere with tone production or finger agility. This involved finding special procedures and exercises to achieve accurate technique and a different manner of vibrating.

The performer's movements are not just movements in the sense of gymnastics. These movements interest us only in how they are able to ensure a particular sound. Free movement leads to a free sound. Tense movement leads to a poor sound and creates serious technical problems. At the beginning we require a clean and smooth sound that doesn't scratch. But later, when speaking of a musical composition, the sound needs to reflect the musical content. Thus a chain is created that links musical content to the sound, the sound to the movement, and the movement to the setup. Consequently, a problematic setup may negatively affect such important and subtle issues as musical interpretation.

It is common knowledge that the bow must move at approximately a right angle to the string, or that pressing the string too hard with the finger makes the playing heavy. These are general principles. But even in these cases many slight deviations are possible that depend on the player's individual adjustment. The role of the teacher is to select the most effective option by clearly understanding, correcting, and guiding the student.

Discussing different components of a setup, Yankelevich would begin by determining the position of the violin in relation to the player's body. This depends on many factors, the most important of which is the height at which the instrument is held, since that then determines the relative position of the right and left arms.

If the violin is too low, then the bow slides to the fingerboard and causes the E string to "whistle." This is a sign that the violin needs to be raised! The length of the right arm also affects the position of the violin in relation to the torso. If the arms are too long they need to be drawn further apart, and if they are short they should be brought together so that the bow is always perpendicular to the string. However, there is another factor that should be taken into consideration: the movements of the left hand that allow for the correct adjustment are more diverse than those of the right hand. This is why one should start by ensuring the possibility of normal movement in the right hand.

Thus, Yankelevich viewed right-hand technique to be the foundation for violin technique in general. He believed that a correct setup must accommodate free movement in the right arm: "The essence of integrated movement is free movements in the arms."

Turning to details of positioning, Yankelevich paid a lot of attention to the placement and function of the fingers on the bow. He maintained that the thumb and the opposite finger "work together" in a unified network, and their activity should not be separated. Freedom in the fingers allows freedom in the wrist, which is key to mastering off-the-string bow strokes. At the frog, the thumb is bent slightly and positioned perpendicular to the stick. At the tip, the thumb straightens and lies at a sharp angle to the stick.

The role of the little finger is very important. From the frog to the middle of the bow it counterbalances the weight of the bow and should be curved (this position also allows the *fingerstriche*). From the middle to the tip of the bow, the little finger's role is less important. Should the little finger always remain on the stick? This depends on the length of the arms. For the most part it is unnecessary, and may even be harmful by causing the wrist to bend excessively when playing in the upper half and making it difficult to get out of this position on an up-bow. It is more correct to use a modifiable position of the pinkie. The thumb should be placed approximately 1 to 1.5 centimeters above the frog, but not in the corner with the bow stick since, as Yankelevich explained, this "restricts the necessary turn in the thumb as the bow moves. If the thumb remains always bent, then the wrist is restricted, for the thumb must act together with the other fingers that lie gently on the stick." The index finger should lie no deeper than its first joint, otherwise playing in the lower half becomes difficult. The index, middle, and ring fingers all regulate the pressure of the hand on the bow stick.

Yankelevich considered excessive pressure to be the most widespread problem in positioning the fingers of the right hand on the bow. All too often, the student does not know if he or she is pressing excessively. Once the teacher turns the student's attention to this, the student is able to check his or her sensations and get used to controlling them. The bow should be held in the fingers as lightly as possible. This allows a subtle feeling for the elastic pressure of the bow on the string, resulting in a better tone.

Yankelevich would tell the following story of Abraham Yampolsky as an example of the importance of correct finger pressure on the bow: "A student played with a beautiful *mezzo forte*, but when he wanted to move to *fortissimo*, suddenly it sounded *piano*! I finally got to the bottom of the problem—the student applied his strength incorrectly and all the pressure went into holding the stick very tightly, which actually lessened the contact of the bow with the string."

Yankelevich considered the position of the right elbow to be very important in transferring the weight of the arm onto the bow stick. When the elbow is too low ("the old-fashioned way," as he would say) the transfer of weight is more difficult, if not impossible, and the amount of sound and energy in the accents is diminished. But if the elbow is too high then the shoulder might lift excessively, which may also be associated with a tense bow hold and tight wrist.

It is extremely important to develop the feeling of a free shoulder and "hanging" arm. This sensation is often absent because of too much pressure or holding the bow too tight. This is why it is absolutely essential to pay attention to the sensations of movements while practicing, striving to understand and refine them.

Regarding the positioning of the left hand, Yankelevich believed it important to determine the variable points of support:

The violinist uses both one and two points of support. When playing in one position the instrument is often held with two points of support, while during shifts the left hand needs to be freed and the violin transfers to one point of support. This is done intuitively.

Regarding the first point of support, between the jaw and the collarbone, Yankelevich noted the efficiency of using a pad or shoulder rest (with preference for the latter). He believed that without a shoulder rest or pad, it is usually very difficult to support the violin when the left hand is moving. The shoulder rest facilitates the movements of the left hand along the fingerboard and relieves the need to lift the shoulder, which causes tension in the hands:

I observed one of my students who managed to even tense his leg when playing extensions! This is why I start students with a shoulder rest (a cushion may dampen the sound). If someone who is already in command of a solid technique wants to play without one (especially in the case of a short neck or high shoulders) I don't mind, although I always monitor that the shoulder doesn't lift or turn.

The second point of support is in the left hand. Here the difficulty is twofold for the violin needs to be both held and played on at the same time. Ideally, this should become one unified process.

The main problem in holding the violin is that the neck of the violin is squeezed, which restricts and interferes with free movement. It is necessary to develop the psychological sensation that the thumb does not seem to support the violin. This can relax it to an effective degree and, incidentally, also helps the vibrato. For the thumb plays an entirely supportive role and its position depends solely on the other fingers. If the other fingers lie correctly on the strings, then the thumb settles into its natural position. Most importantly, the thumb should not get in the way.

Yankelevich cited many examples of different ways to support the violin with the thumb that were recommended by various violinists. He explained their discrepancies through different artistic intentions depending on various eras and the individual particularities of each violinist. Yankelevich believed the thumb should be very dynamic and that it should be placed differently in the lower and higher positions. Moreover, it is the thumb's role to prepare the shift to another position and modify the position of the wrist when vibrating. In these cases, the thumb makes a round, circuitous movement as the hand is brought around to the new position. This type of unified and supple movement is the most effective.

In theorizing the mechanics of the movement in the left hand, Yankelevich sought a coherent model of the most economical movement that follows the simplest trajectories and requires minimal effort.

Ideally, one should imagine the left hand to work the same way as it does on the piano, where each finger drops from above to the corresponding key. The hand remains immobile while each finger is positioned where it naturally falls down onto the keys. If the violinist's fingers are positioned so they can naturally drop onto the string without the need for the hand and wrist to rotate, then there is much more potential in developing left-hand technique.

In determining the role of the wrist, elbow, and forearm, he believed that the most important factor is to provide optimal conditions for accurately and reliably grouping the fingers above the string and placing them correctly. All components of the arm need to be coordinated in making the preparatory and anticipatory movements. He said, "The position of the wrist is especially important, since it should be a natural extension of the forearm." These conditions are essential for ensuring technical freedom and developing the correct sensations of movement.

According to Yankelevich, the correct setup should stem from a basic positioning of the wrist and fingers in relation to the fingerboard.

Beginners often have problems with the fourth finger—the pinkie. It is difficult for them to play a simple tetrachord because of the fourth finger. In this case many teachers recommend extending it. However, it is better to draw back the index finger than to stretch forward the little finger. One should begin by adjusting the hand to the third and fourth fingers—this is the correct position to start from.

Beginners were recommended to use the following setup of the left hand in first position. The wrist would be situated slightly higher than the first position, somewhere between the first and second position, and then it would draw backward to accommodate the first two fingers. This type of setup not only makes the little finger more comfortable but also releases tension in the wrist.

This setup also ensures that the wrist does not bend too far in the opposite direction, which is sometimes observed in practice. This is also the setup advocated by Auer. The slight bend in the wrist, which naturally should not be exaggerated, helps in developing a good vibrato and keeps the fingers grouped correctly above the string. Yankelevich said, "The fingers must be grouped at the interval of a fourth, and retain that placement so they may drop when needed to the corresponding note in any given position. This is especially important in fast passagework." '

Yankelevich believed one of the essential problems of violin playing, affecting both technical agility and tone quality, is the appropriate degree of finger pressure on the string. He noted that many violin methods and treatises recommend not only applying a lot of pressure to the string but also developing strength in the fingers, even "hammering" the fingers on the fingerboard. He found it paradoxical to recommend that the fingers press strongly while at the same time suggesting that the thumb should touch the neck very gently. Strong finger pressure leads to "clenching the fingerboard, since every action has an equal reaction. This instinctive clutching reflex, which has been problematic throughout the history of violin playing, needs to be eliminated. Instead, a professional reflex that is based on the optimal pressure of the fingers needs to be developed."

Yankelevich believed the clutching reflex to be reinforced by spending too much time in first position when the beginner's hand is "fixed" in a static position. Later, when learning to shift, the student is surprised to discover "that the hand must move along the fingerboard. Not only are the student's psycho-physiological perceptions disrupted, but a whole series of difficulties ensue. Firstly, the student, who has already become used to holding the violin with the left hand, finds it now needs to release in order to move along the fingerboard. Then it also turns out the violin needs to be supported at the shoulder, and the student is not used to that. Consequently, the student is confronted with an entirely new set of questions and problems because of the need to move the hand along the fingerboard. I believe it is important to find a different setup at the beginning so these types of problems do not arise."

Yankelevich considered it incorrect to simply avoid the clutching reflex by entirely changing the setup. He was critical of Campagnoli's suggestion to bring the left elbow to the middle of the chest so that the violin neck can rest on the thumb: "Ease in one spot here unavoidably creates tension in other places. The elbow needs to be brought out as little as possible and remain as close as it can to its natural position." He rejected Mikhailovsky's theory of holding the violin neck in the hollow between the thumb and index finger. He was also skeptical of Voiku's recommendation to position the violin on the base of the index finger, since in this case one unnatural position replaces another and the setup restricts the development of the professional techniques that are required later.

He pointed out that Voiku was incorrect in considering the thumb to be "problematic" and believed he underestimated its role. At the same time he agreed with Voiku in the need to bring the left elbow back. "It is better to draw the elbow back than to bring it forward, for the latter is the more unnatural position."

To determine the correct amount of finger pressure, Yankelevich proposed the following solution:

A string that is not pressed firmly enough creates a fuzzy and distorted sound. By gradually increasing the pressure, we arrive at a sound that is clean and has quality. Here it is important to stop. Further pressure causes the sound to get worse, the finger technique suffers, and tension arises that leads to jerky shifts and a tight sound. Tension is always the result of excess energy.

However, the degree of finger pressure is variable and depends on many factors. The further the distance the hand travels during a shift, the weaker the finger pressure needs to be. The pressure may increase slightly in the higher positions, where the strings are more taut and further from the fingerboard, and it may release in the lower positions. The pressure also depends on the tempo; in a fast tempo the fingers lift slightly less above the string. Yankelevich believed that the player's intuition serves an important role in regulating finger pressure. He linked this to "being able to adjust to and have a feel for the instrument, for this is what we call talent." When possible, he recommended aiming for a "uniform degree of pressure, correcting it according to the tone quality and feeling of elasticity in the fingers, and adjusting the finger pressure to the pressure of the bow."

However, one cannot always rely on intuition. Yankelevich would demonstrate the necessity of lightly placing the fingers using the following exercise: "Place the palm of your hand on the table, and press lightly," he would say. "Now move it over here. Now try pressing it harder and then moving it. More difficult, no? It is the same on the string!"

Yankelevich believed there to be two paths in developing technique—developing strength or developing agility. "In playing the violin we only need to use the latter, since we already have sufficient strength." He would go on to explain that there are two types of muscular tension. The first is related to the size of the movement, such as when the entire wrist is involved in finger-work in the left hand or when the entire right arm becomes tense when playing spiccato. The second type is related to an impulse, when the moment of tension seems to "discharge" in the movement. It is this second type that is most effective.

He illustrated these two types of tension through trills. He differentiated the tense "inborn" or "electric" trill, which resists conscious musical intent, from a controlled trill in which the fingers drop without requiring the weight of the entire hand. The latter example allows one to trill slowly and then rhythmically accelerate.Yankelevich would use Szigeti's trill as an example: "Some violinists have a trill that initially seems not very brilliant. Szigeti had a trill that was slow, but also very rich, rhythmical, and precise. I was struck by the brilliance and artistry he displayed when playing Paganini's sixth caprice. At a concert in Moscow he had to repeat it as an encore three times."

Yankelevich believed that uniform movement in the fingers is always associated with light finger technique: "The start of all finger movement lies in the first joint. Any flexion or extension in the other joints must be avoided. This is precisely what allows the most possibilities in developing violin technique."

It was this kind of multifaceted analysis and pedagogical vision that led Yankelevich to many interesting conclusions that enriched the methodology and broadened the horizons of violin technique.

TONE PRODUCTION

Yuri Yankelevich possessed a special ability to develop an individual sound in each of his students. He believed every concertizing violinist should possess a sound palette of many colors and that the process of perfecting tone quality could be limitless. He would often repeat the words of his teacher: "Every violinist reaches limits in the left hand. Sometimes they may be temporary or illusory, such as problems with vibrato or agility. But in terms of the right hand and tone production, there is no limit." Yankelevich stressed Yampolsky's idea that tone is not simply an inborn characteristic but something that can be nurtured.

According to Yankelevich the foundation of sound is the "correct, clean, full, free process of tone production. There are different ways to change the timbre: modifying the sounding point where the bow comes into contact with the string, changing the actual character of the stroke, increasing or decreasing the angle of the bow, changing the type of vibrato, and so forth. A varicolored sound depends on the student's imagination and artistic understanding of the music."

He believed in the importance of determining objective laws of tone production. He particularly noted the following points: developing the feeling of contact between the bow and the string; awareness of the feeling of pressure on the string; and being able to start the notes in different ways, combining the initial contact with subsequent movement.

Yankelevich likened the bow to a lever, with different parts of the bow pressing the string unequally. Less pressure at the tip of the bow requires compensation, but it is "simplistic" to make this solely by pressing more with the index finger as is often recommended. Using the weight of the arm on its own also does not solve the problem.

> The pressure must be specific—both supple and delicate. The elasticity of the bow must be taken into account. The performer must develop and refine his of her sensations, and feel not just the elasticity of the bow but also the elasticity of the string and how it reacts to pressure. This is connected to the weight of the arm. It is necessary to help the student find this sensation, and to proceed as pianists do by letting the sound come from the weight of the arm and adjusting the elbow height accordingly. However, the starting point is to feel the weight of the bow.

The angle of the bow in relation to string is also important:

> Some insist that the bow be drawn entirely flat to the string to create more sound, and that it be drawn at an angle when playing *piano*. This

causes a lot of confusion. The essence of the problem is that the string is stretched at a slight angle from the nut and is most rigid near the bridge. Consequently, when the bow is inclined it helps orient the force in the direction of the bridge and creates better conditions for tone production; otherwise, the bow risks sliding in the direction of the fingerboard.

Yankelevich also noted that when the bow is drawn entirely flat along the string, the sound becomes hoarse and the tone quality suffers.

Yankelevich often lamented that many modern violinists have lost the culture of playing cantabile. This is why some players avoid long legato and frequently change the bow. "In my opinion this is a mistake. One cannot deprive the violin of its most valuable asset—its lyricism. For of all the instruments, it has the greatest ability to sing." He believed a singing tone to be associated, in part, with the ability to draw the bow slowly. He recommended a series of exercises to help develop the so-called everlasting bow. He advised starting these exercises in *piano*, drawing the bow for eight quarter-notes per direction and gradually increasing to twenty quarter-notes. "Some violinists are able to keep the bow moving for one minute. However, it is important to produce a sound that has quality and not just engage in gymnastics."

After achieving a quality *piano*, one can move on to playing *forte*. Yankelevich recalled Auer's important observation that a large sound requires mastery and skill. He believed that the strength of the sound depends on the correct pressure of the bow on the string. To achieve a rich, full, unforced tone the hand must retain the same elasticity and freedom developed when playing *piano*. Therefore the bow must be held freely without the fingers ever tensing. The index and middle fingers transfer the minimal amount of necessary pressure from the shoulder. In *fortissimo*, the bow must be held extremely lightly with the fingers, as if it were just a pencil, in order to feel the string's response. Here it is important to also note Flesch's observation on sensing the distance to the bridge. At the frog there is more support from the little finger, while at the tip of the bow there is more pressure on the index finger. However, this feeling of pressure in the hand is purely internal, something similar to how pianists play "from the shoulder." Most importantly, one needs to maintain the equilibrium between density and power in the sound.

The next step is to change the dynamics from *forte* to *piano* and vice versa and then intensify and release the sound in the middle ($p <f> p$; $f> p < f$). Aside from leading to a mastery of cantilena, these exercises develop a "big breath" and the skills of *messa di voce*, making the sound supple and vocal. These exercises are excellent material for working on unnoticeable bow changes. Although they are very useful, for some reason they are not so common in practice. This is surprising, since it is the right hand that is responsible for the artistic component by creating emotional expression and musical meaning. When working on tone quality it is important the student forms an idea of a "good" sound and knows what to aim for. The violinist should be able to hear and analyze not only his or her own sound but the sound of others as well. The violinist should never be self-content, and from the very beginning the teacher should instill the desire to produce the best possible sound.

Yankelevich believed that work on tone quality must be divided into stages. The first stage consists of basic elements of tone production. The next step is to focus on the quality of the sound, beginning by simply making sure it doesn't scratch, and then developing the ability to listen to oneself, recognizing not only the notes that are out of tune but also those that have a poor tone quality. The third stage involves looking for tonal dynamics and colors and the right nuance and character in relation to the thematic material and style of the composition. Finally, the highest level is to find one's own individual tonal "language," a sound that "defines the artist's personality."

After focusing the student's attention on a pure tone, "one should gradually accustom the student to enriching the sound with nuances, such as delicacy, strength, transparency, and so on. This is the essential moment in developing a multicolored palette." Changing the tone's timbre may be accomplished in different ways. Yankelevich recommended a variety of methods: changing the sounding point, increasing or decreasing the amount of bow hair on the string, or finding a particular kind of vibrato. "These modifications lend variety and color to the sound and are limitless in their possibilities," he said. Yankelevich pointed out that developing the student's artistic imagination directly influences the development of a variety of colors in the sound. Shorter pieces are particularly useful in this respect.

If the student does not progress sufficiently in developing tone quality, one needs to determine what the obstacles are and if they are of a mechanical nature (i.e., gripping the bow too much, thus tensing and forcing the sound). It is important to remember that too much pressure from the index finger on the bow stick can make the sound too harsh.

Once the basic gradations of tone are established, there arises the question of a finding a "beautiful" sound that expresses the musical content of a piece or a given episode. This is not at all the same "beautiful" sound that is developed in a scale or etude. Here we are speaking of the purpose of the sound, which is linked to the violinist's imagination as a musician.

Similar to the painter's search for colors on the canvas, the search for tonal shades is a fascinating and limitless endeavor.

Yankelevich believed variety in accentuation to be an important element of tonal color, calling it "the most subtle element that distinguishes musicianship." By accentuation he meant that initial moment of attack when the sound appears, which at times may be barely perceptible. Even if the start of the note is not audible, the problem of starting and attacking the note remains. Yankelevich would explain:

In Gluck's *Melodie*, I suggest not playing the first note note as a beginning, but as if it were a continuation. This is done by having the hand make a circular motion of the bow above the string so there is no accent. This is similar to an upbeat, like a singer taking a breath. Then the sound emerges naturally.

Very often players make a kind of "banal accent," giving a long note an accent at the beginning similar to playing martelé. Yankelevich considered this to be "a classical antiquated mistake, which many turn into dogma." He explained:

They recommend placing the bow on the string, "pinching" it and then continuing the sound with a marked stop. However, in practice the effect does not work and extraneous sounds occur. An energetic accent happens not from "pinching" the note but solely from the energetic movement of the bow using equal pressure. Martelé is developed from détaché, in which pressure and movement occur at the same time. The pressure must be constant in all parts of the bow, otherwise the string will not resonate.

Yankelevich noted that the common effect of the bow shaking when pressed strongly to the string is explained by the performer "not sensing the string and feeling its resilience," and also because the hand does not release its tension at the tip of the bow.

Strong accents are especially difficult. Yankelevich used the beginning of the second movement of Handel's Sonata No. 4 as an example:

This requires lightning-like precision between placing the bow on the string and moving it. When executed correctly the accent should use half the bow! The difficulty lies in making the accent from the air, to be in command of the bow and to be able to start the note both from the string and from above the string. The hand must make a circular movement above the string, which changes depending on whether the accent is on a

down-bow or an up-bow. This type of exercise also helps develop freedom
and energy in the right hand.

THE ROLE OF TECHNICAL EXERCISES

Yankelevich spent a lot of attention on various aspects of violin technique, and
recommended a variety of different methods. He attached particular importance to independent practice, for which he developed special principles.

He believed the main purpose of playing exercises is to develop the necessary skills and to be able to use them on stage:

> The ability to practice is the ability to set a specific goal and develop meth-
> ods to achieve it. Each repetition must have a reason and be absolutely
> essential. It is important to categorically avoid a mechanical approach,
> and as soon as the attention fades it is important to immediately stop
> practicing and take a break. Productive practice occurs only with a clear
> head and relaxed arms. For this reason it is better to split practice over the
> course of the day, taking breaks, rather than practicing a long time all at
> once. I often tell my students that they should never repeat a passage nor
> draw the bow along the string without clearly understanding why they
> are doing so. One must be able to hear, listen, and correct oneself and not
> reinforce any mistakes.... It is important to keep progressing so that what
> is difficult today becomes easier tomorrow. If you feel this, then you are
> on the right path. But this work should never turn into a technical drill,
> which not only has little benefit but also requires continually restarting
> from the beginning.

One of the main methods of Yankelevich and Yampolsky was to assign supplementary exercises and variations for troublesome passages. Yankelevich
would recall, "When a student encountered technical difficulties, Yampolsky
always assigned an etude, exercise, or even a virtuoso variation that was even
more difficult, and before you knew it the problem was solved."

In regards to slow practice, Yankelevich believed that an extremely slow
tempo might be beneficial for meticulously checking quality and finding the
cause of certain problems, but that it did not work for regular practice. It is
important to develop one's attention so as to be able to observe and notice
everything without slowing the tempo too much, "otherwise there is not
enough time to learn a lot of repertoire." It is important to sensibly and gradually move from a slower tempo to a faster one, avoiding sudden changes. "It is

a big mistake to play slowly for a long time and then immediately play quickly. Increasing the tempo incrementally ensures no tension develops in the muscles." He liked to recall the story of the young Spartan whose teacher suggested he carry a calf slowly around the city to build up his strength: "He was going so slowly that at the end of the day he ended up with a bull on his back, since the calf had so much time to grow."

Excessive practice may have negative consequences and lead to professional injuries. Yankelevich advised his students to be very careful about their arms and hands and to never overwork them. He found the main sign of overworked hands to be problems in motor function.

> One has to find the initial cause of the tension. Strict self-control is required to not spend any more effort than an action requires. Naturally, every violinist retains some elements of tension. But the more they are eliminated the wider the horizons open to the performer.

Yankelevich discussed scales as a component of technical training.

> There is a theory that scales cure all problems. But there is also another theory that more attention should be paid to etudes and difficult sections of a piece. My opinion is that scales should still be practiced but that excessive, mind-numbing repetition is detrimental. An hour and a half spent only on scales is too much. It is important to understand the reason behind mastering scales, which is to be in good shape and in command of the fingerboard. Rabinovich suggests a particularly useful method of playing, in fifteen minutes, at a medium tempo, the entire circle of fifths (each scale with four note slurs and the arpeggios with three note slurs). However, to tone and mobilize the entire hand, it is better to work on difficult technical passages.

He noted that basic muscle training is still useful for violinists, though "naturally, not the same as for a ballet dancer."

> The instrumentalist acquires many skills that need to be maintained, and in this respect scales can be very useful. But it is important to initially work out the skills separately, in isolation, and then bring them together in a scale. This is much more productive. The scale should not be turned into a goal itself.

Working on technique using scales, exercises, and etudes is a "difficult and demanding journey for both the student and the teacher."

There exist basic difficulties for both the right and left hands that need to be practiced daily. These include playing "long notes" with the bow, large and small détaché, spiccato, double stops, and so on. All of these need work. Thirds should be accorded ten minutes, but if, for example, one is already playing an etude in thirds they don't need to be repeated. It is helpful to master difficult spots by playing them with different bowings. This also saves time in maintaining technique, so then scales don't need to be played with different bowings.

Yankelevich was wary of the purely technical exercises of Schradieck and Ševčík. He believed them only to be necessary in the early and middle stages of study. "I rarely incorporate Ševčík's exercises, but the first book of Schradieck is compact and contains some very good exercises. Although if it is still needed at the college level, then the student's level is not sufficiently advanced."

The matter of "warming up" is also part of the violinist's technique. According to Yankelevich, warming up before a lesson or performance is a quick means of getting in shape and allowing the hands and arms to be optimally relaxed. But he firmly rejected the necessity of having to warm up in every case.

Some violinists need to warm up, other don't. One shouldn't eliminate a natural dependence, but it is also important not to exaggerate it. If a student possesses a free technique it is usually not necessary to warm up and vice versa. When there is excessive pressure in the fingers and tension in the hands a longer warm-up is needed to free up the "hardened mechanism" and soften the calluses on the fingers (which should never be there in the first place!). Also, it is important to develop technique so that warming up takes a minimal amount of time. However, the warm-up should never become a habit or ritual (such as warming up before practicing at home, not being able to start a lesson without playing scales, and so on). A performer must never be fixed on a rigid system, since this reflects poor training.

Yankelevich noted that warming up is "a necessary evil in the winter when coming in from outside with cold hands. Although, in this case, it is preferable to stretch and warm the hands, gradually bringing them to a playing condition. It is not good to approach the instrument with cold hands and a cold head." He rejected special gymnastic exercises that were removed from the music and failed to supply what is most essential—a feel for the fingerboard. He believed the highest level to be attained when, as Yampolsky would put it, "the hands are ready to fulfill any command." He recalled a student of Yampolsky asking for advice in choosing a fingering for a difficult spot in *L'Etude en forme de Valse* by Saint-Saëns/Ysaÿe:

> Yampolsky took the student's violin and asked, "Do you play it with this fingering?" And he played the difficult passage in tempo. "Or this finger-ing is also possible." And he played the same passage with a different fin-gering in the same tempo. Then he thought for a moment, and said, "and there is also a third way!"—and again played it just as virtuosically. We were all dumbfounded. Then he smiled and explained, "I had previously played the versions through in my mind." All he needed was to under-stand, and then he could play.

Yankelevich also paid attention to the important possibility and necessity of practicing without the instrument.

> The process of practicing is very complicated. It requires elements of physical training (muscle work), coordinating movements (involving the nerve centers in the brain), and developing musical thought. All these different components must be practiced. It is pointless to work on tone quality and muscular sensations without the instrument. However, it is very useful to visually scan the piece as preliminary preparation. Afterward, something familiar stays in the mind that facilitates subse-quent work.... Some recommend practicing with the violin but without the bow, or with the bow and without the violin. This is possible in the early stages, but I don't like to set up the hands separately, even with beginners. In principle, playing and practicing should always rely on the aural conception of the final result. At the same time it is more useful to practice without the violin than without the bow, although this should be reserved for those who are already sufficiently in command of the instrument.

Yankelevich recommended developing the ability to work without the instru-ment in the following order:

1. With the music and the violin and the bow.
2. With the violin and bow, without the music.
3. With the music, but without the violin, and then without the bow.
4. To imagine playing the violin without the violin or bow.

The last stage is the highest. It reflects an inner understanding of sound and movement. This stage is similar to the so-called autogenic training used in psychology. Yankelevich always insisted on developing the student's inner perceptions.

> By just looking at the score it is possible and necessary to learn to imag-ine the music and "pre-feel" the movements. This is very important. For example, when preparing a long program for a concert or competition, when it is not possible (and not recommended) to play excessively, it is better to sit on a bench in a park and imagine the music and pre-feel the movements. It is also possible to learn a new piece this way, with only the eyes and without the instrument.

Yankelevich found sight-reading to correlate with the ability to connect aural perceptions and movements.

> Sight-reading is the ability to quickly glance at the music and grasp the necessary movements. The speed of reading depends on the agility of the nerve processes (according to Pavlov). Meanwhile, it is necessary to look not at the measure being played but the one that is coming up. This is precisely where the role of anticipatory perception of sound and move-ment comes in—this is what needs to be developed. Another factor is that students generally learn too little repertoire. Sight-reading ability is influenced by the amount of material covered—etudes, sonatas, and so on. The more music one is exposed to, the easier the process of reading unfamiliar music. However, reading is one thing, but technical mastery and knowing the fingerboard is another. The mobilization of technical skills requires the fingers to instantly submit to given commands. In these cases it is helpful, for example, to "grasp" the contour of the passage or be in possession of "basic technical formulas."

The personal organization of practice habits was important for Yankelevich.

> Studying a piece of music, studying the instrument, studying oneself—this is the basis for creating a system of practicing at home, a system of acquiring technique and preparing for the stage.

Yankelevich advised against unnecessary fragmentation and recommended playing large sections until a natural break occurs. It is very important "to be able to combine the whole and the parts, to separate what is most important and what is secondary. One cannot stop for every mistake, for on stage that is impossible. One must be able to continue playing, remember the mistake, and later analyze and correct it."

In Yankelevich's opinion, the method of practicing at home should be almost identical to that of practicing with the teacher: "A good, thoughtful teacher often changes his or her method of working depending on the student's stage of development, the level of preparation, and on the immediacy of the problem they are confronted with. The student should do the very same when practicing at home."

INTONATION

"The process of playing in tune is both complicated and, at the same time, relatively simple," Yankelevich would say.

> Mostras wrote a lot about how problems in positioning and technique affect intonation. But this is not what is most important. Looking at the issue in its entirety, to play the violin in tune it is first necessary to possess a sufficiently musical ear. Secondly, the ear needs to be developed and be active. Thirdly, the ear needs to be coordinated with the physical movements, that is, a "reflex for distance" needs to be developed in relation to aural perceptions. And fourthly, the technique of the movement needs to be correct.

Only a combination of all these factors ensures perfect intonation. If there is a problem in intonation he advised carefully analyzing where in the chain the problem might occur. It may be because of insufficiently accurate aural control, which is a common problem:"The ear needs to be active in matters of basic intonation and clean phrasing; one must be able to regulate and listen to oneself." In his work on intonation, Yankelevich referred to the opinions of Joseph Joachim, Carl Flesch, and Iosef Lesman as well as the theory of aural zones developed by Nikolai Garbuzov.[3]

He would describe the usual process of how a student practices as follows:

> A note is played without pre-hearing it, and the ear assesses the note only after it has sounded. Then the faulty note is corrected. If the hand is able to gradually adjust and the fingers fall where they're supposed to, it naturally becomes easier to play more in tune. But if the positioning of the hand is problematic then extra corrective movements are always required and the ear becomes accustomed to poor intonation (for as Auer points out, the ear can easily become clogged).

Yankelevich noted that any corrective movements in the fingers are audible, and therefore they are not the way to achieve clean intonation. He also considered Flesch's theory of "quickly correcting" intonation with extra movements to be incorrect. "This may sometimes work in a slow tempo, but what about in a fast tempo? If one practices using corrective movements, there will still never be enough time to make them work in a fast tempo, and the intonation will be approximate."

Yankelevich saw the solution to the problem of intonation to lie not in positioning (although it is important) and not even in solely aural perception, for intonation has to do with more than just the ear. He believed the solution must take into account the musical aspect of intonation, the style, and the tonality.

It is absurd to speak of "absolute intonation," for it is an abstract concept. The natural tuning of the violin allows more accurate intonation than the piano and more expressive possibilities. The contradictions of intonation already are apparent when playing double stops. For example, the notes B and C on the A string in first position sound differently in relation to the E string than they do when played on their own. Instrumental ensembles use "tempered intonation," a quartet uses "mean intonation," and so on. There is no way to "measure" intonation. Only musical aural control can be the trustworthy criterion.

Yankelevich believed that problems in intonation are solved by developing conditioned reflexes to auditory stimuli (with the ear as a control):

The performer must *anticipate* the pitch of the note. The control of the ear helps to develop a specific reflex for distance, a feel for the character of the movement and a pre-feeling of this movement. In contrast, Flesch's theory does not encourage the reflex for distance to be conditioned. It is important to always go back and attempt the shift again, instead of simply correcting the false note. In this way the hands adjust to the ear.

Yankelevich noted that sometimes problems in intonation occur when a passage was learned cleanly in a slow tempo but then sounds false in a fast tempo. This is because "the feeling of the fingers as a group and the interrelationship between them changes depending on the tempo. It is easier to establish their relationship in a faster tempo. Also, the interrelation between different parts of the hand and arm changes depending on the tempo." He suggested starting to learn the passage by playing it a few times up to tempo so as to have an idea of the unified movement and grouping of the fingers. Moreover, he noted that "the faster the tempo, the further the reflex for distance. Consequently, the intonation of a particular note is not tied as closely to the previous and subsequent notes as it is in a slow tempo, but involves much wider intervals." He added: "The laws of auditory perception and physiology must also be taken into account; in a faster tempo accurate movement has a different nature, and even the perception of the musical movement changes."

VIBRATO

As Yankelevich himself noted, the question of vibrato was always addressed in his discourse.

The pedagogical process must provide the prerequisites for a free vibrato even when it has not yet been introduced. As the student achieves a certain artistic maturity, a desire arises to produce a sound with a different timbre and hence the need for vibrato. At this point the hand must be completely free and relaxed, ready to follow the artistic impulses that have naturally emerged.

Yankelevich liked to joke that, "it is harder to ruin vibrato than to establish it." He noted that, from a psychological perspective, vibrato is one of the most complicated and difficult problems in violin playing. He explained this firstly by the fact that the speed and small amplitude of a vibrating movement make analysis and external control very difficult. And secondly, the player's vibrato turns into a subconscious habit, making it very difficult to comprehend. Serious obstacles arise in controlling the vibrato and musically modifying its parameters. It becomes difficult for the student not only to change the vibrato movement but also to stop vibrating in those places he or she is used to.

According to Yankelevich, the specific nature of vibrato necessitates a special approach in the early stages of developing it. All the conditions, both technical and musical, must be in place so that vibrato emerges naturally, without constraint. "What is meant by 'naturally'?" Yankelevich would ask.

It means that the teacher must foresee the difficulties that the violinist's left hand will encounter and envision the condition of the hand, the positioning of the fingers, and so on. If the hand is relaxed and the fingers are flexible there should be no obstacles to vibrato emerging, since to a certain extent this is an automatic and natural process. When the student tries to imitate the teacher or other students who can already vibrate, then the hand will naturally be able to vibrate as long as it is not restricted. Consequently, special exercises are unnecessary.

Examining the different types of vibrato, beginning with the two main types—the wrist and the arm vibrato—Yankelevich favored the wrist vibrato from both an artistic and a technical point of view.[4] "I am more inclined to the wrist vibrato, for the arm vibrato entails a large expense of muscular energy. A constant arm vibrato may sometimes even affect the player's technical development. The wrist vibrato allows more possibilities for variation than the arm vibrato, which is generally more standardized and uniform."

At the same time he explained that it is relatively rare to encounter both types of vibrato in their pure state; usually they are combined, or transition from one type to another. This is preferable and produces quite an artistic effect. "Some violinists use one form of vibrato in the higher positions and another in the lower positions. Heifetz employed both types of vibrato. Oistrakh's vibrato with his index finger was even circular in nature." The transition from one type of vibrato to another has to do primarily with the degree of "cohesion" in the joints. In an arm vibrato, the wrist and shoulder are fixed, and in the wrist vibrato the shoulder and forearm are fixed.

From a technical perspective, he believed the initial impulse to be more important than the hand's movement:

The impulse may come from the wrist, the elbow, or a mixture of the two. But it is always the finger that transfers the impulse to the string. Therefore it is essential that the joints in the finger are free and the hand is flexible and relaxed. The finger cannot press too firmly to the string, since this restricts the freedom of the oscillating movement. The feeling of flexibility and suppleness needs to also occur throughout the other parts of the arm, for the smallest bit of tension anywhere is immediately reflected in the vibrato.

Yankelevich believed in the importance of the beginning impulse and the ability to simultaneously make sure there is no tension in the arm (without letting it get lethargic). The preference for one type of vibrato appears depends on the general condition of the arm and how the tension is dispersed. More tension is likely to lead to an arm vibrato, while more flexibility leads to a wrist vibrato. However, at a later stage, one type of vibrato is able to transfer to another type, resulting in mixed transitional forms. The teacher must catch and support this process in time, since this is not only when the tone becomes enriched but also when a "correction" of earlier problems might occur. This is why Yankelevich said, "It is easier to change a type of vibrato than to 'correct' the type already established." Yankelevich indicated the following method as one way of increasing the vibrato's intensity: "Vibrate only in the direction of the bridge, take away the other half of the amplitude toward the nut, and the brilliance and intensity of the vibrato will increase."

Yankelevich associated problems with vibrato primarily with uncorrected tension in the wrist: "As a rule, tension makes the vibrato heavy and dull. When the vibrato turns into a reflex and enters the subconscious, it becomes difficult to control since at that point only the general sensations are regulated, whereas the vibrato needs to be correct from the beginning." He noted one reason for problems with vibrato might be that the teacher started developing it too early. It is important to make sure that tension in the hands, which is to a certain degree natural at the beginning, is eliminated and that the subconscious desire for an expressive tone is established.

To correct these problems, Yankelevich recommended first eliminating the habit of gripping the violin neck and pressing the fingers too hard on the fingerboard. He suggested special exercises to free the left thumb as it moves along the fingerboard and changes positions as "the best means of liberating and freeing the left hand." He also recommended the following exercise: "Move the bow slowly along the string and simultaneously freely move the left hand along the fingerboard, without placing the fingers on the string." It is also possible to "bring the thumb to the top of the fingerboard or to tuck it underneath. If there is equal freedom in both directions then the placement of the thumb is correct." Another exercise is to "ease and develop the finger joints by playing chromatic scales using sliding fingers." All these exercises attempt to remove extra tension, which consists of two aspects: "excessive effort in the movement that is required and the unnecessary participation of other muscles during the movement."

An extremely narrow or "trembling" vibrato is corrected by making wide, oscillating movements in the wrist. An excessively wide vibrato is corrected by intensifying the movement in the elbow and activating the initial impulse. However, one first must "be able to notice a problematic vibrato and have an aural perception of how the vibrato should ideally sound, first with the help of the teacher and then independently." In especially difficult cases when the special exercises don't help, he recommended playing without vibrato for a certain time, as though it never even existed.

Yankelevich believed it is important to develop vibrato in all the fingers, including the fourth finger in the high positions, since each finger gives the sound a different color. If some of the fingers are not sufficiently strong to vibrate, then they need to be strengthened. For example, this may be accomplished with exercises for dexterity or exercises in double stops.

Sometimes it takes the student a long time to develop a vibrato, not because of lack of ability, but as a result of an *insufficient need* to express his or her emotions through vibrato. In this case, it becomes necessary to strengthen the *desire* to vibrate.

In response to the question of whether it is necessary to always use a continuous vibrato, Yankelevich remarked, "the use of vibrato is limited in technical sections. It cannot be used while shifting or on every note in a fast passage. I do not recommend using vibrato in scales and technical exercises." But he also noted how continuous vibrato is used significantly more often than in the past. Consequently, it follows that it should be more diverse so it does not become monotonous and lose its musical purpose. This is why Yankelevich tried to develop various types of vibrato in his students based on the main type of vibrato that determines the student's individual sound. He described the highest form of mastery as "being able to use vibrato at will, to be able to produce the sound one wants to hear, and not to passively enjoy the sound that is being produced, no matter how beautiful it may be."

One of the exercises Yankelevich suggested to develop different types of vibrato is the following: the student plays with vibrato in a lower position, and then uses the same finger to vibrate in a very high position (or vice versa) while trying to retain the identical form of vibrato. Since the natural form of the movement is different in various positions, this exercise helps achieve a controlled movement as well as a different type of sound.

The worst type of vibrato is a "habitual" one, without any conscious auditory preconception or musical expression.

FINGERINGS AND BOWINGS

Yankelevich did not believe in a single system of fingerings and bowings. He always encouraged his students to be creative in their search. While the solution they discover may not always be the best, nonetheless it is "personal," reflecting their capabilities, and therefore logical to retain. The quality of playing is most important, for "even with the best fingerings and bowings it is still possible to play poorly."

Occasionally the concrete goals facing the student require the teacher to change plans and provide more space for the student's creativity: "If the student suggests something musical, I welcome it. But if it is simply for the sake of invention, I suppress it." Yankelevich always emphasized the musical element in bowings and fingerings. If the musical content requires a more difficult technique, then the difficulty of the bowing or fingering needs to be overcome, rather than trying to find an easier option. As an example he illustrated the difficult fingerings Szigeti used in Bach in order to better bring out the voice leading. According to Yankelevich:

Matters of fingerings and bowings deserve flexibility. They are constantly problematic in works by the Classical composers. Take, for example, Mozart. After newly discovered research, and the appearance of Mozart's original manuscripts, much needs to be revised. There are no fixed principles—this is a living process. We see new editions, new ideas, new students.

He went into more detail regarding bowings in Bach.

In Bach, generally the strokes are on the string. Today, off-the-string bowings are also used, although this is not in the best of taste. It is more correct to employ a heavy "Bach" spiccato. It has been calculated that a lifetime would not suffice to rewrite all of Bach's works by hand, and yet Bach managed to compose them all! His thought process was faster than his notation, and he made sketches very quickly. In this kind of creative process, he physically could not write down all the bowings, and there are many pages without any bowings at all. This is why Bach's manuscripts should not be considered absolute references. Moreover, in the last centuries both bowings and fingerings vastly evolved and became more complex. This should be taken into consideration. I think Bach would appreciate a good modern interpretation of his music.

To develop bowing technique, Yankelevich considered it important to be able to clearly imagine the character of the stroke and the functions of the right hand.

Drawing the bow requires a specific sequence of movements in the hand and fingers that stem from one integral movement. For example, sometimes one encounters difficulties when playing spiccato near the frog. How can they be avoided? It is always necessary to integrate each movement into the unified movement of the arm. Each small specific movement needs to maintain a form that "fits into" the general arm movement. It is possible to also find separate forms of movement, but these are not natural.

Yankelevich worked with students according to these general principles, taking into account their individual characteristics. He followed a system of studying bowings he developed in practice, which corresponded approximately to the age and level of the violinist. Bowings were divided as follows:

(1) Long, held notes
(2) Détaché
(3) Transitions to other bowings

The first group was already discussed earlier in the section on tone production, so let us only address the matter of legato. Yankelevich would always stress that legato is not simply what happens when the bow glides over the string while the left hand plays several notes. "Legato is also a bow stroke," he would say, "and as a stroke it has its own beginning, middle, and end." In his opinion the main difficulty of legato consists of uniting the lyrical character of the sound in general with the lyrical character and roundness of each individual note. Thus, one cannot just rely on the right hand since "a lyrical legato requires both hands to be active."

When evaluating a violinist's playing, Yankelevich would first pay attention to tone production and the expressivity of legato:

> We have, to a great degree, lost the art of this stroke. A smooth legato is a color. Cantilena, a long melodic line—these are the violin's strengths. The charm of legato must not disappear.

Elaborating on specific characteristics of legato in the repertoire, specifically in the Beethoven concerto, Yankelevich would remark:

> Legato is prevalent in Beethoven. Some notes may be emphasized more than others, naturally within the confines of good taste. However, they should not be separated. The emphasis is determined by the musical phrase and should be more of an internal rather than an external action.

Yankelevich recommended starting to learn détaché using large sections of the bow, first with the upper half of the bow and then the lower half. Only after this should one move on to playing with the whole bow and combining different parts of the bow. There was a reason he preferred starting with the upper half of the bow, for this is where the right hand is the most comfortable and relaxed. This sequence of studies helps define the functions of each part of the bow. In the course of playing, the student observes the position of the forearm, shoulder, and wrist. The ear is geared primarily to ensure the same quality of sound in all parts of the bow. Kreutzer's Etude No. 1 and Paganini's *Perpetual Motion* are excellent material for working on bowings.[5] He recommended to "always play in different parts of the bow without a noticeable change in sound. This is what allows freedom in playing and provides a wonderful quality and richness to the stroke."

After the basic détaché stroke has been mastered, Yankelevich proposed working on different combinations of the stroke. One example is playing one note détaché and three notes legato, which provides the possibility of alternating slow and fast movements. He considered the following exercise to be especially useful: The bow is conditionally divided into six parts, and the student practices in each of them using different combinations (taken from Yampolsky's edition of the Kreutzer etudes). "This allows the student to 'search for comfort,' and develops light, agile movements and a 'feel for the bow.' Such a method allows this feeling to be developed much faster."

Yankelevich recommended many exercises to develop freedom in the fingers and wrist, something he considered "the key to being in command of all the bow strokes." The wrist is involved both vertically and horizontally. "It should be developed, for example, using Kreutzer's Etude No. 11 in A major played with different combinations of bowings, and also on two strings." For developing elasticity in the fingers on the bow he recommended *fingerstriche* exercises near the frog that also incorporate a slight movement in the hand.

In détaché, he attached a lot of importance to "the initial moment the bow is drawn (i.e., the attack of the note), which affects the energy of the stroke." He recommended the following exercise, originally devised by Yampolsky: The bow is placed on the string at the frog and then taken off the string with an accent. This is repeated a few times with the goal of achieving a sharp "metallic" sound. After this "pinching" with a down-bow at the frog, the bow is placed at the tip and the same "pinching" is made with an up-bow. Then this is done not from the string, but from above. Finally, the bow does not lift after the pinch, but makes a fast movement both down-bow and up-bow. Transitional strokes arise as a strong détaché turns into martelé. These exercises cultivate a feeling for the initial attack; the ability to place the bow on the string and immediately move it; control of the bow in the air; liberation of the hand; and breadth in the movement. The transition to other strokes occurs naturally, as in this case the détaché turns into martelé.

All strokes originate in détaché. This principle is often repeated, but rarely understood and even more rarely utilized. And yet, this is the key to mastering different bowings. On the violin the bow must be drawn, which is the essence of détaché. And spiccato? This may be considered a "more complex" détaché. The corresponding movements of both a small détaché and spiccato need to be controlled. Spiccato is a détaché above the string, in which the bow touches the string in the middle of the stroke. However, the manner of drawing the bow remains the same.

"The manner of playing martelé," Yankelevich would say, "causes many disagreements. "Some believe that the arm must always remain tense while others believe that pressure should be applied to the string (that it should be 'pinched') and then quickly released. If the bow trembles when playing martelé, then the method is incorrect. It is both wrong to just 'pinch' the string and to play the stroke with a tense arm. To eliminate any trembling, the bow needs to be drawn firmly along the string the entire time, with the bow feeling contact with all parts of the string." He recommended learning the stroke by playing a short détaché with rests. Then as the movement is accelerated and amplified, the rests are shortened, and gradually a compact, rich martelé is achieved. "The rests here are just as important as the sound. The bow should not make any noise during the rests. It should lie gently on the string and the arm must be relaxed."

In the "Viotti" stroke, where the martelé notes are connected, it is important to accent the second note. In a "punctuated" or "dotted" bowing, the silence is crucial. "It must absolutely be held its full value," Yankelevich said. "Strange as it may seem, the accent occurs on the short note, which gives the stroke clarity and character."

Regarding staccato, Yankelevich believed that "of all types of staccato, the flying staccato is the easiest to develop, though with perseverance the other types may be mastered as well." He did not see any obstacles to staccato, save perhaps only psychological blocks, which an experienced teacher could easily remove: "Staccato firstly requires that the right hand be set up correctly, and then for the other bowings to be developed, so the muscles in the arm and hand (especially in the wrist) are relaxed and flexible."

If a student had even the slightest trace of tension in the arm, Yankelevich would turn his attention away from staccato. Otherwise, a type of convulsive tension arises that makes free and flexible movement impossible. He believed the tension could be removed through "quick bow changes that liberate the right hand in the same way that shifting liberates the left hand."

In keeping with his concept of the interconnection between bowings, Yankelevich viewed staccato as a special type of martelé. He recommended learning staccato by making a quick down-bow (an accented détaché, almost martelé) and then trying to play six notes staccato on the up-bow. The beginning of the staccato should match the character of an energetic martelé. Moreover, "one should capture the feeling of the required movement without being afraid of a certain harshness in the sound." Yampolsky even once noted that "scratchiness is staccato's traveling companion. Sometimes, the right imagery or example at a lesson is enough for staccato just to take off. Though the stroke emerges more easily if the hand follows its natural course of development."

As already noted, spiccato is closely related to détaché. In spiccato the bow seems to spring from the string. "All the springing movements must be made holding the bow lightly with the fingers, for the movements are based on the flexibility of the bow stick, the vibration of which brings the subsequent note to life. Holding the bow too tightly restricts free movement." Yankelevich emphasized that the wrist is involved relatively little in this movement. "The essential action occurs in the forearm and the fingers. The wrist is also involved, but only indirectly." One method he used to help release the right arm and prepare it for different types of spiccato was to work on moving the bow near the frog. Then he advised crossing over strings using the same movements, as this helps to "unbind" the shoulder.

There are two things to look out for when playing sautillé. "The first is to not hold the bow too tightly with the fingers, and the second is to not press the bow too much on the string." This stroke does not always work immediately. It is better to develop it by playing détaché with a small bow and to accent a group of notes, for example, every fourth, then every eighth, and so on. According to Yankelevich the quality may be improved by taking note of the following: (1) determine the ideal part of the bow where it begins to bounce (this depends both on the bow's weight and the stick's flexibility); (2) take account of the tempo (in a faster tempo the stroke should be played further from the frog); and (3) change the angle of the bow hair (although in principle the angle of the hair should remain the same, for many bows it may be more effective to increase the angle of the stick). Once the stroke is played confidently, it is necessary to establish coordination between the right and left hands. In this case, the right hand is the reference since it establishes the rhythm of the stroke. This is why it is useful to begin by repeating each note four times, then two, and, finally, three times. Only then should the notes be played separately in a moderate tempo.

The ricochet stroke similarly retains the basic motion of détaché. The difficulty here consists of retaining freedom in spite of the momentary impulse. The stroke should be played with the bow held as freely as possible, just like a feather. The main goal is to start the movement and then make use of the springiness of the bow and the string. It is helpful to practice gradually, increasing the number of notes to a bow, starting with triplets, then quadruplets, and so on.

Yankelevich considered the technique of playing chords to fall into the category of bow strokes. While it might be possible to play three or four strings simultaneously, the middle string (of a three-note chord) will inevitably be forced.

> The art of mastering chords is not to play the strings simultaneously, but to make them sound as if they are played simultaneously.

He referred to Yampolsky's advice to "always play chords lightly, with the same principle of tone production as when playing in *piano*. The moment the bow leaves the string is particularly important."

Yankelevich recommended students work daily on all aspects of bowing technique using Kreutzer's Etudes Nos. 1 and 11.[6] "This should take on average forty-five minutes per day. Once all the strokes have been learned this becomes an "ideal warm-up" for the bow arm, and can replace similar material found in other etudes or repertoire." He emphasized that at the beginning, when the technique and different movements of the arm are still being worked out, it is better to play the strokes on a single note. Otherwise, problems of coordinating the hands can divert the student's attention: "I assign bowing exercises for Kreutzer's Etude No. 1 with every note to be played four times so as to avoid any additional difficulties in the left hand. Later, as the stroke develops, it is possible to make it more complicated and include new elements." He did not find it efficient to practice bowings using scales, even though this is often recommended. "A scale involves continuous movement of the left hand along the fingerboard, making it difficult for the right hand and requiring complex coordination." The scale is useful only at the highest level of coordinating bowings with aspects of left-hand technique, such as shifting or string crossing. This becomes "the final step in complicating the skill." Yankelevich also did not find it useful to learn bowings using various etudes, aside from those etudes expressly designed for this purpose. "Etudes help to polish not the actual execution of the stroke, but its musical goal and the limits of how it is used."

This is the way Yankelevich worked out a coherent system of learning bow strokes that stemmed from two principles: progress from the more simple to the more complex, and from a general movement to a more specific movement. He saw a deep internal connection between the various bow strokes and the principal movement of the right hand, which is to draw the bow along the string. He also attached a lot of importance to being able to feel "elasticity in the bow stick and in the strings," and to treat these as active forces in moving the bow. He viewed the strokes as interdependent, since mastering one stroke may help another. This is why he advised to at least touch upon all the different strokes on a daily basis: "This helps to keep the right hand active and saves time mastering technical spots in the repertoire." If technical difficulties persist, different bowing variations not only help overcome them more quickly but also lead to long-term virtuosic mastery of right-hand technique.

SELECTING REPERTOIRE

As we already mentioned, Yankelevich chose repertoire and created individual plans based on a detailed study of the student according to a specific system. This cannot be done solely using intuition, since every detail needs to be examined and clarified to make the right conclusion. He was closely aligned with the methods of Abraham Yampolsky, who in his time created a special questionnaire of sixty questions. These included observations on the student's general development, family cultural background, interests outside of music, personality traits, emotional and nervous disposition, reaction to critique, retention, initiative, and so on. One of Yampolsky's well-known lectures, "Methods of Working with Students," was based on a detailed "deciphering" of a student's individual characteristics. Yankelevich assisted Yampolsky in elaborating sections of the questionnaire and developing its general outline. He believed that precisely this kind of detailed analysis of the student's psychological and artistic qualities (physiology and physique were not as decisively important) determined the following: how quickly or slowly the teacher should move the student forward and precisely which aspects needed to be developed and nurtured.

Foremost, Yankelevich believed it necessary for the teacher to "capture in every student the essential seed and develop that first. Gradually the other aspects are incorporated, but never at the cost of what is most essential, or else all the students will be similar and sound like twins." The second stage is to create a long-term plan for the student's development, and not just restrict the focus to current problems. The student's path of development should be envisioned for four to five years ahead, and the corresponding repertoire determined. However, the formulated plan should not always be adhered to blindly, for life creates its own revisions. Sometimes what has been planned becomes unnecessary if the student already surpasses the goals that were set. Sometimes the opposite may happen if the projected plan turns out to be too difficult.

Yankelevich believed that half of the teacher's success depends on pedagogical flexibility.

It is important not only to see the student integrally, but also to note the tendencies of musical life and the direction the audience is headed. Only then is it possible to create a plan for the student's education. It is easy to make a serious mistake by only dealing with the current issues. This is why I set aside space in my plans for violin miniatures. I know that today they are not "in fashion," and big concertos and sonatas are more popular. But this will change, and it is important to take such a possible future shift into consideration.

In his lectures Yankelevich analyzed the most common pedagogical methods of choosing repertoire and noted that they often stem from an inadequate knowledge of the learning process. One such example is an incorrect understanding of how to "skip" repertoire.

Some teachers use the following "method": "Why don't I assign my student Paganini's Caprices! Even though he will not play them well, they will still give him a push forward." This principle of "throwing the dog into the water so he learns to swim" is deeply flawed. Trying to execute a skill beyond one's ability inevitably leads to tension, poor tone quality, and an absence of artistry (i.e., the opposite of everything the teacher is trying to achieve). However, this does not mean that the idea of "skipping" repertoire should always be rejected, for sometimes it may be necessary. The student may often make a jump, but only if this is structured correctly and there has been a sufficiently long period of accumulating technique. Indeed, if the student is ready for a skip forward and the teacher misses the moment, the student's progress may even be hindered.

Another method Yankelevich analyzed in his lectures is when the teacher focuses his or her attention solely on musical problems.

There are some teachers who insist violinists should only brought up on "good" music of the Classical composers. However, this music is not always the best material for violinistic and virtuosic development. This is why virtuosic pieces, such as those by Dancla, de Bériot, and Vieuxtemps, should be assigned early on. It is essential to create a true violinistic technical foundation that is parallel to the artistic development provided by a gavotte by Bach, a minuet of Mozart, and other arrangements of the classics.... The original works of Bach and Mozart present such difficult musical problems that a young child cannot come even close to solving them properly. Children should still be introduced to the classics, but they should start with simple arrangements. Naturally, Goethe's *Faust* or Beethoven's Symphonies are not meant for children. A child requires fairy tales and material that is simple and accessible.

It is unfortunate that many teachers exclude works of de Bériot, Vieuxtemps, Spohr, and other virtuoso-romantic pieces from the student repertoire, dismissing them as "bad music." However, Yankelevich said, "even if pieces by de Bériot are simplistic, they are also melodic, as are works by Vieuxtemps. These are easily accessible to children and evoke a feeling for artistry. I only assign Mozart in the advanced classes, after the Vieuxtemps concerti and even after the Tchaikovsky concerto. What is important is to find the right proportion of material for both artistic and instrumental development."

Yankelevich believed the teacher should be stricter with technical aspects than with musical aspects.

Only then can the student freely reveal his or her own artistic qualities. It is important to correctly analyze which classical composition to assign a student. For example, if assigning Mozart's Violin Concerto No. 3 to a Year 4 or Year 5 student, one should remember that the performance would have nothing to do with Mozart. Mozart requires a certain degree of maturity, otherwise the student will have a skewed idea of this music. More accessible material lets the student be more exacting on both the musical material and on him- or herself. This kind of approach makes a huge educational difference.

Yankelevich believed certain pieces and etudes to be irreplaceable in the course of study. These included two concertos by Rode (or at least the first movements of Nos. 6 and 7), de Bériot's Concerto No. 9 and the last two movements of Concerto No. 7, and Kreutzer's Concertos Nos. 12 and 13. Yankelevich especially liked Spohr's concerti, and recommended all three movements of Nos. 7 and 9 and the first movement of No. 11. He concluded this list with Concertos Nos. 2 and 4 by Vieuxtemps. He also recommended *La Scène de Ballet* by de Bériot and the Goldmark concerto. He found all these pieces to "provide such mastery of the instrument, which would be impossible to achieve by only playing Mozart's sublime concerti."

Students always play the rather theatrical concerti of de Bériot with a lot of enthusiasm, and this helps them to grow. Spohr helps to cultivate tone quality, correct bow movements, and technical mastery. Spohr instills discipline. He is not nearly as "academic" as many believe. Auer would assign his students three Spohr concerti, and Szigeti considered Spohr's music to be good, respectable, and useful. Szigeti said he couldn't imagine a violinist's education without them and I am of the same opinion. As for the works of Vieuxtemps and Wieniawski, they develop taste, temperament, phrasing, and a sense of fantasy.

At a certain stage Yankelevich believed one can and should assign many classical works. The included Martini's *Gavotte*, Lully's *Gavotte*, Haydn's *Minuet*, and so on as well as older Italian works of Corelli, Tartini, Vivaldi, Geminiani, and Torelli. But these should be assigned "only when the student is ready for them and can play them properly from an artistic point of view. In order to arrive at a true understanding of both classical and contemporary music, the student's instrumental mastery needs to be developed by assigning pieces appropriate to the student's age and taking into account the student's intellectual and emotional understanding."

In the more advanced classes, Yankelevich found the works of Ernst to be especially beneficial for technique. "In terms of motor skills, they help more than works by Paganini." Yankelevich recommended first learning Ernst's *Othello Fantasy* and *Hungarian Airs* and then his concerto. In response to comments that Ernst's compositions are musically lacking, he always replied, "There is no bad music, only those unable to find the music in these works." He recalled the words of Auer who told one student who resisted playing Ernst's *Othello*: "You will keep playing this piece until you are able to make good music out of it!"

In the more advanced classes the repertoire was different, and included Mozart, Beethoven (except for the concerto), and Bach. The latter can be studied "once the student has a certain degree of skill and is able to perceive the depth of these works," Yankelevich said. "It is most important that the teacher is very exigent in maintaining high artistic standards. The more complicated contemporary and classical works need to be approached gradually. Only by mastering the right tools for expression and by becoming musically, and no less importantly, generally educated, do the doors open for the violinist." He would affirm that "two concerti by Vieuxtemps and two sonatas by Mozart are enough to develop both technique and musicality."

But just choosing the correct repertoire is not enough, for every drop must be "extracted" from the piece so it has the maximum benefit. This is why the teacher must know precisely what may be "extracted" from any given piece, as well as from the student playing the piece. The Kreutzer etudes are a good example. They may be used "to improve the quality of bow strokes, intonation, tone, tempo, and so on. In terms of improving technique Kreutzer gives just as much as Dont, and possibly even more in terms of quality. The Kreutzer etudes, followed by Rode and Dont, provide an essential technical foundation. They must be covered very thoroughly, always maintaining a high level of quality. Later, all the other etudes may be played such as Fiorillo, Dancla, and so forth. For developing right-hand technique (the wrist, various bowings), one can take two or three etudes by Gavigné, as well as certain etudes of Schradieck and Rovelli." In the beginning classes he recommended etudes by Kayser and Mazas (especially for those needing extra musical development), followed by the "baby" Dont etudes.

Yankelevich generally attached a lot of importance to etudes, but he did not see them as a goal unto themselves. He believed that the more etudes are covered, the more pieces need to be studied in order to maintain a balance between technical and musical development. It is also important to know the extent to which etudes should be perfected and what is a good "average" number of etudes to be covered. Yankelevich believed that one of the main problems in pedagogy, aside from overwork, inefficiency on the part of the teacher, and laziness on the part of the student, is that too few etudes and pieces are studied in general.

The student's technique is established through etudes. However, the etudes need to be learned correctly and, most importantly, with quality. The difference between a good and bad violinist seems obvious—the good one plays better, the bad one plays poorly. Continuing this train of thought means a good violinist creates a beautiful tone, makes good shifts, and so on. Consequently, good technique, good sound, and good bowings need to be cultivated and developed. What material to use for this—pieces? Well, in this case everything must be learned anew, for each piece is unique. Instead, pieces should make use of technical skills that have already been established and are best acquired through etudes. A student cannot progress normally without covering at least two or three etudes per month, with different goals set for each one. This comes to about twenty-five to thirty etudes per year. Therefore, regular practice should always include at least two etudes, with two or, even better, three lessons devoted to each etude.

Yankelevich noted that, "if the student maintains this rhythm of learning, he or she will be able to assimilate repertoire quickly. This helps develop the professional skills of being alert and being able to quickly orient oneself in new repertoire. These are essential qualities for a violinist, for without them even the best technique cannot be used to its maximum potential."

The criteria for perfecting a piece or etude are also important. This includes being able to play from memory, in a concert setting, up to tempo. "Attempting to bring each piece to absolute perfection can slow the student's progress," Yankelevich said. "It is important to achieve the main goal or concrete purpose of the etude or composition. For example, Ries's *Moto Perpetuo* is targeted at developing sautillé and coordinating the bow with the fingers. Once the piece is played in tempo with good intonation, good tone, and basic phrasing, the goal may be considered accomplished." He advised setting aside the more difficult etudes and pieces and returning to these works later to polish them for performances. The others do not need to be so thoroughly perfected. He also temporarily "forgave" musical deficiencies if the student did not yet understand the depth of the piece, although he would always come back to the piece later since he liked to complete everything he started.

Yankelevich would always point out the importance of taking into account the personality and desires of the student.

Some students are easily able to perfect pieces without losing interest, whereas others quickly "wilt" and lose motivation. The first may be kept on the same repertoire, while the others need the repertoire to be frequently updated, although still in line with the same goal. The teacher can, and should to a certain degree, take into consideration the student's requests for repertoire, but only if they do not conflict with the general plan that the teacher must always have in mind.

Another important matter is the repetition and assimilation of repertoire.

The teacher may occasionally lose sight of this goal. It can happen that the student is unable to really play anything—the old repertoire is forgotten, and the new is not yet learned. It is necessary to regularly repeat pieces that have already been covered and accumulate "baggage." The teacher must be involved in this process. I always ask that at least one piece from the old repertoire be repeated each month. Some students postpone this until vacation, but I consider it more useful to work on scales, etudes, and technique during the holidays.

Yankelevich also did not neglect to continue working with former students after they started concertizing: "Any performer is in need of friendly advice. It is better that this advice comes from a qualified pedagogue, who has already analyzed him or her better than anyone else." In giving advice to concertizing violinists, Yankelevich said: "One should be able to play everything and master every style. It is a mistake that so many players consider virtuoso pieces by Paganini, Vieuxtemps, Wieniawski, and Kreisler to be 'superficial.' These pieces not only provide a means of perfecting violin mastery but also the opportunity to showcase it."

He observed many competitions in which a violinist was able to perform the classics with quite good taste and understanding, but turned out to be helpless in the virtuoso-romantic works, which are an obligatory part of any competition.

If a violinist is a true artist, he or she must be versatile and, just like an actor, be capable of transforming from drama to vaudeville! The interpretation of a subtle and charming short piece by Kreisler requires its own particular approach. There may only be three or four phrases, but each note, each turn, assumes a paramount importance. Today, the art of playing short pieces is being forgotten, and yet nothing opens a violinist more than playing these kinds of works. They not only condition musicality but also develop the ability to express more profound and powerful sentiments.

WORKING ON REPERTOIRE

Yankelevich would often discuss how to work on repertoire in his lectures and appearances, and believed it to be one of the most central themes in pedagogy. He found this issue to encompass not only the process of working on a piece but also the more general process of educating a student through this work and preparing him or her for a future musical career. He saw the process of working on a piece not just in terms of capturing the composer's intent and uncovering the deeper artistic subtext (although naturally he never lost sight of this), but also as a discovery of the student's own capabilities, imagination, and feel for artistry as well as the student's ability to assimilate different styles, forms, genres, and expressive devices. In other words, he saw the methodological-pedagogical aspect of this work.

Yankelevich did not always distinctly separate the stages of working on a piece, since they would unite in the closely knit pedagogical process. Nonetheless, he considered it necessary to focus on the few "key points" of whichever problem he considered to be most important in correctly structuring the lesson.

Yankelevich emphasized not only the methodological and technical side of this process but also thoroughly explored the psychological and creative side. For him, mastering a composition meant the student creates his or her own conception (with the teacher's help) and is then able to transmit that conception to the public. For this reason Yankelevich always included the matter of psychological preparation before performance when addressing the topic of "how to work on a musical composition." In this way Yankelevich tied together the entire process of the musician's education.

Yankelevich distinguished three stages in learning a piece. The first consisted of "learning about the composer, the style, the epoch, and the milieu in which the composer worked, as well as the performers with whom the composer was in contact."

> One must remember that the works of each composer undergo development. Generally, composers are under certain influences in their younger years. Then they forge their own path and later may be ahead of their time, looking toward the future. Thus it is important to know at which stage of development a composition belongs and to understand what the composer was interested in. This may also determine which aspects of the composition need to be brought out.

> The second stage is to analyze the piece, including its content, style, and genre. This stage should begin when the piece is initially being discovered, but

not by playing it on the violin as is usually done. Yankelevich suggested listening to a good recording, but never more than twice to avoid any risk of copying it. Even better is to play the piece at the piano, or for more advanced musicians, to visually read the score and analyze its elements.

If the student has not yet played the piece with instrument in hand, then there are no customary habits and the student can perceive the piece as music and not just as another technical exercise. Thus, the composer's intentions become clearer as does the character of the piece, which is important in guiding a good musician. This also makes it easier to imagine how the composer heard his or her own piece. For the character and emotional structure of the piece, the colors and nuances, are beyond the limits of transcription, since all that the composer heard and understood cannot be expressed solely in notes. And yet, one may find a student already playing a piece from memory without being fully aware of the composer's indications.

The third stage is to "realize an individual interpretation." This stage is itself divided in two: working on details and achieving unity. This division is possible if the student has already worked out the musical goals in the first stage of learning the piece. This method helped Yankelevich's students achieve such resounding success and demonstrate a variety of musical interpretations after what would seem to be uniform technical work in the lessons. In this system any work on details is always subservient to a preliminary musical idea.

It is very difficult to develop a unified representation of the piece. Both the technical and the musical challenges need to be reconciled. This process must be flexible, and sometimes may deviate from the preliminary plan. But constant mechanical repetition leads nowhere, not even in terms of technical development. The form and character of the musical idea become lost in such "drilling." Yampolsky would always discourage this type of work. He recommended one keep in mind the musical character of the section and try to determine the reason behind the problem. Then he recommended making up an exercise for the problematic movement or technique so that it is not worked out on the piece itself. He was very creative in developing these kinds of exercises and taught his students how to do this. Using the material in tricky passages, it is possible to make up different bowings, fingerings, and other kinds of variations. If a few difficult passages still create problems for the entire piece, it is better to start working on a new piece while gradually finishing work on the former one.

After working in detail on technical and expressive problems, it is necessary to unify the piece by balancing the character, tempo, dynamics, and, finally, achieving an individual artistic interpretation. And this is where Yankelevich felt the preliminary artistic conception to be most important, for it had already been polished and enriched with details, although it had yet to assume its unified form.

At this stage it is very useful to leave the instrument and work on tying together all that has been achieved and again search for the character, tempo, and dramatization of the piece. Only then should the piece be played again—though not immediately in its entirety, but in large sections marked by rests. If the piece has no rests, it should still be played with stops, but the stops should be always changed so as to avoid mechanical habits. And finally, the whole piece should be rehearsed with accompaniment.

Yankelevich saw the process of achieving continuity as being twofold. On the one hand, all the details are consolidated and become part of the larger form in the process of playing the piece through many times without interruption. "It is important to be able to carry on after a mistake, but still to remember it and fix it later," Yankelevich said. And at the same time, it is necessary to continue working on details that become clearer given the perspective of the entire work.

Yankelevich considered one of the main ways to achieve unity is by determining the exact tempi of separate sections as well as the general tempo from beginning to end. He believed this to account for at least half the success. He understood a unified tempo not as something strictly uniform but as an artistic combination of the main tempos within the piece—a clear structure of tempi held together by a pulsating rhythm.

One must determine the main sections of the piece and make sure the tempo is metronomically exact. All the refrains in a rondo (if there are no contrary indications in the score) must be played absolutely precisely. I can give you an example when Szigeti plays the first movement of the Brahms concerto. His opening establishes a very precise tempo. Then, after various fluctuations, the return of the principal theme brings us back to the exact tempo of the beginning. Later, there are more fluctuations, but the chords return to the initial tempo, which is also maintained for the principal theme in the development, whereas the second theme is played more freely. Szigeti created the impression of a flexible, yet unified, monolithic form with a continuous tempo that was easy to follow. Another example is in Ravel's *Tzigane* where the allegro alternates with moderato. It is very important to clearly establish the relationship between these tempi and then attempt to stabilize it.

Yankelevich illustrated how the performer needs to develop a specific sensation of "feeling the tempo" and being able to determine it. There are two components to this. Firstly, one needs to find the tempo that best matches the musical intent of the work, taking into account any augmentation. For the tempo will be slightly different depending on whether the work is played with piano or orchestral accompaniment or if the piece is performed solo. Secondly, one must be able to remember the discovered tempo and able to reproduce it with relative accuracy. He recommended working on tempo in the following order:

1. Create an internal idea of the tempo that optimally suits the musical excerpt, taking into account the genre, style, and so on.
2. Verify the tempo with the instrument, and establish the metronome marking.
3. Play something else, then return to the excerpt and compare the tempo with the metronome marking. Do this a few times, trying to accurately match the tempo.
4. Try to play the entire piece through and maintain the tempo, if possible with a recording device. Go back and check the tempos, taking into consideration the entire form.

Yankelevich found this method helps to learn how to accurately return to the tempo relatively quickly.

Another important means of creating musical meaning is phrasing. In his opinion, work on expressive phrasing should begin only when the style and general unified contour of the piece is perfectly clear. At the same time, purely intellectual work is not always enough since intuition plays a huge role in phrasing. This is what differentiates the "artist" violinist from the "artisan" violinist. Intellect alone is not enough, for talent arises from intuition. Therefore it is necessary to combine intuition with understanding.

In the final stage of unifying a piece, it becomes necessary to polish and correct one's own conception. Yankelevich advised returning to listen to a variety of recordings but with a critical ear. "It is necessary to determine the differences in the interpretations, why the performers play differently, what they are trying to say, and how this is tied to their particular way of playing. This is how one's own understanding is enriched, through clearly understanding the interpretations of other performers."

And lastly, Yankelevich noted the psychological components of performing on stage and engaging the audience. He compared the finished piece to a painting:

A small painting may be perfectly appropriate for a small room, but in a public space only a poster will do. In order to interest and captivate the audience, it is important to have a clear idea of the impression one desires to create. Playing that is fast and technical does not work well in the concert hall; it blurs together and becomes trivial. The stage requires expansive and expressive playing, exaggerated accents, a powerful sound, and articulate technical passagework. Therefore, when playing with piano, it is necessary to make everything more pronounced and play on a larger scale, but at a slightly slower tempo so that everything may be controlled. This ensures a feeling of calmness on the stage, whereas fast playing creates instability.

Yankelevich was especially attentive to preparing the student psychologically for the stage. This is also the teacher's responsibility, for the teacher must ensure the student does not break down on stage, and not let the student perform a piece that is not yet ready or without preparing the student for the new sensations that arise when performing. "Part of the task is to cultivate a businesslike approach to performance and to the results of one's efforts," Yankelevich said. "It is necessary to notice and analyze all one's mistakes, and not just superficially. Only a serious and objective discourse is helpful, whether at home, in the lesson, or on stage."

This type of professional attitude is acquired throughout the course of the entire pedagogical process, long before going on stage. For the stage is like a microscope, revealing the entire learning process with all its successes and failures. Yankelevich did not agree with those who claimed the performer's inspiration occurs only on stage in front of an audience.

Emotion must be already created when first studying the piece. A musician must always be engaged and living the music without waiting for "inspiration" on stage. I can't remember Victor Tretyakov ever playing anything at the lesson without being completely involved, he never "saved" anything extra for the stage. When Isaac Stern was asked how he practiced at home—with complete involvement or more analytically— he replied: "How do you say in Russian? ... Like a cow's husband!"

Everything needs to be directed toward performance, for this is the final goal of our work.

Yankelevich believed the most important part of this process is nurturing calmness, confidence, and a feeling that everything will work out. This depends on knowing the piece, knowing one's limits, and being confident that the work is within the scope of one's capabilities. One must understand that something can always happen on stage, but the mistakes should be ignored and treated as trifles: "One should not lose self-control because of a false note or even a more serious mistake." Good instrumental mastery lessens the likelihood of this happening.

The instrument must be played well, with sufficient technical preparation. The best psychological preparation for going on stage is feeling completely in control of the instrument.

He recommended the following advice of Yampolsky: Before a performance, play through the piece without stopping, at a slightly slower tempo, with complete involvement and following all nuances. "It is important to be able to exaggerate the musical idea, but without ever becoming too excited or flustered," Yankelevich said. This also helps to "grasp the form as a whole, consolidate the transitions and sequences, precisely control all the details and improve the coordination between mental conception and physical realization."

It is important to not lose oneself on stage. The performer should think only about the music and not notice anything else. Nothing unexpected should interfere with the violinist's fundamental goal, which is artistry and a musically convincing whole.

According to Yankelevich, the most important outcome after working on a piece is not just its realization or performance, but the step forward made by the student.

Studying a piece is inextricably linked to studying the violin and studying oneself. Only on this basis should practice at home and preparation for the stage be structured.

Yankelevich placed an additional responsibility on the teacher. "The student must not only understand the musical value of the piece, but also understand his or her own capabilities at any given moment. Otherwise, the student will always feel deficient."

Yankelevich was interested in all aspects of the pedagogical process, including the educational importance of grades and assessments that are given by teachers and committees. He even gave a special lecture on this topic at the Central Music School and later at the Moscow Conservatory. He spoke of the fact that grades or marks often do not fulfill their main educational purpose. Biases and inflated grades discredit both teachers and committees, and are mocked by students. This is evidence of "the absence of strict guidelines in respect to grading." In his opinion, a good grading system should consist of specific criteria that let a student be graded fairly and with an "educational" result. Yet teachers often do not understand this educational aspect, and he provided examples of incorrect grades that were given with the best of intentions.

For example, some teachers believe grades should sometimes be elevated to encourage the less capable student who tries hard, the youngest in the class, or those students playing difficult programs. Other times grades are lowered when students play a program that is much easier than their capabilities, or in order to "stimulate" a student who is talented but lazy.

Yankelevich considered all these deviations to be fundamentally wrong. If a student received a lower grade when playing a program that was too difficult, then he believed it should be the teacher who receives the lower grade. He believed, "Life will make its own corrections sooner or later. The talented student will find his or her place and a mediocre student will remain on the sidelines, despite excellent grades."

The sole correct approach is to only grade the *performance of the piece*. The pedagogical effect is greater if the grade accurately reflects musicality and interpretation. This develops the student's creativity, which is the fundamental musical element that guarantees his or her future development. At the same time this kind of grade educates not just the particular student but all the others as well.

If the piece is too difficult for the student this will inevitably be reflected in the grade. However, this is a sign for the teacher that this piece should never have been assigned in the first place. "This kind of approach increases the teacher's responsibility in choosing the student's repertoire," Yankelevich said.

Another criteria in grading should be the frequency of the student's performances over the course of the year and the efforts made to perform and assimilate repertoire. He believed that the yearly grade should take into consideration all the year's performances and be lowered if there are too few of them.

Regarding specific grades, he made the following observations: "a grade of excellence ('A') requires good rhythm, intonation, tone quality, musicianship, and adherence to the score.[7] The absence of any of these elements must lower the grade, and an 'A' must be given only to a good musician and instrumentalist." Requiring "artistry" in a performance, although desirable, is beyond the scope of beginners and should only apply to exceptional children. However, the standards in this respect should be raised at the conservatory level.

Meanwhile, the meaning of a grade of "B" or "C" needs to be elevated. "Often teachers will give a 'C' when the student really deserves a 'D,' and a 'B' is sometimes misconstrued as a complete misfortune. This all results in 'A's being handed out a dime a dozen."

For Yankelevich, performing on stage was a fundamental component to becoming an artist.

> There are talented violinists who appear to be capable of playing brilliantly at the highest level, but who do not end up fully developing their abilities. For, at a certain professional stage, the artist's development is determined by factors that, to a certain degree, lie beyond the confines of the classroom. In this respect performing in public is very important, since the stage provides something that no teacher in a classroom can. If the teacher always treats the student as a student, he or she will forever remain a student. I often reproach teachers, myself included, for being too narrow in our judgments. We need to give our students more trust and creative freedom.

CONCLUSION

In his book *Didactica Magna*, John Amos Comenius wrote that the educational process should be "brief, pleasant, and thorough." Yankelevich liked to repeat this often, and it became something of a motto for his own work. For him, "brevity" consisted of finding the optimal path for the student's formation and eliminating anything superfluous in the pedagogical process. All his actions were to the point, never losing sight of the long-term goal. However, the long-term goal that was so characteristic of his pedagogy did not just consist of creating a prospective plan for the student. He believed in foreseeing the student's entire development, so that the tactical goals did not eclipse the long-term strategic goals that were much more important. Yankelevich was always waiting (and waiting impatiently) for the hidden capabilities of the student to emerge. He believed these to "emerge more readily in an atmosphere of mutual understanding and friendship that dispels any inhibitions." With incredible tact and perseverance he managed to create a wonderfully creative atmosphere in his classroom, which naturally brought out the better musical and personal qualities in his students.

Yankelevich proceeded from the very correct and contemporary under-standing of the two-sided nature of the pedagogical process. The teacher not only acts as a leader by giving suggestions and sharing his or her experience but also serves as a kind of "objective mirror" for the student. This way the teacher provides the student with essential objective information on the state of the student's apparatus and whether or not it functions to realize the stu-dent's musical goals. This constant and painstakingly corrective process of working helps to explain the quick and natural mastery of the instrument that distinguished so many of Yankelevich's top students.

Yankelevich clearly understood what fosters a creative atmosphere in the studio, and he was able to establish the ideal conditions for his concise remarks to resonate. He believed that vivid and aphoristic comments are remembered better than narrow instructions that can block the student's imagination, and which he always avoided.

Yankelevich always strove to "optimize" the student's mental state, but never to the point of overworking it. This applied to both lessons and per-formances. He understood that optimal conditions without exertion make the student more receptive so that the teacher's comments are absorbed cre-atively rather than mechanically. This helps the student to utilize his or her reserves, take initiative, and establish an individual plan of study, which, in interacting with the teacher's plan, creates the ideal fusion that forges the stu-dent's individual personality. Yankelevich insisted on achieving an "inverse relationship" between the teacher and the student (something that is often declared but rarely achieved). This meant not only mutual understanding and a good "reaction" to comments, but also the emergence of the creative "I" in the student, which in turn eventually enriches the teacher. This is probably why Yankelevich wanted his class to have a spectrum of talent, remarking that the more students differ, the more they influence each other. "The greater the diversity of talent in the studio, the more successful the development of all the students."

Yankelevich considered the "pleasure" of the learning process for the teacher to lie in gaining new and interesting experiences by nurturing interesting stu-dents. For the student it lies in generating interest not just in the final goal but also in the creative learning process itself. He believed any curtailing of the student's creative capabilities inevitably causes boredom. That is why he believed in and used the method of experimentation: "Achieving a difficult goal that initially seemed impossible is a motivating stimulus that helps the student progress faster. The student starts to believe in him- or herself and trust the teacher."

Yankelevich helped his students to remove any obstacles in their way; he elim-inated tension, made their playing more dynamic, and accelerated the process of learning new repertoire. He always saw a connection between the amount of material covered in the lessons (without compromising quality), between "the stream of music that flows through the student" and the development of the student's talent and abilities. "This is how to nurture an artist, for this develops memory, sight-reading, and the ability to quickly master new repertoire."

And finally, the thoroughness of his teaching was evident through his constant research into contemporary practices and his compilation of the experience of the leading pedagogues. He was able to discover and determine all the elements of the playing process, be they mechanical-acoustic, physiological, psychological, or aesthetic-artistic. He not only determined them but also linked them together by understanding their interaction, and then used this insight in his practice.

It was this multifaceted vision, this profound knowledge of the pedagogical process, which caused Yankelevich to abandon formulaic systems in favor of wider synthesis. This helped him to be extremely accurate and precise in his corrections, even in the most difficult cases. He enabled students by giving them complete information on their own abilities and future paths, which endowed them with a high degree of self-control. He developed remarkable cohesion of all the links in the pedagogical process and the methodological principles he recommended. This cohesion stemmed from his accurate understanding of the parts and the whole, both their differentiation and their hierarchy. In any part Yankelevich could see the whole, and in the whole he saw the individual components. This explains the solid technical foundation of his students and also his ability to delegate work between the teacher and the assistants. Yankelevich's assistants were always allowed a lot of independence in solving specific problems, which were based on the main goals set forth by the teacher.

In conclusion, it should be added that Yankelevich continued serious work with his students even after they became concertizing artists. He developed a transitional program to move them from student to independent creative artist. His experience with all aspects of violin pedagogy, from the beginning child to the recognized artist, allowed him to see all that was new—all that was replacing the old traditions, methods, and dogmas.

Many teachers are guilty of resisting all that is unusual and different from their customary established ideas. This kind of inert thinking does not allow them to see what is new. Their students continue to play the theme of Bach's Chaconne entirely in chords, they don't want to take a look at the urtext score and discover Mozart's original bowings ... they stubbornly cling to the past.

Yankelevich was an innovator, and his work was at the heart of the battle to modernize violin teaching and methodology. Through his relentless, gargantuan efforts he contributed enormously to the Russian violin school and developed valuable traditions that will nurture more than one generation of violinists to come.

NOTES

1. As already noted in the Introduction, it is important not to confuse Abraham Yampolsky with his nephew, Israel Yampolsky (the author of *Principles of Violin Fingering*). Throughout this text the single name "Yampolsky" will refer only to Abraham Yampolsky. —*Translator's note.*
2. Ivan Petrovich Pavlov (1849–1936) was a renowned Russian physiologist, psychologist, and physicist largely known for his work on conditioned reflexes. — *Translator's note.*
3. Nikolai Garbuzov, *Zonnaia priroda zvukovysotnogo slukha* (Natural Zones of High-Frequency Hearing) (Moscow: Izd-vo Akademii nauk SSSR, 1948).
4. "Wrist" vibrato is also known as "hand" vibrato. —*Translator's note.*
5. Etudes in different editions of the Kreutzer etudes are numbered differently. In this case, Kreutzer No. 1 refers to the etude in sixteenth notes in C major (often listed as Kreutzer No. 2) and Kreutzer No. 11(often listed as No. 13) refers to the etude in sixteenth notes in A major. —*Translator's note.*
6. See n. 5.
7. In the original text Grigoryev designates the grades according to the Russian numerical system, with 5 being the highest and 1 the lowest. —*Translator's note.*

Selected Students and Assistants of Yuri Yankelevich

Below is the list of Yankelevich's students taken from the latest Russian edition of *Pedagogicheskoe Nasledie* (Pedagogical Legacy).[1] Further biographical information on Yankelevich's students, including select interviews and essays, are available on the companion website to this book www.oup.com/us/therussianviolinschool.

Ruben Aharonyan
Levon Ambartsumian
Felix Andrievsky
Boris Belkin
Mikhail Bezverkhni
Irina Bochkova
Alexandre Brussilovsky
Eugenia Chugaeva
Lydia Dubrovskaya
Arcady Futer
Boris Garlitsky
Alexander Gelfat
Tatiana Grindenko
Ilya Grubert
Lina Guberman
Vladimir Ivanov
Pavel Kogan
Mikhail Kopelman
Bogodar Kotorovych
Vera Kramarova
Vladimir Landsman
Lev Markiz

Albert Markov
Irina Medvedeva
Anatoliy Melnikov
Gayane Pogosova
Anna Rosnovskaya-Leikina
Zare Saakyants
Sergey Sapozhnikov
Dora Schwarzberg
Nelli Shkolnikova
Lidia Shutko
Dmitry Sitkovetsky
Valery Slutsky
Evgeny Smirnov
Vladimir Spivakov
Sigvard Stenberg
Victor Tretyakov
Valeria Vilker-Kushment
Gregory Zhislin
Valery Zvonov

Assistants to Yuri Yankelevich:
Felix Andrievsky
Irina Bochkova
Evgenia Chugaeva
Inna Gaukhman
Zinaida Gilels
Maya Glezarova

NOTE

1. Yuri Yankelevich, *Pedagogicheskoe nasledie* (Pedagogical Legacy), 4th ed. (Moscow: Muzyka, 2009).

APPENDIX B

Methodological Writings and Lectures by Yuri Yankelevich

Problema zvuchaniia v skripichnoi igre: Analiz raboty Karla Flesha (The Problem of Tone in Violin Playing: An Analysis of the Work of Carl Flesch). Manuscript, 1932.[1]

Pravaia ruka skripacha i rabota nad shtrikhami (The Right Arm of the Violinist and Work on Bow-Strokes). Manuscript, 1940.

Tekhnika levoi ruki skripacha (Left-Hand Technique of the Violinist). Manuscript, 1940.

O vibratsii (On Vibrato). Manuscript, 1940.

Nekotorye cherty metoda prof. Iampol'skogo (Certain Aspects of the Method of Prof. Yampolsky). Manuscript, 1951.

Ostsilograficheskii analiz smen pozitsii (An Oscillographic Analysis of Shifting Positions). Manuscript, 1952.

Smeny pozitsii, priyomy ikh vypolneniia i vospitanie sootvetsvuiushchikh navykov (Shifting: Means of Execution and the Cultivation of Corresponding Skills). Manuscript, 1952.

O metodah ovladeniia pozitsiiami (On Methods of Mastering the Positions). Manuscript, 1955.

Smeny pozitsii, v sviazi s zadachami khudozhestvennogo ispolneniia na skripke; opyt obobshcheniia nekotorykh polozhenii sovetskoi skripichnoi shkoly (Shifting Positions in Conjunction with the Musical Goals of the Violinist; Experience Reflecting Certain Views of the Soviet Violin School). Doctoral dissertation, 1955.

Voprosy pervonachalnoi postanovki ruk skripacha (Matters of Initially Positioning the Violinist's Hands and Arms). Manuscript, 1956.

O metodakh A. I. Iampol'skogo v formirovanii skripacha muzykanta (On Yampolsky's Methods in Developing a Musician-Violinist). Manuscript, 1957.

Ob intonatsii (On Intonation). Lecture at the Moscow Conservatory, October 29. Manuscript, 1958.

Lecture at the conference of the orchestral faculty at the Moscow Conservatory November 28th, 1958. Manuscript.

Lecture at the 3rd conference of the association of Russian pedagogue-musicians March 25th, 1959. Stenogram.

Lecture at the conference dedicated to the technical development of the violinist Manuscript, 1960.

Cycle of lectures at the Moscow Conservatory and Gnessin Institute: On Vibrato; On Notation; System of Intervals; Temperament. Manuscript.

"Smena Pozitsii" v sbornike *Ocherki po metodike obucheniia igre na skripke* ("Changes of Position" in *Essays on Violin Pedagogy*) Moscow, 1960.

"O pervonachalnoi postanovke skripacha" v sbornike *Voprosi skripichnogo ispolnitelstva i pedagogiki* ("On the initial positioning of the violinist" in *Matters of Violin Performance and Pedagogy*) Moscow, 1968.

Konkurs, problemy i opyt (Competitions; problems and experience) *Sovetskaya kultura*, No 5, 1970.

Na muzikalnykh seminarakh v Yaponii I GDR (At musical seminars in Japan and the German Democratic Republic) *Masterstvo muzikanta-ispolnitelya*, Moscow, 1972.

NOTE

1. This is a reproduction of the list published in Yuri Yankelevich, *Pedagogicheskoe nasledie* (Pedagogical Legacy), 4th ed. (Moscow: Muzyka, 2009).

Compositions Edited by Yuri Yankelevich

Published Compositions

M. Bruch	*Scottish Fantasy.* Moscow, 1962.[1]
H. Vieuxtemps	*Concerto No. 1.* Moscow, 1968.
H. Vieuxtemps	*Concerto No. 5.* Moscow, 1958.
G. F. Handel	*Aria.* Moscow, 1955.
G. F. Handel	*Sonata No. 2.* Moscow, 1951
K. Goldmark	*Concerto.* Moscow, 1970.
E. Grieg	*Sonatas 1–3.* Moscow, 1971.
W.A. Mozart	*Concerto No. 5.* Moscow, 1983.
S. Prokofiev	Three Pieces from *Romeo and Juliette.* Moscow, 1956.
P. Sarasate	*Carmen Fantasy.* Moscow, 1956.
C. Saint-Saens	*Havanaise* (reconstruction of A. Yampolsky's edition). Moscow, 1957.
P. Tchaikovsky	*Meditation* (reconstruction of A. Yampolsky's edition). Moscow, 1957.
L. Spohr	*Concerto No. 7.* Moscow, 1968.
L. Spohr	*Concerto No. 9.* Moscow, 1959.

Unpublished Compositions

J. S. Bach	*Partita in E minor.*
J. S. Bach	*Sonata in C minor.*
L. Beethoven	*Sonatas Nos. 3, 5, 8, 10.*
J. Brahms	*3 Sonatas.*
Handel/Thomson	*Passacaglia.*
A. Glazunov	*Concerto.*
M. Glinka/Sher	*Fantasia on Themes from "Ruslan and Ludmila."*
C. Dittersdorf	*Scherzo.*
M. Karlovic	*Concerto.*

E. Lalo	*Symphonie Espagnole.*
S. Lyapounov	*Concerto.*
A. Machavariani	*Concerto.*
W. A. Mozart	*Sinfonia Concertante.*
A. Nikolayev	*Sonata.*
N. Rakov	*Three Pieces.*
N. Rimsky-Korsakov	*Mazurka.*
A. Sabitov	*Concerto.*
A. Flyarkovsky	*Concerto.*
C. Franck	*Sonata.*
A. Khachaturian	*Dance.*
P. Tchaikovsky	*Scherzo.*
F. Schubert	*Duo in A Major.*
A. Exaudet	*Minuet.*

NOTE

1. This is a reproduction of the list published in Yuri Yankelevich, *Pedagogicheskoe nasledie* (Pedagogical Legacy), 4th ed. (Moscow: Muzyka, 2009); complete reference information for compositions is sometimes missing.

Alard, Jean Deplhin. *Polnaia shkola dlia skripki, priniataia dlia rukovodstva v parizhskoi konservatorii* (Complete Violin Method in use at the Paris Conservatory). Translated from French to Russian by A. Sokolova. Moscow: n.p., 1909.[1]

Alekseev, V. *Gammy i arpedzhii dlia skripki: Opyt ritmizatsii protsessa ih izucheniia* (Scales and Arpeggios for the Violin: The Rhythmic Process of Their Study). 2nd ed. Moscow: n.p., 1937.

Andrievskii, Felix. "Sovetskaia skripichnaia shkola. Professor Iurii Iankelevich" (Soviet Violin School. Professor Yuri Yankelevich). Manuscript.

Asaf'ev, Boris. *Muzykal'naia forma kak protsess. Kn 2. Intonatsiia* (Musical Form as Process, Vol. 2: Intonation). Moscow: n.p., 1963.

Asaf'ev, Boris. *Muzykal'naia forma kak protsess.* Leningrad: Gosudarstvenoe muzykal'noe izdatel'stvo, 1963. Trans. James Robert Tull as "Musical Form as a Process." Ph.D. diss., Ohio State University, 1977.

Asoian, E. "O kontsertakh pamiati I. Iankelevicha i I. Shvartsberg" (On the Concerts in Memory of Y. Yankelevich and I. Schwartzberg). *Novoe Vremia* 20 (1990).

Auer, Leopold. Graded Course of Violin Playing: A Complete Outline of Violin Study for Individual and Class Instruction. New York: Carl Fischer, 1926.

Auer, Leopold. Interpretatsiia proizvedenii skripichnoi klassiki (Violin Masterworks and Their Interpretation). Moscow: n.p., 1964.

Auer, Leopold. Moia dolgoia zhizn v muzyke (My Long Life in Music). St. Petersburg: Kompozitor, 2003.

Auer, Leopold. *Moia shkola igry na skripke* (Violin Playing as I Teach It). Moscow: Muzyka, 1965.

Auer, Leopold. *My Long Life in Music.* New York: Frederick A. Stokes , 1923.

Auer, Leopold. *Violin Masterworks and Their Interpretation.* New York: C. Fischer, 1925.

Auer, Leopold. *Violin Playing as I Teach It.* New York: Frederick A. Stokes, 1921.

Bai, O. "Kontsert, zapozdavshii na 15 let . . . vystuplenie skripacha Vladimira Lantsmana na Moskovskoi stsene" (A Concert 15 Years Overdue . . . the Appearance of Vladimir Landsman on the Moscow Stage). *Novoe Vremia* 50 (1988).

Baillot, Pierre Marie François de Sales, P. Rode, and Rodolphe Kreutzer. *System for the Violin.* New York: Firth and Hall, 1800. *See* Rode-Baillot-Kreutzer

Baillot, Pierre Marie François de Sales. *L'art du violon: nouvelle méthode*. Mainz 1834.

Bekker, Hugo. *Tekhnika i estetika igry na violoncheli ((perevod s nem.)* (Technique and Aesthetics of Cello Playing, translated from German)). Moscow: n.p., 1977.

Belenky, Boris (Belenkii, Boris). *Pedagogicheskie printsipy L. M. Tseitlina* (Pedagogical Principles of L. M. Tseitlin). Moscow: Muzyka, 1990.

Berezin, V., ed. *Ispolnitel'skie i pedagogicheskie traditsii Moskovskoi konservatorii: Sbornik statei* (Performance and Pedagogical Traditions of the Moscow Conservatory: A Collection of Articles). Moscow: Moskovskaia gos. konservatoriia im. P. I. Chaikovskogo, 1993.

Bériot, Charles de. *Méthode de violon*. Mainz: B. Schott, 1910.

Bériot, Charles de. *Shkola dlia skripki* (Violin Method). Moscow: n.p., 1938.

Bernandt, Grigorii. *Sovesteskie kompozitory i muzykovedy: spravochnik v trekh tomakh* (Soviet Composers and Musicologists: An Encyclopedia in Three Volumes). 3 vols. Moscow: Sovetskii kompozitor, 1978.

Blok, M. C., ed. *Ocherki po metodike obuchenie igry na skripke* (Essays on Violin Pedagogy). Moscow: Gossudarstvenoye muzikalnoye izdatelstvo, 1960.

Borisiak, A. *Shkola igry na violoncheli* (School of Cello Playing). Moscow: n.p., 1949.

Brozh, B. *Nachal'naia shkola skripichnoi igry* (Beginning School of Violin Playing). Moscow: n.p., 1930.

Burlakov, B. "Stenogramma vystuplenia po povodu eissertatsii I. T. Nazarova na temu: 'Psikhofizicheskii metod dostizheniia i sovershenstvovaniia muzykal'noi tekhniki'" (Stenograph of a Report on I. T. Nazarov's Dissertation:"Psychophysiological Method of Acquiring and Perfecting Musical Technique'"). Stenograph. Leningrad, 1946.

Campagnoli Bartolomeo. *Neue Methode der fortschreitenden Fingerfertigkeit*. Leipzig:Breitkopf und Härtel, 1797.

Campbell, Margaret. *The Great Violinists*. New York: Doubleday, 1981.

Campbell, Margaret. "Last of His Line." *Strad* 109, no. 1295 (1998): 248–53.

Chugaeva, Eugenia. "Pamiati uchitelia" (Memory of a Teacher). *Sovetskii muzykant*, October 2, 1973.

David, Ferdinand, and Waldemar Meyer. *Violinschule*. Leipzig: Steingräber, 1900.

Davidov, Karl. *Shkola dlia violoncheli* (School of Cello Playing). Ed. and rev. by S. M. Kozolupov and L. S. Ginzburg. Moscow: n.p., 1947.

Dulov, Georgy. *Sistematicheskii kurs gamm dlia skripki* (Systematic Course of Violin Scales). Moscow: n.p., 1924.

Eberhardt, Goby, and Gustav Saenger. *My System for Practising the Violin and Piano Based upon Psycho-Physiological Principles*. New York: Fischer, 1906.

Eberhardt, Siegfried. *Absolute Treffsicherheit auf der Violine* Berlin: Fürstner, 1912.

Flesch, Carl. *Die Kunst des Violinspiels Bd. 2*. Berlin: Ries & Erler, 1929.

Flesch, Carl. *Etuden-Sammlung für Violine*. Kopenhagen: Wilhelm Hansen, 1921.

Flesch, Carl. *Gammy i arpedzhii* (Scales and Arpeggios). 3rd ed. Moscow: n.p., 1971.

Flesch, Carl. *Iskusstvo skripichnoi igry* (The Art of Violin Playing). Moscow: n.p., 1964.

Flesch, Carl. *The Art of Violin Playing*. Boston: C. Fischer, 1924.

Gaidamovich, Tatiana. "Iurii Iankelevich" (Yuri Yankelevich). *Sovetskaia muzyka* 9 (1985).

Gaidamovich, Tatiana. "V rastsvete Sil" (At the Height of His Powers).*Sovetskaia muzyka* 12 (1966).

Gaidamovich, Tatiana. "Zamechatel'nyi Pedagog" (A Wonderful Pedagogue). *Muzykal'naia zhyzn'* 2 (1974).

Gaidamovich, Tatiana. "Zhizn' pedagoga v tvorchestve ego uchenikov" (The Pedagogue's Life through the Creative Work of His Students), in Yuri Yankelevich, *Pedagogicheskoe nasledie* (Pedagogical Legacy), 4th ed., Moscow: Muzyka, 2009.

Gaidamovich, Tatiana, ed. *Muzykalnoe ispolnitelstvo i pedagogika* (Musical Performance and Pedagogy). Moscow: Muzyka, 1991.

Garbuzov, Nikolai. *Zonnaia priroda zvukovysotnogo slukha* (Natural Zones of High-Frequency Hearing). Moscow: Izd-vo Akademii nauk SSSR, 1948.

Gill, Dominic, ed. *The Book of the Violin*. Oxford: Phaidon, 1984.

Glezarova, Maya. "Iarkii talant pedagoga. K 70—letiyu so dnia rozhdeniia I. Iankelevicha" (Exceptional Talent of a Pedagogue: Commemorating the 70th Anniversary of Y. Yankelevich's Birth). *Sovetskii Muzykant*, April 11, 1979.

Glezarova, Maya. "On dumal o sud'be vospitannikov" (He Thought about His Students' Destiny). *Sovetskii Muzykant*, April 4, 1964.

Gofman, R. *Bol'shaia i podrobnaia shkola tekhniki igry na skripke, v progressivnom sistematicheskom raspolozhenii ot pervyh shagov obucheniia do visshego ssovershenstvovania. Perevod s Fr.* (Large and Detailed School of Violin Technique, in Progressive Systematic Format from the First Steps to the Highest Mastery, translated from French). Moscow: n.p., 1959.

Gotsdiner, Mikhail. *Kratkie ocherki o skripichnom iskusstve* (Short Essays on the Art of the Violin). Moscow: Klassika-XXI, 2002.

Greene, Lynnda. "Staying Home." *The Strad* 115, no. 1376 (2004): 1314–21.

Grigoryev, Vladimir Yurevich (Grigor'ev Vladimir Iurevich). "A. I. Iampolskii i ego metodicheskie vzgliady" (A. I. Yampolsky and His Methodological Views). In *Ispolnitel'skie I Pedagogicheskie Tradicii Moscovskoi Konservatorii*, 100–12.

Grigoryev, Vladimir Yurevich (Grigor'ev Vladimir Iurevich). *Leonid Kogan: tvorcheskii portret* (Leonid Kogan: Portrait of an Artist). Moscow: Muzyka, 1984.

Grigoryev, Vladimir Yurevich (Grigor'ev Vladimir Iurevich), ed. *Problemy muzykal'noi pedagogiki, sbornik trudov* (Problems of Musical Pedagogy, a Collection of Articles). Moscow: Moskovskaia gosudarstvennaia konservatoriia im P. I. Chaikovskogo, 1981.

Grigorian, A. *Nachal'naia shkola igry na skripki* (Beginning School of Violin Playing). Moscow: n.p., 1951.

Gruenbaum, J. "Change of Position." *The Strad* 690 (1947).

Grum-Grzhimailo, T. *Muzykal'noe ispolnitel'stvo* (Musical Performance). Moscow: n.p., 1984.

Guhr, Carl. *Paganini's Kunst die Violine zu spielen*. Berlin: B. Schott's Söhne, 1929.

Guth, P. *Die Moderne Russische Violinschule Und Ihre Methodik Aus Violinspiel Und Violinmusik in Geschichte Und Gegenwart*. Vienna: n.p., 1970.

Hakobian, Levon. *Music of the Soviet Age: 1917–1987*. Stockholm: Melos Music Literature, 1998.

Heiles, Anne Mischakoff. *Khandoshkin and the Beginnings of Russian String Music*. Ann Arbor, MI: UMI Research Press, 1983.

Hřimaly, Jan. *Scale Studies for Violin*. New York: G. Schirmers, 1905.

Hřimaly, Jan (Grzhimali, I). *Uprazhneniia v gammakh dlia skripki* (Scale Studies for Violin). Moscow, 1935.

Jacobsen, Maxim. *100 technische Paraphrasen über Kreutzer-Etüden zur höchsten Ausbildung der Violintechnik*. Leipzig: Zimmermann, 1929.

Joachim, Joseph, and Andreas Moser. *Violinschule*. Berlin: N. Simrock, 1905.

Jockisch, Reinhold. *Katechismus der Violine und des Violinspiels*. Leipzig: J. J. Weber, 1900.

Kayser, Heinrich Ernst. *Neueste Methode des Violinspiels, op. 32 Th. 3*. Leipzig: Cranz, 1900.

Kharlap, M. "'Ispolnitel'skoe iskusstvo kak esteticheskaia problema" (Art of Performance as an Aesthetic Challenge). *Masterstvo muzykanta-ispolnitelia* 2 (1976).

Klopcic, Rok. "Shift Work." *The Strad* 115, no. 1372 (2004): 814–17.

Koch-Rebling, Kathinka. *Violinspiel Und Violinpedagogik*. Leipzig: VEB Deutscher Verlag für Musik, 1979.

Koeckert, Gustave. *Rationelle Violintechnik*. Leipzig: Breitkopf & Härtel, 1909.

Koneder, Walter. *The Amadeus Book of the Violin*. Trans. Reinhard G. Pauly. Portland, OR: Amadeus Press, 1998.

"Kontsert pamiati I. I. Iankelevicha. K 75—letiyu so dnia rozhdeniia" (Concert in Memory of Y. I. Yankelevich Marking the 75th Anniversary of His Birth)." *Muzykal'naia zhyzn'* 3 (1984).

Korguev, Sergei. *Uprazhneniia v dvoinykh notakh* (Exercises in Double Stops). Moscow: n.p., 1949.

Kreutzer, Rudolph, and Emil Kross. *42 Etüden oder Capricen*. Mainz: Schott, 1884.

Laurencie, Lionel de la. *L'école française de violon de Lully à Viotti v. 3*. Paris: n.p., 1909.

Lefort, Narcisse Augustin. *Méthode complète de violon*. Paris: E. Leduc, P. Bertrand et Cie, 1910.

Leonard, Hubert. *Ecole Leonard pour le violon*. Paris: Richault et Cie, 1877.

Lesman, Iosef. *Ob igre na skripke* (On Violin Playing). Petrograd: n.p., 1914.

Lesman, Iosef. *Puti razvitiya skripacha* (Paths of the Violinist's Development). Leningrad: n.p., 1934.

Lesman, Iosef. *Shkola igry na skripke* (School of Violin Playing). Leningrad: n.p., 1924.

Lesman, Iosef. *Skripichnaia tekhnika i ee razvitie v shkole prof. L. S. Auera* (Violin Technique and Its Development in the School of L. Auer). St. Petersburg: n.p., 1909.

Liberman, M., and M. Berlianchik. *Kul'tura zvuka skripacha: puti formirovanii i razvitiia* (The Violinist's Tone Quality: Paths of Formation of Development) Moscow: Muzyka, 1984.

Loginov, V. A., ed. *Istoriia, tvorchestvo, ispolnitelstvo, pedagogika* (History, Creativity, Performance, Pedagogy). Orenburg: Izd-vo Orenburgskogo gos. instituta iskusstv, 2001.

Lubotsky, Mark (Lubotskii, Mark). "A. I. Ampolskii—muzykant, pedagog, vospitatel'" (A. I. Yampolsky—Musician, Pedagogue, Mentor). *Sovetskaya Muzyka* 24, no. 11 (1960): 117–23.

Lvov, Alexei. *Sovety nachinaeshemu igrat' na skripke* (Advice to a Beginner on Playing the Violin). St. Petersburg: n.p., 1859.

Mařák, Jan, and Viktor Nopp. *Housle, dějiny výroje houslí, houslařstvi a hry houslove. Methodika. 3. vydáni, dopiněné až do doby přitomné*, upravil Viktor Nopp. Praha: Hudebni matice umělecké besedy, 1944.

Markov, Albert. *Sistema skripichnoi igry* (System of Violin Playing). Moscow: Muzyka, 1997.

Markov, Albert. *Violin Technique*. New York: Schirmer, 1984.

Merkulov, A. M., ed. *Professora ispolnitelshkikh klassov Moskovskoi konservatorii* (Professors of the Perfomance Classes at the Moscow Conservatory). 2 vols. Moscow: Moskovskaia gos. konservatoriia im P. I. Chaikovskogo, 2000.

Mikhailovsky, B. (Mikhailovskii, B). *Novii put' skripacha* (New Direction for the Violinist). Moscow, 1934.

Milshtein, A., ed. *Masterstvo muzykanta-ispolnitelia* (Artistry of the Musician-Performer). Moscow: Izd-vo Sov. kompozitor, 1972.

Minster, M. "Iz zamechanii I. I. Iankelevicha o proizvedeniiakh Bakha i Motsarta" (From Y. Yankelevich's Notes on the Works of Bach and Mozart). Manuscript. Archive of I. I. Iankelevich.

Mironov, N. A., ed. *Moskovskaia konservatoriia: ot istokov do nashikh dnei: istoriko-biograficheskii spravochnik* (Moscow Conservatory: From Its Origins through Today: A Histo-Biographical Encyclopedia). Moscow: Progress-Traditsiia, 2005.

Montague, David. "The Principles of Violin Fingering." Review of *The Principles of Violin Fingering*, by Israel Yampolsky. *Notes* 25, no. 3 (1969): 500.

Moser, Andreas. *Methodik des Violinspiels*. Leipzig: Breitkopf & Härtel, 1920.

Mostras, Konstantin. *24 kaprisa dlia skripki solo N. Paganini. Metodicheskii Kommentarii* (24 Caprices for Violin Solo by N. Paganini: Methodological Commentary). Moscow: Gosudarstvenoe muzykalnoe izdatelstvo, 1959.

Mostras, Konstantin. *Dinamika v skripičnom iskusstve* (Dynamics in the Art of Violin Playing). Moscow: Gosudarstvenoe muzykalnoe izdatelstvo, 1956.

Mostras, Konstantin. *Intonatsiia na skripke* (Intonation on the Violin). 2nd ed. Moscow: Gosudarstvenoe muzykalnoe izdatelstvo, 1968.

Mostras, Konstantin. "Kurs metodiki u Strunnikov." (Course in String Methodology) *Sovetskoye Iskusstvo* 30 (May 1938).

Mostras, Konstantin. "Lektsii po metodike igry i prepodavaniia na skripke" (Lectures on Methodology of Playing and Teaching the Violin). Manuscript.

Mostras, Konstantin. "Nasha Piat'erka" (Our Group of Five). *Izvestia* 2 (April 1937).

Mostras, Konstantin. *Ritmicheskaia distsiplina skripacha* (Rhythmic Discipline of the Violinist). Moscow: Gosudarstvenoe muzykalnoe izdatelstvo, 1951.

Mostras, Konstantin. *Sistema domashnykh zaniatii skripacha* (System of Practicing at Home for the Violinist). Moscow: Gosudarstvenoe muzykalnoe izdatelstvo, 1956.

Mostras, Konstantin. "Vidy tekhniki" (Types of Technique). In *Ocherki po metodike obuchenie igry na skripke* (Essays on Violin Pedagogy), ed. M. C. Blok. Moscow: Gossudarstvenoye muzikalnoye izdatelstvo, 1960.

Mozart, Leopold. *A Treatise on the Fundamental Principles of Violin Playing*. London: Oxford University Press, 1951.

Mozart, Leopold. *Osnovatel'noe skripichnoe uchilishche/perevod s nem* (Fundamental Violin Treatise, translated from German). St. Petersburg: n.p., 1804.

"Muzykant. K 75-letiyu professora I. I. Iankelevicha." (Musician. Commemorating the 75th Anniversary of Professor Y. Yankelevich). *Sovetskaia muzyka*, no. 8 (1984).

Nazarov, Ivan. "Psikhofizicheskii metod dostizheniia i sovershenstvovaniia muzykal'noi tekhniki" (Psychophysical Method of Attaining and Perfecting Musical Technique). Diss., Leningrad 1946.

Nemirovsky, L. (Nemirovskii, L). *Mekhanicheskie i psikhologicheskie momenty v osnovnykh priemakh skripichnoi tekhniki* (Mechanical and Psychological Moments in the Fundamental Skills of Violin Technique). Moscow: n.p., 1915.

"Otkrytoe pis'mo vospitannikov professora I. I. Iankelevicha v redaktsiiu zhurnala *Sovetskaia Muzyka*" (Open Letter from Y. I. Yankelevich's Students to the Editors of *Sovetskaia Muzyka*). *Sovetskaia muzyka* 9 (1988).

Pennequin, Jules Charles. *Nouvelle méthode de violon, théorique et pratique: en deux parties.* Paris: Enoch, 1900.

Pribegina, G. A. *Moskovskaia konservatoriia, 1866–1991* (Moscow Conservatory, 1866–1991). Moscow: Muzyka, 1991.

Raaben, Lev. *Istoriia russkogo i sovetskogo skripichnogo iskusstva* (History of Russian and Soviet Violin Art). Leningrad: Muzyka, 1978.

Rabinovich, A. *Ostsillograficheskii metod analiza melodii* (Oscillographic Method of Analyzing Melody). Moscow: Gosudarstvenoe muzykal'noe izdatelstvo, 1932.

Radmall, P. "Change of Position." *The Strad*, no. 689 (1947).

Rezvetsov, Aleksandr. *Melodicheskaia elementarnaia shkola dlia skripki* (Elementary Melodic School of Violin Playing). 3rd ed. Moscow: n.p., 1897.

Rode-Baillot-Kreutzer. *Skripichnaia shkola* (Violin School). 2nd ed. St. Petersburg: n.p., 1829.

Rodionov, Konstantin, ed. *Mastera skripichnoi pedagogiki* (Masters of Violin Pedagogy). Moscow: Gosudarstvenii muzykal'no pedagogicheskii institut im Gnessinih, 1974.

Rodionov, Konstantin, ed. *Nachal'nye uroki igry na skripke* (Beginning Violin Lessons). Moscow: n.p., 1950.

Rudenko, V. "80 let so dnia rozhdeniia I. I. Ankelevicha (1909–1973)" (80 years from the day of Y. Yankelevich's Birth). *Ezhegodnik pamiatnyh muzykal'nykh dat i sobytii*, 1988.

Sapozhnikov, R. *Shkola igry na violoncheli* (School of Cello Playing). Moscow: n.p., 1951.

Sapozhnikov, S., ed. *Voprosy skripichnogo ispolnitel'stva i pedagogiki. Sbornik Statei* (Matters of Violin Performance and Pedagogy: A Collection of Articles). Moscow: Muzyka, 1968.

Sass, August Leopold. *Neue Schule für Geiger.* Leipzig: Steingräber Verlag, 1920.

Schwarz, Boris. *Great Masters of the Violin.* New York: Simon & Schuster, 1983.

Schwarz, Boris. *Music and Musical Life in Soviet Russia.* New York: W. W. Norton, 1972.

Seitz, Diana I. *The System of Effective Violin Practice according to Konstantin Mostras.* Thesis (D.M.A.), University of Oklahoma, 2008.

Ševčík, Otakar. *Skripichnaia shkolà dlia nachinaiushshih/perevod s cheshskogo* (Violin School for Beginners, translated from Czech). Moscow: n.p., 1928.

Ševčík, Otakar. *Shkola skripichnoi tekhniki/perevod s cheshskogo* (School of Violin Technique, translated from Czech). Moscow: n.p., 1929.

Sibor, Boris. *Skripichnaya technika dvoinih not* (Violin Technique of Double Stops). Moscow: n.p., 1928.

Singer, Edmund, and Max Seifriz. *Grosse theoretisch-praktische Violinschule.* Berlin: Cottaschen Buchhandlung, 1887.

Sitkovetskii, Dmitrii. "Skripka daetsia neprosto" (The Violin Does Not Come Easily). *Yunost',* no. 1 (1974).

Smirnov, M. A., ed. *Problemy muzykal'noi pedagogiki, sbornik trudov* (Problems in Musical Pedagogy, a Collection of Articles). Moscow: Moskovskaia gosudarstvennaia konservatoriia im P. I. Chaikovskogo, 1981.

Soboleva, G. "Pleiada zvezd—iunym Skripacham" (Galaxy of Stars—to the Young Violinists). *Vechernaia Moskva,* May 27, 1992.

Spivakov, Vladimir. "Skripka i vsia zhizn'" (Violin and All Life). *Moskovskii komsomolets,* 1987.

Spivakov, Vladimir. "Uchitel' i shkola" (Teacher and School). *Muzykal'naia zhyzn',* no. 12, 1979.

Spohr, Louis. *Violinschule.* Wien: T. Haslinger, 1832.

Stetsenko, V. "V tvorcheskoi laboratorii mastera skripichnoi pedagogiki" (In the Creative Laboratory of the Masters of Violin Pedagogy). Manuscript. Archive of Yuri Yankelevich.

Struve, Boris. *Puti nachal'nogo razvitiia iunykh skripachei i violonchelistov* (Beginning Paths of Development in Young Violinists and Cellists). Moscow: Gosudarstvenoe muzykal'noe izdatel'stvo, 1952.

Struve, Boris. *Tipovye formy postanovki ruk u instrumentalistov: Smichkovaia gruppa* (Typical Forms of Positioning the Hands of Instrumentalists: Bowed Instrument Group). Moscow: n.p., 1932.

Struve, Boris. *Vibratsiia kak ispolnitel'skii navyk igry na smichkovykh instrumentakh* (Vibrato as a Performance Skill on Bowed Instruments). Leningrad: n.p., 1933.

Tessarini, Carlo. *Nouvelle methode pour apprendre par theorie dans un mois de tems à jouer du violon divisée en trois classes, avec des leçons à deux violons par gradation.* Paris: n.p., 1750.

Tret'iakov, Victor. "Uroki masterstva" (Lessons in Mastery). *Sovetskaia kul'tura,* May 22, 1984.

Tsypin, G. "Trudnoe tainstvo" (Secrets of the Craft). *Sovetskaia kul'tura,* August 18, 1988.

Tumanin, N. ed. *Vospominaniia o Moskovskoi konservatorii* (Recollections of the Moscow Conservatory). Moscow: Muzyka, 1966.

Valter, Viktor (Val'ter, Viktor). *Kak uchit' igre na skripke* (How to Teach Violin Playing). 3rd ed. St. Petersburg: n.p., 1910.

Voiku, Ion. *Postroenie estestvennoi sistemy skripichnoi igry (tekhnika levoi ruki). Perevod s Nem. V. N. Rimskogo-Korsakova* (The Formation of a Natural System of Violin Playing (Left-Hand Technique). Translated from the German by V. N. Rimsky-Korsakov). Moscow: n.p., 1930.

Voldan, Bedřich. *Nová škola poloh: (analogická soustava skupinová).* Praha: Neubert 1924.

Yampolsky, Abraham (Iampol'skii, Abram). "K voprosam razvitiia skripichnoi tekhniki: shtrikhi" (Concerning the Development of Violin Technique: Bowings). In *Problemy Muzykal'noi Pedagogiki, sbornik trudov* (Problems of Musical Pedagogy, a Collection of Articles), ed. Vladimir Grigor'ev. Moscow: Moskovskaia gosudarstvennaia konservatoriia im P. I. Chaikovskogo, 1981.

Yampolsky, Abraham (Iampol'skii, Abram). "K voprosu o vospitanii kul'tury zvuka u skripachei" (Concerning the Development of Sound in Violinists). In *Voprosy skripichnogo ispolnitel'stva i pedagogiki, sbornik statei* (Matters of Violin Performance and Pedagogy, a Collection of Articles), ed. S. Sapozhnikov. Moscow: Muzyka, 1968.

Yampolsky, Abraham (Iampol'skii, Abram). "O metode raboty s uchinikame" (On Methods of Working with Students). In *Voprosy skripichnogo ispolnitel'stva i pedagogiki, sbornik statei* (Matters of Violin Performance and Pedagogy, a Collection of Articles), ed. S. Sapozhnikov. Moscow: Muzyka, 1968.

Yampolsky, Abraham (Iampol'skii, Abram). "Pedagog—tvorcheskii rukovoditel', a ne repetitor" (Pedagogue as Creative Mentor, Rather Than Tutor). *Sovetskii Muzykant*, no. 28 (1953).

Yampolsky, Abraham (Iampol'skii, Abram). "Podgotovka pal'tsev i ostavlenie ikh na strunakh." (Preparing the Fingers and Leaving Them on the String). In *Ocherki po metodike obuchenie igry na skripke* (Essays on Violin Pedagogy), ed. M. C. Blok. Moscow: Gossudarstvenoye muzikalnoye izdatelstvo, 1960.

Yampolsky, Israel (Iampol'skii, Izrail). *David Oistrakh*. Moscow: Muzyka, 1968.

Yampolsky, Israel (Iampol'skii, Izrail). *Osnovy skripchnoi applikatury* (Principles of Violin Fingering). Moscow: Gosudarstvenoye muzykal'noe izdatelstvo, 1955.

Yampolsky, Israel (Iampol'skii, Izrail). *Russkoe skripichnoe iskusstvo: ocherki i materialy* (Russian Violin Art: Essays and Materials). Moscow: Gosudarstvenoe muzykalnoe isdatelstvo, 1951.

Yampolsky, Israel. *The Principles of Violin Fingering*. Translated by Alan Lumsden. London and New York: Oxford University Press, 1967.

Yankelevich, Yuri (Jankelewitsch, Juri). "Grundatzliches Zu Haltungsfragen Beim Violinspiet." In *Violinspiel Und Violinpedagogik*, ed. Kathinka Koch-Rebling. Leipzig: VEB Deutscher Verlag für Musik, 1979.

Yankelevich, Yuri (Iankelevich, Iurii). "Konkurs, problemy i opyt" (Competitions: Problems and Experience). *Sovetskaia kul'tura* 5 (1970).

Yankelevich, Yuri (Jankelewitsch, Juri). "Lagenwechsel." In *Violinspiel Und Violinpedagogik*, ed. Kathinka Koch-Rebling. Leipzig: VEB Deutscher Verlag für Musik, 1979.

Yankelevich, Yuri (Iankelevich, Iurii). "Na muzykal'nyh seminarakh v Aponii i Gdr" (At musical seminars in Japan and the German Democratic Republic). *Masterstvo muzykanta-ispolnitelia* (1972).

Yankelevich, Yuri (Iankelevich, Iurii). "O pervonachal'noi postanovke skripacha" (On the Initial Positioning of the Violinist). In *Voprosy skripichnogo ispolnitel'stva i pedagogiki, sbornik statei* (Matters of Violin Performance and Pedagogy, a Collection of Articles), ed. S. Sapozhnikov. Moscow: Muzyka, 1968.

Yankelevich, Yuri (Iankelevich, Iurii). *Pedagogicheskoe nasledie* (Pedagogical Legacy). Moscow: Muzyka, 1983.

Yankelevich, Yuri (Iankelevich, Iurii). *Pedagogicheskoe nasledie* (Pedagogical Legacy). 2nd ed. Moscow: Postskriptum, 1993.

Yankelevich, Yuri (Iankelevich, Iurii). *Pedagogicheskoe nasledie* (Pedagogical Legacy). 3rd ed. Moscow: Fond podderzhki molodyh rossiiskikh skripachei imeni I. I. Iankelevicha (Foundation Supporting Young Russian Violinists in the Name of Y. Yankelevich), 2002.

Yankelevich, Yuri (Iankelevich, Iurii). *Pedagogicheskoe nasledie* (Pedagogical Legacy). 4th ed. Moscow: Muzyka, 2009.

Yankelevich, Yuri (Iankelevich, Iurii). "Smeni pozitsii" (Shifting Positions). In *Ocherki po metodike obuchenie igry na skripke* (Essays on Violin Pedagogy), ed. M. C. Blok. Moscow: Gossudarstvenoye muzikalnoye izdatelstvo, 1960.

Yankelevich, Yuri (Yankelevitch, Yuri). *Yuri Yankelevitch et l'ecole russe du violon.* Trans. Anna Kopylov. Fontenay-aux-Roses: Suoni e colori, 1999.

Yurev, A. (Iurev, A). *Ocherki istorii i teorii smychkovoi kultury skripacha: iz tvorcheskogo naslediia skripichnogo pedagoga* (Essays on the History and Theory of the Violinist's Bowing: From the Artistic Heritage of a Violin Pedagogue). St. Petersburg: Peterburgskaia gos. konservatoriia im N. A. Rimskogo-Korsakova, 2002.

Zaletova, I. *Ruben Agoronian.* N.p.: Yerevan, 1989.

Zhislin, Grigorii. "Ia ne mog by zhit' inache" (I Could Not Live Otherwise) *Sovetskaia muzyka*, no. 10 (1989).

Zhivov, L. "Master skripichnoi pedagogiki" (Masters of Violin Pedagogy). *Muzykal'naia zhyzn'*, no. 12 (1969).

NOTE

1.. The references provided here are largely based on the list compiled in Yankelevich, Yuri (Iankelevich, Iurii). *Pedagogicheskoe nasledie* (Pedagogical Legacy). 4th ed. Moscow: Muzyka, 2009. In certain cases complete bibliographic information is unavailable.